A *Philip E. Lilienthal* Book

The Philip E. Lilienthal imprint honors special
books in commemoration of a man whose work at
the University of California Press from 1954 to
1979 was marked by dedication to young authors
and to high standards in the field of Asian Studies. Friends, family, authors, and foundations
have together endowed the Lilienthal Fund,
which enables the Press to publish under this imprint selected books in a way that reflects the taste
and judgment of a great and beloved editor.

The Meeting of Eastern and Western Art

MICHAEL SULLIVAN

UNIVERSITY OF CALIFORNIA PRESS   BERKELEY   LOS ANGELES   LONDON

TO KHOAN

University of California Press
Berkeley and Los Angeles, California

University of California Press, Ltd.
London, England

© 1989 by
The Regents of the University of California

First Paperback Printing 1997

Library of Congress Cataloging-in-Publication Data

Sullivan, Michael, 1916–
   The meeting of Eastern and Western art.

   Bibliography: p.
   Includes index.
   1. Art—Chinese influences.   2. Art—Japanese
influences.   3. Art, Chinese—Occidental influences.
4. Art, Japanese—Occidental influences.   I. Title.
N7429.S93   1989   709   88-4788
ISBN 0-520-21236-3 (alk. paper)

Printed in the United States of America
1   2   3   4   5   6   7   8   9

Contents

Plates

(*following page 170*)

Acknowledgments

One of the pleasures of authorship is the contacts it brings with people who share one's interests and enthusiasms. In the writing of this book, I am happy to acknowledge the help I have had from old friends and new, from colleagues, students, collectors and many others who have been fascinated by one aspect or another of the East-West confrontation in art, and in various ways have helped me to bring this diverse material together.

Among those to whom I am especially grateful are Madeleine Barbin of the Bibliothèque Nationale, Paris; Chiang Fu-tsung, Chuang Yen and Marshall Wu of the National Palace Museum, Taipei; Kurata Bunsaku of the National Museum, Tōkyō; Homma Masayoshi of the National Museum of Modern Art, Tōkyō; Orimo Yasuo of the Kōbe Municipal Museum of Namban Art; Alan Fern and K. T. Wu of the Library of Congress, and Philip Stern and Thomas Lawton of the Freer Gallery, Washington; Graham Reynolds and R. W. Lightbown of the Victoria and Albert Museum, London; Chandler Kirwin; and Max Loehr at Harvard.

Information and suggestions have also been most kindly given to me by John Addis, Edith Dittrich, George Loehr, Fang Chao-ying, Richard Barnhart, Laurence Sickman, Roderick Whitfield, the late Rudolf Wittkower, Tadashi Sugase and members of my graduate seminar at Stanford, especially Mayching Kao. I should like to express my gratitude to all the individual collectors and museum directors who have permitted pictures in their collections to be re-produced. Without their kind help this book would never have appeared.

The manuscript has been read by F. E. McWilliam, to whom I am indebted for some valuable comments and suggestions in the parts dealing with modern Western art, and by Donald Davie, who at some critical points in the text helped me to express what I wanted to say with far more clarity and grace than I myself could command.

Once again, Carmen Christensen has spent many devoted hours in typing the final draft, and I am happy to acknowledge the help that she and her hus-band, Allen, have given me towards the writing of this book and towards other activities connected with the study of Oriental art at Stanford. I should like to thank Michael Graham-Dixon, Elizabeth Clarke, Alan Wilbur and Jean Ellsmoor for the thought and care they have given to the production of the book.

My research has also been aided by grants from the Carnegie Foundation and from the Center for East Asian Studies at Stanford, to which my thanks are due.

Of the part played in this book by my wife I can give only a hint. Quite apart from the work she has put into every stage of its making, this is, in a very special sense, her book. Not only has she opened doors and built bridges for me everywhere, but in our often strenuous discussions of her civilisation and mine, her own experience, understanding and depth of feeling have helped me to see the meeting of East and West not as a conflict, or even as a reconciliation, of opposites, but as a dynamic and truly life-enhancing dialectic. Seldom can an author have been so blessed.

Stanford, April 1972

Acknowledgments to the Second Edition

To the debt of gratitude I owe to all those who helped to make the first edition possible, I should like to add my thanks to Eva Neurath and Stanley Barron of Thames and Hudson for making available to the University of California Press the illustrations that they provided for the first edition.

I should also like to thank the following artists, collectors, scholars and mu-seum directors and staff members who have supplied me with additional in-formation and illustrations: Adachi Kenji, National Museum of Modern Art, Tōkyō; Hugh Adams, London; Atarashi Kukuo, Museum of the Tōkyō Univer-sity of Art; Patrick Conner, Art Gallery and Museums and the Royal Pavilion,

Brighton; Susan Casteras, Yale Center for British Art, New Haven; Fumiko Cranston, Fogg Museum of Art, Cambridge; Rupert Faulkner, Victoria and Albert Museum, London; the late Dr. Calvin French, University of Michigan, Ann Arbor; Pat Hui, Minneapolis; Hanz Hinz, Allschwil; Honda Akihiko, Hakone Open Air Museum; Jiang Xuan and the staff of the Chinese Artists' Association, Peking; Kazu Kaidō, Tōkyō; Chu-tsing Li and the Spencer Museum of Art, Lawrence, Kansas; Constance Naubert-Riser, Montreal; Patricia Lui, Toronto; Max Hutchinson, Director, Max Hutchinson Gallery, New York; Akiko Murakata, Kyōto; The National Gallery of Scotland, Edinburgh; The Royal College of Physicians, London; Takehiro Shindō, Tōkyō; Jerome Silbergeld, University of Washington, Seattle; Henry Trübner, Seattle Art Museum; Martie Young, Cornell University, Ithaca; Tseng Yü, National Palace Museum, Taipei; Franco Vannotti, Lugano; W. Veit, Museum für Ostasiatische Kunst, Berlin; Wang Keping (Wang K'o-p'ing), Paris; Marc Wilson, Nelson-Atkins Museum of Art, Kansas City; Wu Guanzhong (Wu Kuan-chung), Peking; Yang Yanping (Yang Yen-p'ing), Stony Brook, New York; Yuying Brown, British Library, London; Nakano Shōzo, National Diet Library, Tōkyō; Kishida Toshiko, Monash University, Victoria, S. Australia; Lucy Lim, Chinese Culture Center, San Francisco; Mr. and Mrs. Peter Quennell, London; and Colin Mackay, Sotheby's, London. I should also like to thank Betsey Scheiner, Jeanne Sugiyama and Steve Renick of the University of California Press, Berkeley, for the care they have given to the design and production of the book.

Since the book's inception Allen and Carmen Christensen have continued to give my work their generous support, and I am glad once more to express my gratitude to them.

The last words of the new edition were written in the peace of a beach house beside Puget Sound in deep winter. I should like to thank George and Jane Russell and their family not only for providing us with the ideal setting in which to finish the book, but also for the generous help that they have given towards its production.

Oxford, December 1987

A Note on the Romanisation of Chinese Names

In this new edition, I have retained the Wade–Giles system so long familiar to Western readers, for, while it is not perfect, it is easier to pronounce than the official *pinyin* system. Both forms will be found in the index. For well-known place names (e.g., Peking, Canton), I have followed the usual, and I think correct, custom of using the Anglicised form, as is done, for instance, with Rome, Athens, Munich.

In the case of some modern Chinese artists, I have given the names in the form they themselves adopted in the West: e.g., Zao Wou-ki (Chao Wu-chi), Chang Dai Chien (Chang Ta-ch'ien).

Introduction

More and more thinking people today are coming to believe that the interaction between the cultures of Asia and the West is one of the most significant events in world history since the Renaissance. Both East and West accept the flow of Western ideas and forms to the Orient, which has been gathering pace since the sixteenth century. The westward flow from East Asia has not yet penetrated so deeply into our culture. But in recent years we have seen a deep interest in Oriental thought and religion and, on the material plane, Japanese experts showing Westerners how better to apply in their steelworks and electronics factories techniques that the Japanese had learned from the West. The implications of this cross-fertilisation for the future go beyond what we can yet imagine.

If the importance of my theme needs no justifying, I still feel that I owe it to the reader to explain the scope of the book and why it covers the ground it does. To the Western reader the 'East' is everything from the Islamic world, which begins on the Atlantic coast of Africa, to the northernmost islands of Japan; Oriental rugs mean Persian or Turkish, not Chinese. So a book that fully justified the title I have chosen would need to include Islamic art and its influence on the West, greater India and the whole of the Far East. In a work of several volumes this might be possible, but I have chosen not to paint so huge a canvas, partly because I do not know enough, and partly because to have embraced the whole of Asia and the Islamic world would have shifted the balance of the book from 'fine art', and particularly painting, to the decorative arts and even to archaeology.

I will have little to say in this book about chinoiserie. Not only has the story been well and often told, but it is clear that chinoiserie has very little to do with China. The arrival of Chinese arts and crafts in the seventeenth century worked no transformation in French art; rather, the exotic imports were themselves transformed beyond recognition into something entirely French. Chinoiserie is, more than anything else, a part of the language of Rococo ornament. Even Watteau, who certainly saw Chinese paintings and claimed on occasion to be painting in the Chinese manner, merely played with pseudo-Chinese motifs in a decorative way. So far as we know, he never examined Chinese paintings for what he could learn from them, nor did any European painter or critic in the eighteenth century say anything interesting or perceptive about them. It was quite otherwise with the writers and philosophers of the Enlightenment, whose thinking was profoundly affected by their reading of the Confucian classics in translation. Yet Chinese concepts did eventually come to influence eighteenth-century European taste, though in a very indirect and subtle way.

My concern is with artistic influences at the higher creative levels. Here, the interaction between East and West, though intermittent and fraught with mis-understandings, has been no mere matter of motifs and techniques. It has significantly enlarged the vision of artists, and sometimes of their public as well. At this level, the protagonists have not merely borrowed ornamental motifs from each other; they also have been at least partly aware of each other's aims and artistic ideals. Chinese scholars and Japanese painters have written from time to time very discerningly about European art, comparing it with their own, and if Europeans have been less discerning about the art of China, they have neverthe-less been conscious of it as a manifestation of the great civilisation they admired for other reasons and have taken from it what they could use. In fact, as any study of eighteenth-century taste must show, Europeans were more deeply affected than they realised, while in the nineteenth century Japanese influence was decisive. This is more than can be said of the interaction between Europe and the Indian subcontinent, where European art merely had the effect of cor-rupting a great tradition without enriching it. Today, the dialogue between India and the West is just beginning, but it is still chiefly in the sphere of music and the dance that contact has been made and a vital spark struck. For the plastic and visual arts—the film excepted—truly fruitful cross-fertilisation has yet to come.

This may suggest that I believe that the interaction between one civilisation and another, or indeed between one artist and another, must produce 'better' art than either would achieve alone. I do not believe this, and would insist that in making aesthetic judgements it is only the quality of the work of art that matters. In the final analysis, it is the dialogue of the painter with his medium, not of one painter with another painter, that determines whether he paints a good picture or not, whatever may have been the influences upon him. The historian, however, is concerned not only with the quality of human action but also with its results. He must often deal with works of art that are not in themselves of high quality but are historically important. The reader will certainly recognise a number of works of this kind among my illustrations. Most art lovers, for example, would agree that Fu Pao-shih, the modern master of Chinese painting in the literary style, was a far better and more sensitive artist than Hsü Pei-hung. But in this book Fu Pao-shih, in whose work Western influence is scarcely perceptible, finds no place, while Hsü Pei-hung must be acknowledged as the most important figure in the introduction of conservative Western painting techniques into China in the twentieth century.

I have been influenced too by the almost simultaneous appearance in East and West in the mid-twentieth century of Abstract Expressionism and Action Painting. We need not worry too much about definitions; it is enough to say that the movement that linked East and West was nonfigurative and based on the dynamic or calligraphic gesture, whether the hand that made the gesture held a brush or a dripping paint can. It includes Pollock, Soulages, Kline, for example, and sometimes Tobey and de Kooning, but not Rothko, Dubuffet or Appel. The breakthrough achieved by the New York School in the 1950s, immediately followed by the rediscovery by Chinese and Japanese painters of the Abstract Expressionist elements in their own tradition, provided a dramatic climax to this dialogue between East and West. Now, suddenly, painters of the East and the West seemed to be speaking the same language, or at least to be listening to each other. Whether this meeting of minds was momentary or purely illusory, or whether it was the beginning of a deeper understanding, no one would then have dared to predict. But it put the dialogue of the last four centuries in a special relationship with the present. The appearance since the heyday of Abstract Expressionism of other new movements such as Environmental Art and Photorealism makes the event no less significant, for Abstract Expressionism in its many forms became a vital strand in contemporary art the world over.

Just as important as Abstract Expressionism in breaking down barriers between Eastern and Western art has been the rejection of the idea of the avantgarde. As long as it was thought that the cutting edge of modern art could be identified and localised in New York, Paris, or Tōkyō, it was natural to see the latest movement as something that the less advanced countries must somehow catch up with if they were to be taken seriously by the critics and art historians. But by the 1980s the idea of progress in art had been virtually abandoned. Today in America, Europe and Japan an enormous variety of styles and techniques in art, and views of what art is, happily coexist; in Kandinsky's phrase, everything is permitted. Echoes of this idea have been heard even in the People's Republic of China, although in China the resistance to so ethically neutral a view of art is far older than Mao Tse-tung, and acts as an effective curb on the more outlandish manifestations of contemporary art.

The effect of this ecumenical attitude has been to make many people, in East and West, receptive to almost anything that claims to be art. Does this reflect an uncertainty, a lack of conviction, about what is true and real? Perhaps it does, but this very uncertainty creates an atmosphere in which ideas and forms in the arts can flow more freely than ever before between country and country, artist and artist, while deeply entrenched prejudices melt away.

The active dialogue between Western and Far Eastern art began after 1500. But for centuries before that there had been occasional contacts—if we can call the transmission of a craft, a motif or a technique across Asia 'contact' at all. Chinese silk, rewoven as transparent gauze in Syria, was sold in first-century Rome, whose citizens professed to be shocked by the sight of women clad in this diaphanous stuff, in which 'no woman', Pliny remarked, 'could swear she is not naked'. A Chinese bronze vessel of the fourth century B.C., unearthed in Canterbury, had perhaps been brought there in Roman times. A typically Han dynasty design on a fragment of a third-century fabric from Dura-Europos in Mesopotamia is thought to be the earliest direct imitation of Chinese art in the West. And Chinese dragons adorn fourteenth-century church vestments woven in Lucca and Venice. Across the world, Roman artefacts have been excavated at the site of the ancient port of Oc-éo in southern Vietnam. With the introduction of Buddhism there came to the Far East, by way of Sasanian art, motifs, such as the acanthus scroll, that originated in the eastern Mediterranean world.

We could multiply these instances. But this book is not concerned with random contacts, interesting as they are, or with the appearance at one end of Asia of occasional objects or motifs that originated at the other. It is concerned with interaction between East and West as an active, generative force in art. The events that in a given period caused this interaction may have taken place primarily in the world of art itself, as when the Impressionists, few of whom knew or cared anything about Japan, seized on the Japanese colour print, introduced almost by accident. Or artistic influence may have been the by-product of political, economic or religious pressure, such as that brought to bear on Japan by Portuguese expansion in the sixteenth century. Whatever the initial cause, the result was the historically decisive stimulus and enrichment of the art of a nation, or of an individual painter, that we call 'influence'.

This, finally, is not a definitive history of the East-West interaction in art. Such a work would fill many volumes. There are at least a score, for instance, that deal with Japanese influence on Western art since 1850 and even more (mostly in Japanese) that cover Western influences in modern Japan. Each of these themes is given just one chapter in this book. My aim has been, rather, to try to sum up the effects of East and West on each other's art, to give a brief account of how these effects came about, to compare the responses of China and of Japan to Western art and to consider what 'influence' means, how it operates and how it may sometimes fail to operate at times when it would seem that all the conditions for a fruitful interaction were present.

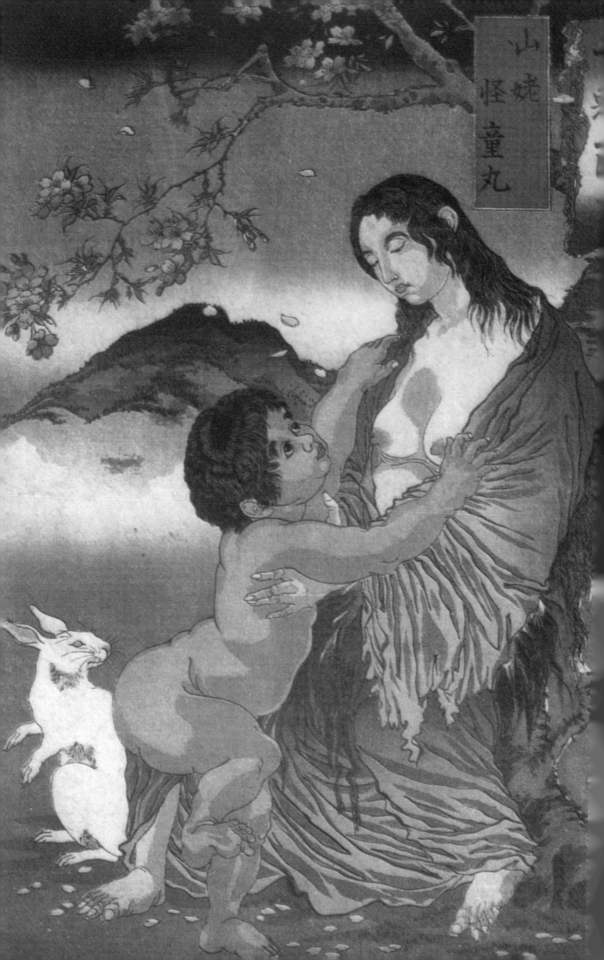

Japan: The First Phase, 1550–1850

The Christian Century

By 1549 several Portuguese ships had visited the shores of Japan, and Portuguese traders had been seen in the streets of Kyōto. In that year the great Jesuit missionary, Francis Xavier, bringing with him a painting of the Annuciation and another of the Virgin and Child, landed at Kagoshima and preached to an audience of feudal lords, or daimyō, who, after two centuries of a rigidly enforced closed-door policy, were avid for foreign contacts and trade. There were no immediate results of Francis Xavier's brief visit—he left in 1552—but by 1568 the Portuguese Jesuits were firmly established in the favour of Shōgun Nobunaga. He and his successors, unable to consort with their vassals on equal terms, welcomed the missionaries as socially acceptable and intellectually stimulating company, and for forty years Christianity prospered under their protection.

But when the Japanese authorities began to observe the rivalry between the Franciscans and the Dominicans and to read the dire lesson of the Spanish conquest of the Philippines, their attitude began to change. By the time Ieyasu became shōgun in 1598, the foreigners were openly quarrelling among themselves and denouncing each other's motives to the government. At the same time, the ruling class was becoming increasingly uneasy about the popular response to the missionaries' teaching that all are equal under God. Within a few years the authorities had decided that any benefit to be derived from foreign trade was not worth the risk of further Western penetration.

When in 1605 Hideteda succeeded to the shōgunate, a brutal persecution was begun. Japanese were forbidden to profess the Christian faith on pain of death, and churches were torn down. Christianity lived on, however, though driven partly underground, and was not wholly suppressed even when, in 1638, Shōgun Iemitsu slaughtered over twenty thousand peasants, many of them Christians, who had rebelled and seized the castle of Shimabara. For our story it is interesting to note that, of the handful of survivors, one was a certain Emonsaku, who had been taught by the Jesuits how to paint in oils.

In 1639 Japan slammed the door to the outside world. Japanese were forbidden to leave the country or to build ocean-going vessels. All foreigners were expelled, except for the Dutch, who were little feared, for their eastward expansion had been confined to the Indies. In 1641 the handful of Dutch traders was herded onto the artificial island of Deshima, forbidden to step beyond it except when the factor paid his annual visit to the shōgun. For the next two hundred years this tiny parcel of reclaimed land in Nagasaki harbour remained Japan's only link with the outside world.

Although the heyday of the Catholic missionaries in Japan was short—the persecution had begun long before in 1638, and the term 'the Christian century' for the period 1542–1638 is somewhat of an exaggeration—it was long enough for the Jesuit seminaries at Nagasaki, Arima, Amakusa and elsewhere to become centres for the copying of European devotional paintings and sculpture. The surviving products of these ateliers have been exhaustively studied. Most of the paintings and images that they turned out were destroyed in the persecution, but enough survived to show how quickly Japanese painters and craftsmen became adept at copying European art.

In about 1561 Queen Catherine of Portugal had sent a painting of the Virgin and Child as a present to Yukinaga, daimyō of Uta, and in the same year another was sent from Portugal to Hirado in Kyūshū. In 1565 Father Luis Froes had Japanese goldsmiths make two retables for his chapel at Sakai near Ōsaka. This is probably the earliest recorded instance of Japanese craftsmen working in the European manner. Not all the originals came from Portugal, however. There is in the Imperial Household Museum, Tōkyō, a painting on copper of the Sacred Face, which had arrived in Japan by 1583 and is a facsimile (without the accessories) of a copy of the well-known work of Quentin Matsys in Antwerp.

As yet there were no European painters to instruct the Japanese, who did the best they could with local materials. But in 1583 the Italian Jesuit, Giovanni Niccolò (or Nicolao; 1560–?), who had been trained in Naples, arrived in Nagasaki from Macao. After two years' illness he established the Academy of St Luke in Nagasaki where he trained young Japanese converts in oil and fresco painting and engraving. In 1587 his principal work was a picture of Christ as

Salvator Mundi, which was sent to the Church in China. Perhaps this is the painting that the great scholar-missionary Matteo Ricci took with him to Peking and presented to the emperor in 1601.

Niccolò had a number of Japanese pupils, among them Fr Leonardo Kimura (1574–1619), who became a painter, engraver and Latinist, and Fr Shiozuka (1577–1616), who was listed as painter, organist and choirmaster at Nagasaki. Shiozuka's Virgin and Child, painted when he was nineteen, drew the favourable notice of Bishop Pedro Martinez on his official visit to the Jesuit college at Arie in 1596. A crucifixion, possibly by Kimura, was thought good enough to be sent to Rome in 1595.

With the arrival of a printing press in 1590, Niccolò began to teach engraving, and a Jesuit father reported in the *Annual Letter* of 1594 that the students in eight of the seminaries were so engaged. He wrote: 'They have already engraved very naturally the pictures coming from Rome, of which many have been printed to the great pleasure and satisfaction of the Christians'. He also remarks that they were so competent that their work was indistinguishable from that of their Jesuit teacher. This was by no means the first, or the last, instance of the eager facility that this island race has shown in copying the latest thing from abroad.

Although the Jesuits summed up Niccolò as 'a man of less than medium intelligence', his influence, until his flight to Macao in 1614, must have been considerable. Not only did he train painters for the large Christian community in Japan, but two of his pupils, Fr Mañoel Pereira (1572–1630) and Fr Jacopo Niva (1579–after 1635), were sent to China, where they were the first artists to instruct Chinese seminarians in European techniques. Of the earliest surviving Chinese works of art that show European influence—four plates in the monograph on ink sticks, *Ch'eng-shih mo-yüan* (1606), discussed on page 000—one is almost certainly copied from an engraving made in Niccolò's atelier after a Flemish original.

After 1638 Christian art was destroyed or went underground. A few specimens survived, touching evidence of the heroism of their owners rather than of the artistic merit of their creators. But secular art that was European in theme or technique may have continued till the middle of the century; indeed, at Nagasaki it never completely died out. This kind of painting the Japanese called *Namban*, the art of the 'Southern Barbarians'—that is, the Portuguese. It was of two kinds. In one kind are Portuguese, and later Dutch, ships, with traders, soldiers and priests, generally depicted as arriving at Nagasaki and mingling with the natives. The foreigners are all immensely tall, with jutting noses, piercing blue eyes and red hair; hence another name for this kind of painting is *kōmō*, 'red-haired', a term applied particularly to the Dutch, and later used, by Chinese as

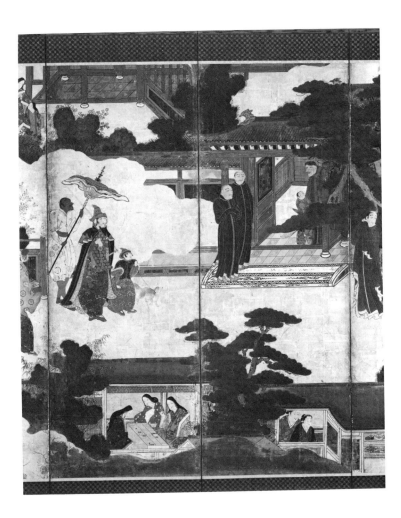

1.
Anonymous. Portuguese and Catholic
Priests. Detail from a *Namban* screen.
Ink, colour and gold on paper. Momoyama period; late sixteenth or early seventeenth century. Asian Art Museum. The
intense curiosity of the Japanese, who
had for so long been starved of foreign
contacts, is shown in this screen, which
combines an attempt at realism with the
Japanese painter's skill as a decorator.

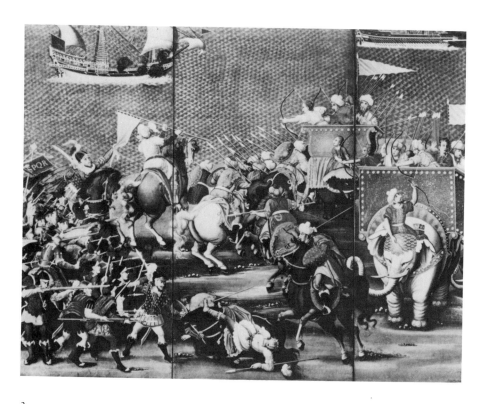

2.

Anonymous. Horsemen at the Battle of Lepanto, 1571. Detail from a *Namban* screen. Ink and colour on paper. Momoyama period; late sixteenth or early seventeenth century. C. Murayama Collection.

The triumph of Catholic Europe over the Moslems at Lepanto (actually a naval engagement) was a theme skillfully used by the missionaries in their propaganda.

well as Japanese, for Europeans in general. These pictures, generally screens (*Namban byōbu,* 'Southern Barbarian screens'), were entirely Japanese in style and technique (Figure 1). Their stylised landscapes, gorgeous colours and gold-leaf backgrounds belong to the tradition of Momoyama period screen painting and owe nothing to European art. The earliest were probably painted in about 1580; the last, forty years later.

Examples of the second type of *Namban byōbu* were copied from European originals. The Jesuits, always eager to impress their hosts with the power and splendour of Europe, brought to Japan engravings of monarchs, battles (the defeat of the Turks at Lepanto is the theme of a famous *Namban* screen [Figure 2]; Henry IV of France on horseback is the theme of another) and scenes of court

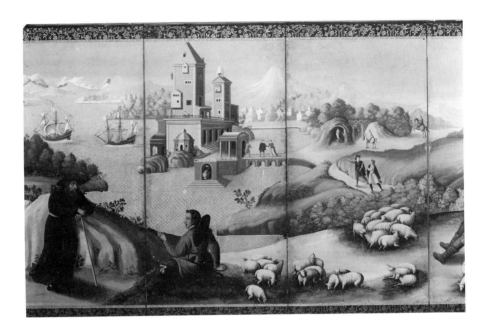

3.

Anonymous. Shepherd and Sheep, with Other Figures. Half of a *Namban* screen. Ink and colour on paper. Late Momoyama or early Edo period; seventeenth century. Kōbe City Museum, Kōbe. Several of these figures, adapted from a print, appear elsewhere with minor changes in this and other *Namban* screens.

and aristocratic life. Among the many sumptuous volumes in the Jesuits' libraries (discussed in more detail in the next chapter) was Ortelius's great atlas of the world, *Teatrum Orbis Terrarum,* published in Antwerp in 1579. The engravings at the back included two depicting the pope and rulers and nobles of the Holy Roman Empire, which were used for figures on several *Namban* screens. Japanese artists were immensely resourceful not only in enlarging the designs from engravings and applying harmonious colours (perhaps taken from devotional oil paintings) but also in making a few figures go a long way: the same courtier or musician might be repeated not only in different screens but also several times with slight variations in the same screen. The artists made discreet use of linear perspective and shading, techniques that they seem to have been reluctant to apply to Japanese subjects. To the more progressive daimyō the *Namban* screens not only provided a sumptuous decoration for their mansions but brought a breath of the outside world to their claustrophobic society.

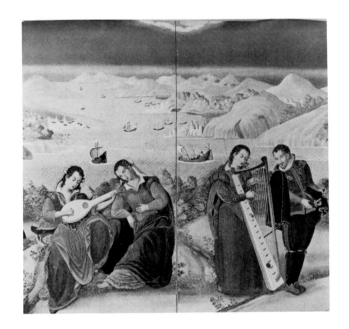

4.

Anonymous. Lutanist and Admirer. Detail of a *Namban* screen of Western social customs. Late Momoyama or early Edo period; early seventeenth century. Hakone Museum, Hakone. The same woman also appears on the companion to the screen in Figure 3 and on an almost identical screen in the Hosokawa Collection. The artist tries to create the texture of oil paint using nut oil as a base with mineral colours.

Although after 1638 the interdiction on Christianity was ruthlessly enforced, some examples of Christian art survived, as has been mentioned above, hidden at great risk by the secret communities of converts. The most remarkable instance must be the painting of the Virgin that hung undetected on the altar of a Buddhist temple in Kyūshū, disguised as the goddess Kannon. Another is the pastoral screen in the Kōbe City Museum that shows a landscape with shepherd and sheep (then unknown in Japan), with, to one side, what looks like a Buddhist monk reading from a book (Figure 3). This is almost certainly a disguised allegory of Christ as the Good Shepherd.

This delightful screen has been attributed to Nobutaka, a Christian painter who had studied under Niccolò at Arima before 1591. Little is known about his career, but several *Namban* screens with European subjects have been ascribed to him, such as the famous fête champêtre in the Hakone Museum, in which young nobles are shown listening to two ladies playing the lute and the harp, with a Flemish-looking village in the background and galleons riding the waters of a broad bay (Figure 4). This can hardly be based on any single European work and was probably concocted from several different engravings.

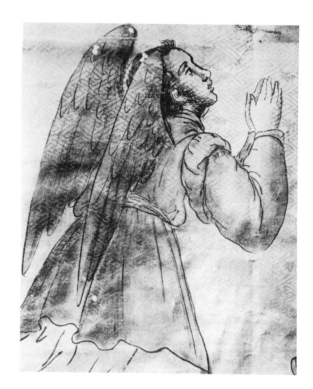

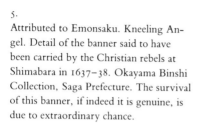

5.
Attributed to Emonsaku. Kneeling Angel. Detail of the banner said to have been carried by the Christian rebels at Shimabara in 1637–38. Okayama Binshi Collection, Saga Prefecture. The survival of this banner, if indeed it is genuine, is due to extraordinary chance.

A fellow pupil with Nobutaka at Niccolò's academy in Arima (where he was known as Justus of Nagasaki) was Yamada Emonsaku, whom we have already encountered as one of the few survivors of the Shimabara massacre in 1638. In 1615 he had entered the service of the Christian daimyō of Shimabara, for whom he painted European-style pictures in oils on a monthly retainer. It is said that Lord Matsudaira, leader of the shōgun's punitive force, spared him because of his well-known talent and took him to Edo, where he put him to work virtually under house arrest. Emonsaku continued to paint in the European manner, though he no longer treated Christian subjects, till the end of his long life in the 1650s.

A few paintings have been tentatively identified as Emonsaku's, the most remarkable, at least as an historical document, being the banner captured at the fall of Shimabara Castle, adorned with two angels adoring the Eucharist and the inscription 'Louvado Seia Sanctissimo o Sacramento' (Figure 5). His painting of the Archangel Michael, probably based on an engraving by the sixteenth-century Flemish artist Jerome Wierix, was hidden for many years by a Christian family in Nagasaki. His most splendid works were the big *Namban* screens, one of which (in the Ikenaga Collection) shows pairs of Christian and Moslem knights in combat: two of the former have been identified by their coats of arms as Antoine de Bourbon (1519–63) and Prince Henry of Navarre. The other screen, in Boston, shows, in six separate panels, a European monarch and members of his court, each standing in an Italian architectural setting.

Had Nobunaga not slammed the door on the West so decisively, art in Japan during the succeeding decades might have taken a very different path. The story of the Nara period, when the arts of T'ang China became virtually the arts of civilised Japan, might well have been repeated, only this time seventeenth-century Japan might have seen the rise of a new school of figure painting in the manner of Rubens and Caravaggio and the Kanō school of landscape painting revolutionised by the impact of Poussin and Claude Lorrain. But after 1640 a new generation of painters grew up who had no contact whatever with European art unless they visited Nagasaki or gained entry to the great castles where the *Namban* screens were kept. Within a short time, what had once been a swiftly flowing stream of Western influence had become a dry riverbed.

While the menace of Western expansion is enough to explain Japan's withdrawal into its fortress, there is another, much more deep-seated factor that helps to account for the recurring pattern in Japanese history of eager acceptance of foreign ideas followed by equally passionate rejection of them. The older major civilisations, all formed at about the same time, were able to lay a deep foundation in philosophy and metaphysics of which the arts became in time one form of expression. Japan, a 'child of the world's old age', as it has been called, inherited no such legacy. The country desperately needed, from time to time, a fresh infusion of ideas and forms for its immense creative energy to work on and a broadening of its comparatively narrow cultural base. At such times, Japan seemed to make a total surrender to foreign influences. Then there followed the inevitable reaction, when these influences were absorbed and sometimes rejected and Japan reasserted and developed its own traditions. The wave of T'ang culture, for instance, was followed by the rise of the native school of painting, *Yamato-e;* the fashion for Sung-style ink landscapes gave way to the glitter of Momoyama screen painting; the sudden impact of European art that we have been describing in this chapter was followed by the rise of the *Ukiyo-e*, the popular art of Edo; and the almost total surrender to Western art in the Meiji period produced a violent reaction and the rise of a 'New National Painting'. Nothing is inevitable in history, but, given the geographical situation of Japan, such a pattern of alternating acceptance and rejection is not difficult to understand. It is, in fact, this dialectical rhythm that gives Japanese art its peculiar power and fascination.

The Eighteenth Century

Not until well after the turn of the eighteenth century did the stream of European art begin to flow once more into Japanese soil—weakly at first, but with a slowly increasing volume until with the Meiji Restoration of 1868 it became a flood that threatened for a few years to engulf the native tradition altogether. In 1720 the total ban on the import of Western books was lifted to allow manuals on science and technology to enter Japan. After a century of seclusion, a door to the outside world seemed suddenly to open. These books were avidly seized upon, their texts haltingly translated and their illustrations copied by many nameless artisans. By the 1770s the contemptuous name *bangaku* (Barbarian studies) had given way to *rangaku* (Dutch studies), which a few farsighted men saw as the way to the regeneration of Japanese culture.

Of this new generation, the earliest Japanese artist to be strongly influenced by European art was Hiraga Gennai (1729–1779 or 1780), a well-known metallurgist, zoologist, potter, novelist and playwright from Shikoku who had been sent by his daimyō to learn the Dutch language and Western science in Deshima. He must have studied oil painting, though the picture most often attributed to him, a copy of a rather dashing portrait of a European woman, is very roughly executed (Figure 6). Very few of his pictures have been identified, and these are of indifferent quality, but he was one of the men chiefly responsible for spreading a knowledge of Western painting in eighteenth-century Japan, especially in the northern city of Akita, which for a time became a centre of 'Dutch' studies.

A more considerable artist was Maruyama Okyo (1735–95). He was embarking on the conventional path as a pupil of a Kanō painter when one day he saw a European peepshow. He was so fascinated by its perspective and illusionism that he began to study Western painting. He became an expert in drawing perspective pictures for peepshows, *megane-e* (eyeglass pictures), and one that he made is preserved, with his camera obscura, in the Namban Museum in Kōbe. He was soon receiving commissions for 'European' landscapes and screens and was probably the first Japanese artist to make life drawings from the nude (Figure 7). That he was also influenced by Shen Nan-p'in, an academic Chinese flower painter who stayed in Nagasaki from 1731 to 1733, is an indication of the indiscriminate enthusiasm with which he, and indeed many of his contemporaries, seized upon any foreign art that was available, no matter where it came from.

Ōkyo's examination of the natural world, inspired by Western science and art, is illustrated by his minutely observed sketches of plants and animals, such as the set of album leaves, now mounted as a handscroll, in the Nishimura

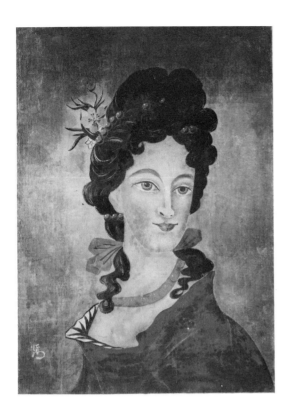

6.
Attributed to Hiraga Gennai (1728–79 or –80). *Young European Woman.* Colour on canvas. Atami Art Museum, Momoyama. This dashing 'portrait' seems to be derived from a copy of a work by an early eighteenth-century French artist, such as J-B. Oudry. It is the only surviving oil painting from Gennai's hand.

7.
Maruyama Ōkyo (1735–95). *Studies of Running Men.* Ink on paper. National Museum, Kyōto. Although these are possibly the first studies of the nude in Far Eastern art that are not erotic, Ōkyo's treatment of the figure is rather perfunctory; he seems more interested in the flow of the drapery over the body.

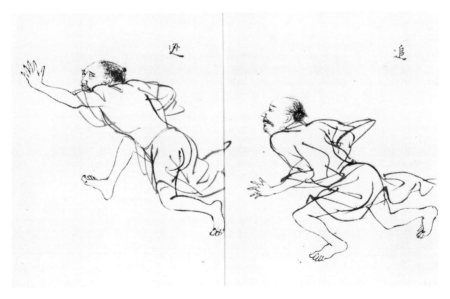

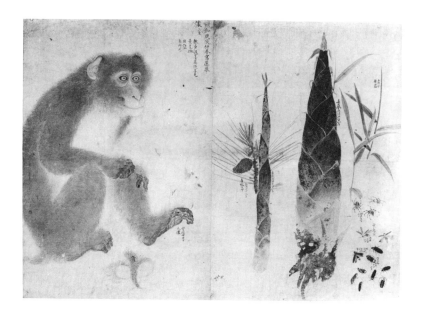

8.

Maruyama Ōkyo (1735–95). Sketches of Animals, Plants and Insects. A page from an album. Ink and colour on paper. National Museum, Tōkyō. The brush technique is Japanese, but Ōkyo's scien- tific interest in nature and the way in which the studies are arranged on the page probably derive from his acquain- tance with European books on botany and natural history.

Collection in Kyōto, in which each creature and plant is carefully labelled after the manner of the European botanical books that he had seen (Figure 8). Ōkyo's triumph was that he was able to exploit his new knowledge of the appearance of things in works on a large scale that were both realistic and decorative in the Japanese way. The most famous of these syncretic paintings is the huge screen, *Pine Trees in the Snow,* in the Mitsui Collection in Tōkyō (Figure 9). Here, per- spective, texture and light and shade are handled in a thoroughly European way, yet the picture as a whole achieves a cool, impersonal decorative splendour that is uniquely Japanese.

One of Hiraga Gennai's best pupils was Shiba Kōkan (1747–1818), who throughout his life was a passionate admirer of Western learning, in the dis- semination of which he saw art as an essential instrument. He had begun his career as a maker of sword hilts and had graduated to forging woodblock prints in the manner of Harunobu. While still a young man, he mastered the Chinese literary style of painting, which the Japanese call *Nanga,* and once gave a daz-

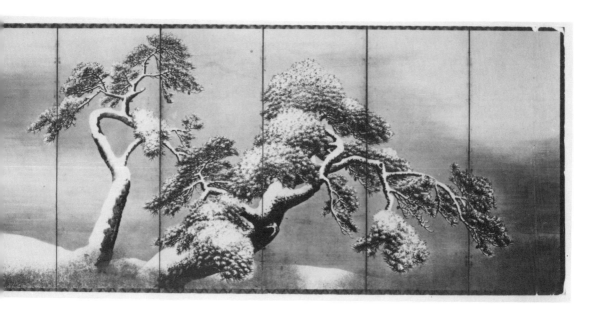

9.
Maruyama Ōkyo (1735–95). Pine Trees in the Snow. One of a pair of folding screens. Ink, colour and gold on paper. Mitsui Collection, Tōkyō. Ōkyo, in this work of about 1785, brilliantly combines the decorative splendour of Kanō screen painting with a restrained westernised drawing and shading.

zling performance of the art, painting for twelve hours without stopping. It was partly his dissatisfaction with the Chinese style as practised in his day that led him to Western art. He was fascinated by European realism and perspective, making in 1784 his own camera obscura, which can still be seen in Kōbe. Before that, he had already learned how to paint in oils.

Shiba Kōkan loved Mount Fuji and longed to paint it, but there was no convention in the Chinese *Nanga* repertory for that famous cone. Why then not use the Japanese style? For Kōkan, there was no such thing. 'Japanese painting', he wrote, 'is derived entirely from China. . . . Nothing whatever has been invented in Japan'. But he also said, 'If one follows only the Chinese orthodox methods of painting, one's picture will not resemble Fuji'. There was only one way out. 'The way to depict Mount Fuji accurately', he declared, 'is by means of Dutch painting'.

In his *Seiyōga Dan* (Discussion of Western Painting), Shiba Kōkan spells out the superiority of Western art. The passage is worth quoting in full because it is

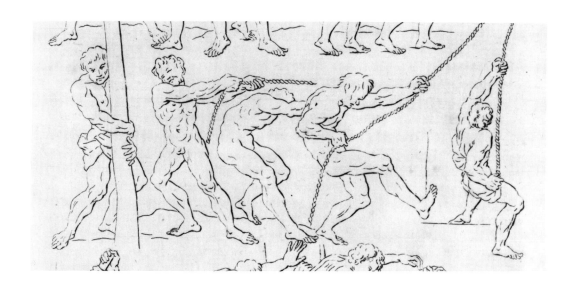

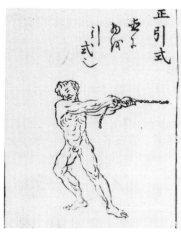

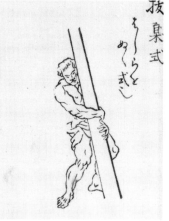

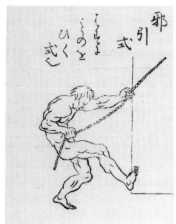

10 (top).
Anonymous. A Page of Figure Studies from the *Groot Schilderboek* of Gérard de Lairesse (1712). Bodleian Library, Oxford. Isaac Tinsingh gave a copy of this widely used manual of art instruction to Shiba Kōkan in about 1780, which he and a number of other Japanese artists studied with intense dedication.

11 (above).
Anonymous. A Page from the *Kōmō Zatsuwa* by Morishima Chūryō (1787). Bodleian Library, Oxford. This shows how faithfully Japanese artists followed their European models. The figure pulling on the rope appears clothed in an oil painting by Shiba Kōkan.

so uncompromising a statement of a position that has been taken by many painters, both Chinese and Japanese, up to the present day:

> A picture that does not represent reality faithfully is not well executed. There is far more to realistic painting than the mere drawing of perspective. Eastern pictures have no accuracy of detail, and without such accuracy, a picture is not really a picture at all. To paint reality is to paint all objects—landscapes, birds, flowers, cows, sheep, trees, rocks or insects—exactly as the original objects appear, thereby actually animating the drawing. No technique other than that of the West can achieve this feeling of reality. When a Western painter looks at the work of an Eastern artist, he must surely see it as the mere playing of a child, hardly worthy of the name 'painting'. But when an Oriental artist, who is used to living with his wretched paintings, has an opportunity to compare his work with the distinctly superior Western art, he stupidly considers the latter merely another school of art, calling it 'perspective painting'. Obviously such categorisation represents an extreme misunderstanding of Western painting.

Kōkan's studies of European painting were spurred on when in about 1784 he discovered a copy of the 1712 edition of Gérard de Lairesse's popular manual on drawing and painting, *Groot Schilderboek,* which he went through with Gennai's help (Figure 10). (The story that it was given to him by the Dutch factor at Deshima, Isaac Titsingh, seems improbable; the dates do not fit.) Some of the illustrations in this manual were published in 1787 in Morishima Chūryō's *Kōmō Zatsuwa* (Miscellaneous Red-hair [i.e., Dutch] Studies) (Figure 11). Just how much Kōkan understood of Western principles of composition, perspective, shading and cast shadows is difficult to tell, for his most famous works in the Western manner, such as the *Barrel Makers* in the Mori Collection (Figure 12), are adapted from Dutch pictures, in this case from another Dutch miscellany, *Iets voor Allen* (Something for Everyone). He liked to sign his paintings horizontally in the Western manner, 'K. Shiba'.

Another 'progressive realist' and pupil of Gennai was Odano Naotake (1749–80), whose landscape with a vase of flowers (Figure 13) is an adroit blend of the kind of landscape that Aōdō Denzen was to make so popular in his etchings and the technique of flower painting that, at about the same time, Giuseppe Castiglione was perfecting at the court of Ch'ien-lung in Peking.

At the middle of the century the Dutch imported several copper plates, but no one knew what to do with them, for the art of engraving had been lost after the closing of the Jesuit Press in 1614. Kōkan obtained, probably from Titsingh, Egbert Buys's *New and Complete Dictionary of the Arts and Sciences* (1769) and studied particularly the parts about engraving. He set to work and in 1783 was able to publish the first print in this medium to appear in Japan after nearly two hundred years. (We illustrate his charming hand-coloured etching of the Serpentine

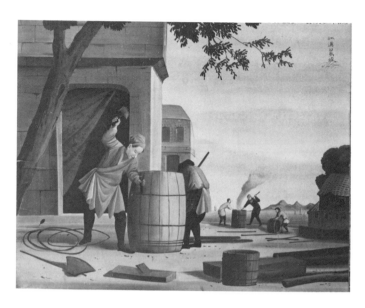

12.

Shiba Kōkan (1747–1818). *Barrel Makers.*
Oil. Mori Collection, Tōkyō. Signed
both 'S–Kokan' and in Chinese characters, this curious painting is adapted from
Abraham van Santa Clara's engraving of
the cooper in *Iets voor Allen* (Something
for Everyone), 1736.

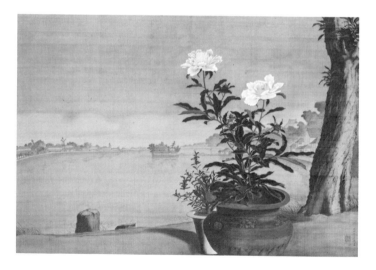

13.

Odano Naotake (1749–80). *Shinobazu
Pond, Edo.* Ink and colour on silk. Museum Yamato Bunkakan, Nara. A number
of painters and printmakers, including
Shiba Kōkan and Tōyōharu, depicted famous beauty spots. Naotake handles a
semiwesternised shading and distance
with great skill.

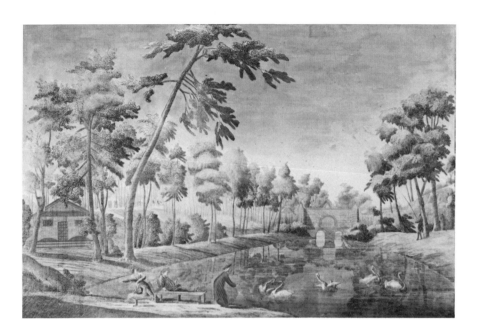

14.
Shiba Kōkan (1747–1818). *The Serpen-*
tine, Hyde Park. Hand-coloured etching.
Municipal Art Museum, Kōbe. A dem-
onstration of Kōkan's skill in handling
reflections in the water, which in the Far
East were attempted only by artists influenced by Western art.

in Hyde Park, adapted from an English print—Figure 14.) Another pioneer was Aōdō Denzen, whose name Aōdō begins with the characters for Asia and Europe. It was given to him by the prime minister, who in 1799 sent him to Nagasaki to learn engraving from the Dutch—although one wonders which of them would have been competent to teach him. He had been a textile designer and liked to make his plates look like pieces of silk with frayed edges (Figure 15).

There is something remarkable in the care these artists devoted to mastering a new and alien art. It is hard to imagine any Chinese or Western artists, apart from mere decorators, doing this. But Japanese painters, even the most prominent of them, were inspired both by an eagerness for anything new and foreign and by a concern for craftsmanship for its own sake. Unlike the Chinese and Europeans, they asked no questions, but humbly met the challenge and did their best. Besides, they lived in an atmosphere of restless curiosity about the world. The newly prosperous and often illiterate urban classes were unmoved by the austere and deeply traditional conventions of the Nō drama, by the Tosa and Kanō schools of painting. They wanted an art that reflected real life. This impulse owed nothing to Western art, but when Western art came, it soon became clear how useful it could be.

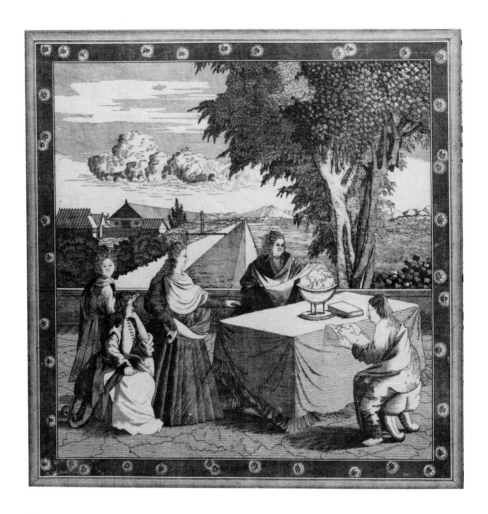

15.
Aōdō Denzen (1748–1822). *The Queen
of Spain Granting an Audience to Columbus*.
Etching. National Museum, Tōkyō.
Denzen is experimenting with effects of
perspective, the rich tapestrylike effect
being aided by the floral border of the
picture drawn on the plate.

European Influence in Nanga *Painting*

The indirect influence of Western realism on the Japanese masters of the Chinese literary style of landscape painting is a remarkable instance of Japanese artistic eclecticism. Japanese painters in the eighteenth century much admired the work of the Chinese gentlemen artists, which they called *Nanga,* (Southern [School] painting). These pictures are often sketchy, sensitive, spontaneous, intimately related to poetry and scholarship and belong to a tradition in which the expression of personal feeling and sensibility means more than the correct representation of nature. Indeed, they are anything but realistic. In the seventeenth century the 'Southern School' of Chinese landscape painting had become the vehicle for political ideals as well, for its scholarly exponents, turning their backs on the corruption of court life and patronage, saw themselves as the heirs of the Confucian scholar-painters of the Yüan dynasty, who had likewise refused to compromise with authority during the Mongol occupation of China.

In the hands of Japanese artists, however, *Nanga* was not always, as it was to the Chinese literati, both an idle pastime and the expression of a whole way of life. They often looked on it as just one more style of painting, which could be learned just as other styles—the Tosa or Kanō, for example—could be learned. So it was not incongruous for a Japanese *Nanga* painter, as it certainly would have been for a Chinese gentleman, to be a student of Western realism as well. Under Western influence these artists, as Kōkan's little treatise shows, had come to realise that the conventional forms of traditional Far Eastern art, however much enlivened by the calligraphic movement of the brush, did not reflect reality. The Chinese literary style was feeding not upon nature but upon itself. Western painting seemed to point the way to the rediscovery of the natural world.

Matsumura Goshun (1752–1811), a follower of the great poet-painter Yōsa Buson, and in his youth a pure *Nanga* painter, became a realist under the influence of his friend Ōkyo. Tani Bunchō (1763–1840), often regarded in Japan as the founder of the 'Chinese style' in Edo, was thoroughly eclectic, although his attempts to marry Chinese brushwork and Western realism were not always very happy. One of his most notable works is a spectacular pair of paintings of flowers in vases (Colour Plate 1), after copies of panels by the Dutch court painter Willem van Royen (1654–1728) which had been given to the shōgun by a Dutch sea captain. Goshun's pupil Watanabe Kazan (1793–1841), working always in the Oriental medium of silk or paper, ink and watercolour, achieved a more successful synthesis. He was a versatile and powerful artist, who saw Western realism not simply as another style of painting but as a means of getting closer

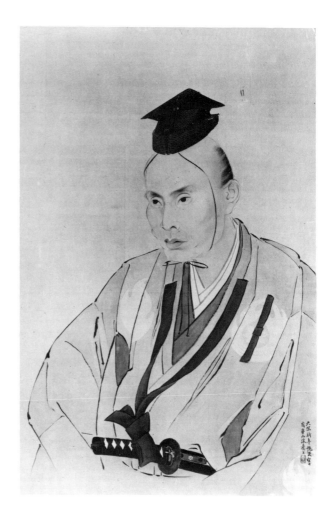

16.
Watanabe Kazan (1793–1841). *Portrait of Takami Senseki* (1785–1858). Ink and colour on silk. National Museum, Tōkyō. This portrait of the scholar, who was exiled for advocating greater intercourse with the West, was painted in 1837 by a follower who was himself later arrested for opposing the shōgun's closed-door policy.

to nature. He was particularly fascinated by the power of Western portrait painting to reveal not only the sitter's features and social role but also the deeper psychological elements of personality, as in his study of Takami Senseki (Figure 16). More than that, Western art was in itself a symbol of the contact with the outside world that an increasing number of Japanese scholars and reformers were working for. Kazan joined the movement of protest against the rigid exclusion laws, was condemned to the 'foreign traitors'' prison, was released under house arrest and committed suicide. His realism, and that of other eclectic artists before the Meiji Restoration, was as much a political gesture as had been the style of the Chinese literati in the seventeenth century. These Japanese painters felt, moreover, that Western realism was a useful tool for the spread of knowledge and education, as the Chinese style could never be. 'Western oil painting', Shiba Kōkan declared, 'is an instrument in the service of the nation'.

Another champion of the spread of Western learning through Western art was Honda Toshiaki, who wrote in his *Tales of the West* (*Seiki Monogatari;* 1798):

> European paintings are executed with great skill, with the intention of having them resemble exactly the objects portrayed so that they will serve some useful function. There are rules of painting that enable one to achieve this effect. The Europeans observe the division of sunlight into light and shade, and also what are called the rules of perspective. For example, if one wants to draw a person's nose from the front, there is no way in Japanese art to represent the central line of the nose. In the European style, shading is used on the side of the nose, and one may thereby perceive its height.

Because the kind of pictures these artists saw were chiefly of a practical kind, they naturally assumed that the sole purpose of Western art was to illustrate and instruct.

Artists such as Ōkyo, Gennai and Goshun were essentially traditional painters who were intrigued by one aspect or another of Western technique. But there were other, on the whole lesser, artists to whom Western subject matter was the most important thing. They clustered in and around the little Dutch settlement at Deshima, where some were servants and interpreters. Their pictures are called *Nagasaki-e*. They translated Dutch books and copied European engravings and maps. Many of their paintings and prints depict the cramped life of the Dutch on Deshima and the annual expedition of the Dutch factor to Edo accompanied by his Indian and Javanese servants and black slaves.

Most of the men who turned out these paintings and prints in such enormous quantities were anonymous craftsmen, but among them were a few whose names are known, such as Araki Genkei (d. 1799), his son, Ishizaki Yushi, who was a skilled oil painter and perspective expert, and Araki Jōgen, born about 1773. Jōgen became an official (that is, Kanō) artist and art connoisseur, but he was also a painter of portraits in oils, an art that he may have learned from the Dutch physician on Deshima, Herman Feilke. The last and perhaps most important of the Nagasaki painters was Kawahara Keiga, whose known works include a portrait of Opperhofd (Factor) Jan Cock Blomhoff and his family, painted in 1818,

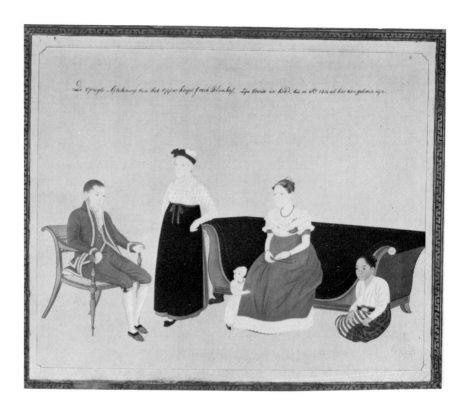

17.

Kawahara Keiga (c. 1786–c. 1860). *The Blomhoff Family*. Free-standing single-panel screen. Colour on silk. Municipal Museum, Kōbe. There are several versions of this picture of the Dutch Factor with his wife, son, nurse and Javanese maid. Keiga's style is cool, detached, more Japanese than Western, reflecting the view of a contemporary, Sato Chū-ryō, that Western women, 'although extremely beautiful, neither talk nor smile'.

of which at least five versions exist (Figure 17). He composed a delightful genre scene called *De Groote Partj,* depicting a grand social gathering at the Dutch Factory, and executed a number of views of Nagasaki harbour thronged with foreign ships. He also drew many original illustrations for von Siebold's *Nippon* (1823–30), notably the flora and fauna japonica section.

The *Nagasaki-e* are a mine of source material on Japan's growing cultural and technological contacts with Europe during the eighteenth and early nineteenth centuries. But few of them are of much artistic merit. The colouring is often crude, and Western techniques such as shading and perspective are adopted for purely utilitarian ends, simply to make the pictures as clear and informative as possible.

Western Influence on the Japanese Colour Print

The Japanese print came into being to record the delights of the theatres and red light district of Edo, a world equally remote from the Dutch at Nagasaki and from the scholar-painters who were using Western art as an instrument of reform. The pioneer printmakers, at least in the early decades after 1680, showed no interest in Western art as such, though they found the new perspective useful for depicting the interiors of teahouses, theatres and brothels. Masanobu claimed, in about 1740, to have been the inventor of these *uki-e,* 'perspective pictures', although they are in many cases careful adaptations from illustrations in Jan Vredeman de Vries's *Perspective* of 1604–5 (Figure 18). Certainly he and Moromasa, the son of a pupil of Moronobu, showed an easy mastery of simple perspective, in which the straight lines of the post and frame construction of a large teahouse not only precisely define the space and the relationships of the figures within the space but also create a striking formal counterpoint to the voluminous rhythmic curves of the figures—a contrast that had already been exploited in earlier Japanese narrative scroll painting. The convincing Western-style perspective of these *uki-e,* moreover, gives a new flavour to the age-old tensions in Japanese art between pictorial depth and two-dimensional pattern making. In the hands of a master such as Moromasa, these conflicting claims are held in subtle balance, for the architectural grid is a semiabstract pattern in itself. Later, when the sense of design was increasingly sacrificed to pictorial realism, this balance was often lost.

Utagawa Tōyōharu (1735–1814) may have been in touch with Kōkan or Gennai or may have known more directly about Western art through a friend in Nagasaki. In any event, the Western flavour in his prints goes beyond perspective, and he was more willing to experiment. Among his adaptations of Western engravings is a curious plate taken from a print of Armenian medicinal herbs, with figures in a Baroque setting on one side and a rather feeble Japanese landscape on the other. A more skilful adaptation is his picture of the Roman Forum (Figure 19), apparently adapted from a print after Pannini.

It was above all in the landscape prints produced after 1780 that Western methods were successfully absorbed. One of the seashore series of prints of Utamaro, poetically entitled *Gifts of the Ebb Tide,* shows people wandering along the beach, searching for shells under an open sky (Figure 20). In this serene landscape, space and depth are fully mastered, and there is little of that tension between two dimensions and three that is so often present in Japanese art. Whether the subordination of decoration to a natural spatial effect is due to Utamaro's study of Chinese art or to his knowledge of Western art, or to both, is hard to say.

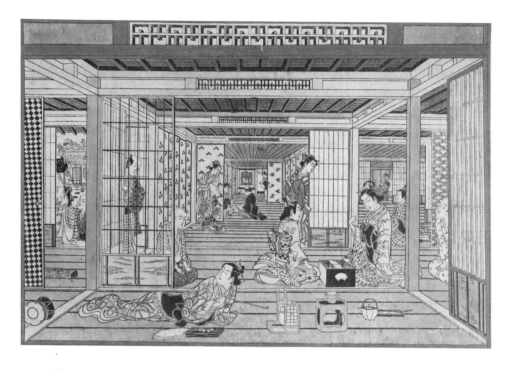

18.

Attributed to Okumura Masanobu (1686–1764). *A Game of Backgammon in the Yoshiwara*. Hand-coloured woodblock print. Hayashi Collection, California Palace of the Legion of Honor, San Francisco. Like other Japanese perspective enthusiasts in the eighteenth century, Masanobu probably learned the art from the study of Jan Vredeman de Vries's *Perspective*.

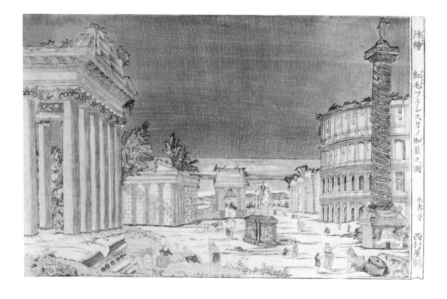

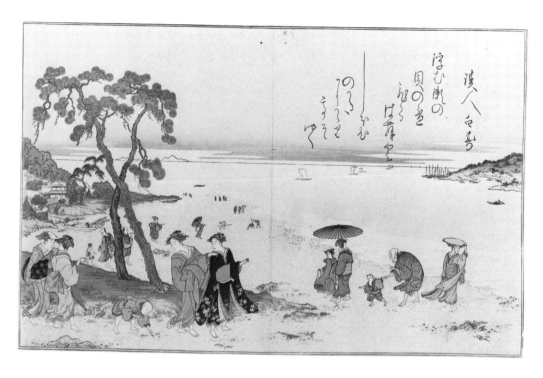

浅人行当
浮む嵐の
貝の音
掬ふ
はれ空
のつ
ちよ
さ子そ
や

20 (above).
Utamaro (1735–1806). *Gathering Shells along the Shore of Shinagawa Bay*. From the *Gifts of the Ebb Tide* series of colour woodblock prints. c. 1790. Arthur B. Duel Collection, Arthur M. Sackler Museum, Cambridge. A Western flavour seldom shows in Utamaro's work, but his handling here of a continuously receding ground line with the figures convincingly diminishing in size may possibly be influenced by Western art.

19 (bottom left).
Utagawa Tōyōharu (1738–1814). *The Roman Forum*. Colour woodblock print. Victoria and Albert Museum. The title to the right refers to a Franciscan church in Holland. Tōyōharu, in making this delightful adaptation from a Western engraving, possibly after Pannini, probably had little idea of what he was depicting.

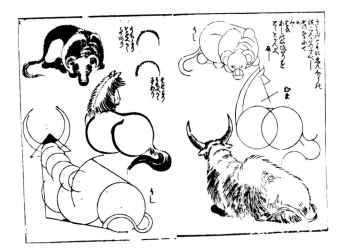

21.
Katsushika Hokusai (1760–1849). A Page
from *Simplified Lessons in Drawing* (*Rya-
kuga Haya Oshi;* 1812). Woodblock reproduction of brush drawing. These
studies are probably inspired by van de
Passe's *Encyclopedia*.

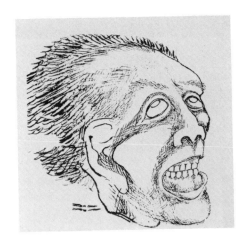

22.
Katsushika Hokusai (1760–1849). *Spectral Face.* Brush drawing. Tikotin Collection, Israel. This drawing is unlike any
other attributed to Hokusai or any of his
contemporaries. It may reflect his constant curiosity about drawing techniques.

Of all the Japanese printmakers, Katsushika Hokusai (1760–1849) seems to
have been the most relentlessly energetic in his search for new material and in his
skill and resource as a draughtsman. One might expect that his curiosity would
have led him into many experiments in Western techniques. He certainly studied
Western paintings and engravings, and in 1812 produced a little manual, *Simplified Lessons in Drawing,* in which he says that lines of designs consist of circles
and squares, a theory that he illustrates with stereometric diagrams and drawings of animals derived from them (Figure 21), after the manner of the section
on drawing in van de Passe's *Encyclopaedia,* which had been circulating in Japan
for some time. He seems to have experimented with oils, for there exists an extraordinary still-life with fishes on a dish, bearing his signature, which antici-
pates Takahashi Yūichi's famous *Salmon* by several decades. Two other experiments in Western techniques attributed to him are the 'spectral faces', one of

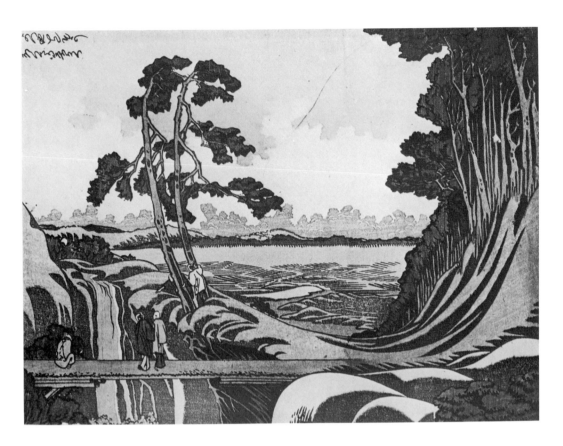

23.
Katsushika Hokusai (1760–1849). *View of Jūnisō in Yotsuya*. Colour woodblock print. National Museum, Tōkyō. One of Hokusai's most satisfying landscapes, brilliantly composed in a manner that echoes the classical compositions of Claude Lorrain and Poussin.

which is obviously an imitation of a Western pen drawing (Figure 22), the other positively Picassoesque in its handling of ink wash.

Hokusai made exaggerated use of Western perspective in his colour prints of the early 1780s, such as the *Fuji from Takahashi,* theatre interiors, and the illustrations to the drama *Chūshingura,* of which Hillier remarks, 'Even the trees with their tall leafless trunks are perfunctorily drawn as if with the trees of the Dutch polders, remembered from the third-rate prints that found their way into Japan, in mind'. The splendid *View of Jūnisō at Yotsuya,* designed in the late 1790s, is perhaps Hokusai's most successful blending of East and West (Figure 23). The composition has the balance and solidity of a Poussin and yet has a swaying rhythmic movement that is purely Oriental. Darker shapes in the foreground provide both depth and chiaroscuro, contributing to the overall design, and Hokusai carries off the daring contrast in texture between formalised landscape and naturalistic sky with great assurance. As if to tease the viewer into thinking that this is a Western landscape, he writes the title and signature sideways in the upper left corner.

In his later work Hokusai moved away from this kind of deliberate synthesis. If he used perspective, as in the first of the famous *Thirty-six Views of Fuji* (about 1822) (Figure 24), in which long receding lines of warehouses along the river lead the eye back to the distant mountain, he did so almost playfully, distorting the perspective and subordinating optical truth to flat decorative pattern-making in colour. It is not the most pleasing of the *Thirty-six Views,* but it restores purely Japanese qualities to the woodcut and represents the triumph of the print designer over the pictorial realist.

Hokusai's passionate 'search for form' shows a kinship with Western art that goes surprisingly deep, yet may not be due to Western influence at all. In the preparatory drawings for some of the prints, such as *The Rape* (Figure 25), he goes over the line again and again in his search for the most telling contour, giving this sheet and the extraordinary *Woman with Octopus* almost the quality of a seventeenth-century Italian drawing. Elsewhere we see him blocking out a figure composition very much in the Western manner. Other Japanese masters of the woodcut did this also, but few of their drawings survived. They too, like Hokusai, must have been concerned primarily with problems of composition in which the design was deliberately worked out, and not preconceived and executed, as in China, in a spontaneous flourish of the brush. In this respect, the methods of the Japanese print designer were closer to Europe than to China, and the question of influence need not necessarily arise.

If Hokusai is the resourceful craftsman, moulding nature to his own ends, borrowing techniques from any source in the interests of greater visual impact and arresting design, Hiroshige (1797–1858) is the lyric poet who seeks to convey the appearance and mood of a scene without undue distortion or technical bravura. His greatest achievement was the *Fifty-three Stages of the Tōkaidō,* produced in 1833 and 1834. Here, Western influence has been so completely absorbed that it never obtrudes, although some of these prints would be impossible to account for without it, notably No. 15, *Mount Fuji from Yoshiwara* (Colour Plate 2). No only are the perspective and foreshortening in this print masterly, but Hiroshige has created a convincing tunnel of enclosed space between the twisted pines that has no precedent in Japanese art. Yet the ultimate effect is unmistakably Japanese. Occasionally, Hiroshige reverts to a cruder Western-style perspective. To the somewhat mechanical recession in the *Night View in Saruwaka-chō* from the *Hundred Famous Views of Edo* published in 1856–58, he adds shadows cast by the full moon overhead. This series, coming at the very end of his life, is among his less inspired works, but the attempt to suggest nocturnal lighting effects foreshadows the night scenes that were to become so popular in the art of the early Meiji period.

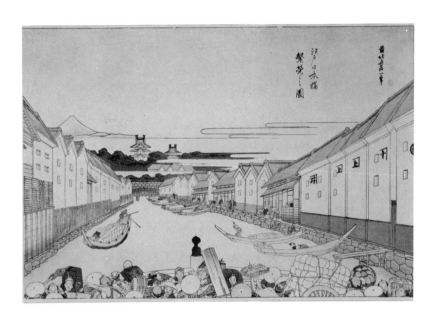

24.
Katsushika Hokusai (1760–1849). *Mount Fuji from Nihonbashi*. From the *Thirty-six Views of Fuji*. Colour woodblock print. c. 1822. Victoria and Albert Museum, London. A successful, if rather tame, exercise in perspective enlivened by the bustling scene on the bridge, which— such is Hokusai's control—is not allowed to disturb the tranquil balance of the scene.

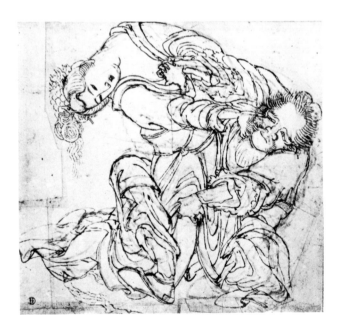

25.
Katsushika Hokusai (1760–1849). *The Rape*. Brush drawing with pentimenti. Collection of John R. Gaines, Lexington, Kentucky. This is a preparatory study for an illustration to the *Himpen Sukio Gaden,* a Japanese version of the epic Chinese novel *Shui-hu-chuan,* published in 1829.

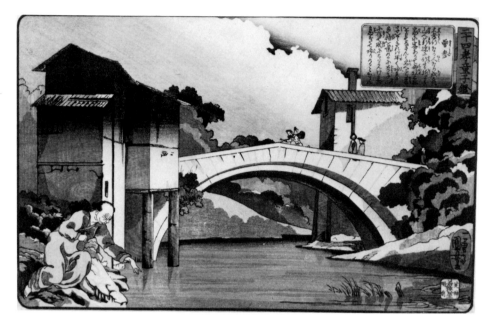

26.

Utagawa Kuniyoshi (1798–1861). *Sōsan Returning to His Mother.* Colour woodblock print. c. 1860. B. W. Robinson Collection, London. Kuniyoshi's setting of the story from the Chinese *Twenty-four Paragons of Filial Piety* in an Italian landscape is a striking illustration of Japanese artists' enthusiasm at this time for European art, no matter how inappropriate to the subject.

The last major printmaker to experiment with Western techniques before the Meiji Restoration flooded Japan with European art was Utagawa Kuniyoshi (1798–1861). Not only did he master perspective, but he also went so far as to take Western pictures as models for subjects drawn from classical Chinese literature. Several of his illustrations for the Chinese *Twenty-four Paragons of Filial Piety* show the result of this extraordinary marriage. The story of Sōsan (Tseng Shen) returning to his mother is set in a conventional Italianate landscape (Figure 26), while the print of the paragon Yü Ch'ien-lou galloping back to his sick father is obviously based on a picture of St George, minus his dragon. To call Kuniyoshi an eclectic is hardly explanation enough. It seems that by the 1840s the hackneyed old Chinese themes could no longer inspire: it was Western art, fresh and exciting, with its hint of a new era about to dawn for Japan, that provided the stimulus. Western art could even give a new glamour to popular Japanese themes. When in 1873 Kuniyoshi's pupil Yoshitoshi Taisō (1839–92) illustrated the story of the mountain woman Yama-uba and her son, the wild Kintarō, his inspiration was clearly a picture of the Virgin and Child (Figure 27).

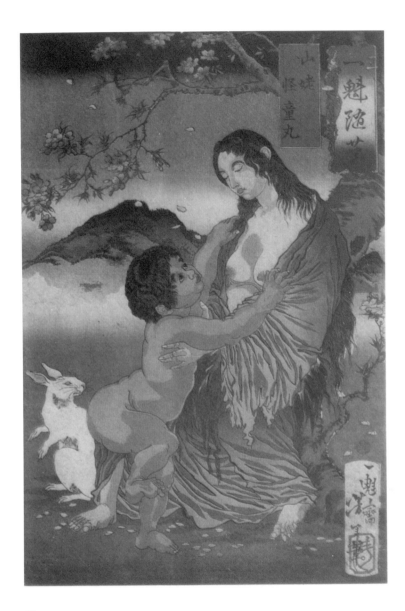

27.
Yoshitoshi Taisō (1839–92). *Yama-uba and Kintarō*. Colour woodblock print. 1873. Achenbach Foundation for Graphic Arts, San Francisco. Another example of the choice of a European model to illustrate a Far Eastern theme. The Virgin and Child are hardly suitable for depicting the wild 'Mountain Mother' and the orphan child of a Minamoto general whom she reared to be a hero, but the result is a bold and effective design.

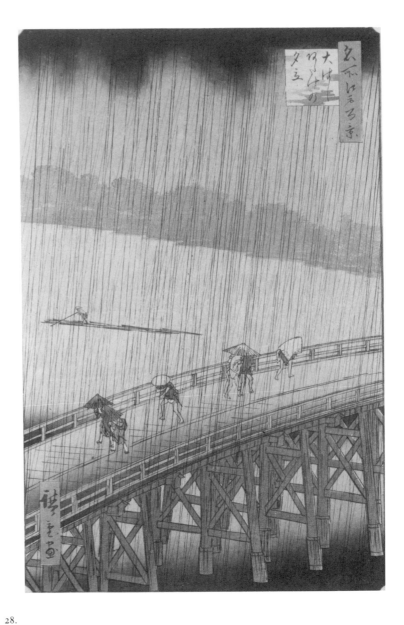

28.
Andō Hiroshige (1797–1858). *Sudden Shower at the Great Bridge at Atake*. From the *Hundred Famous Views of Edo*. Colour woodblock print. 1856–58. British Museum, London. An important print not only because it shows how Hiroshige absorbed Western perspective and atmospheric realism, but also because it was to be copied by van Gogh in oils thirty years later (see Figure 150).

The result is an effective marriage of Western solidity and flat Japanese pattern making.

With the death of Hiroshige and Kuniyoshi the classical 'art of the floating world', *Ukiyo-e,* came to an end. But before they died, their world had already begun to change. In 1854 Commodore Perry returned to Edo to sign with the shōgun the treaty that was to throw open the doors of Japan to the outside world. Is this change reflected also in Hiroshige's later prints, and if so, did photography play any part in it? The painter Sakurada Kinnosuke, who has been called 'the father of Japanese photography', is thought to have taken up that art after seeing a daguerreotype for the first time in 1844. It has been suggested that the influence of photography may be seen in some of Hiroshige's *Hundred Famous Views of Edo,* published in 1856–58. If so, it is hard so discern, and the series as a whole represents a sad falling-off from his earlier work. The designs are mostly uninteresting, the colours crude. The series is chiefly important because it was late, and on the whole bad, prints such as these that were to profoundly influence the Impressionists. Whistler's *Falling Rocket* was inspired by Hiroshige's *Fireworks at Ryōgoku;* van Gogh was to make a careful copy in oils of the *Sudden Shower at Atake* (Figure 28); Gauguin's *Puppies Feeding* is clearly derived from a composition by Kuniyoshi. It is ironic that only with its dying gasp did the traditional Japanese print begin to influence European art.

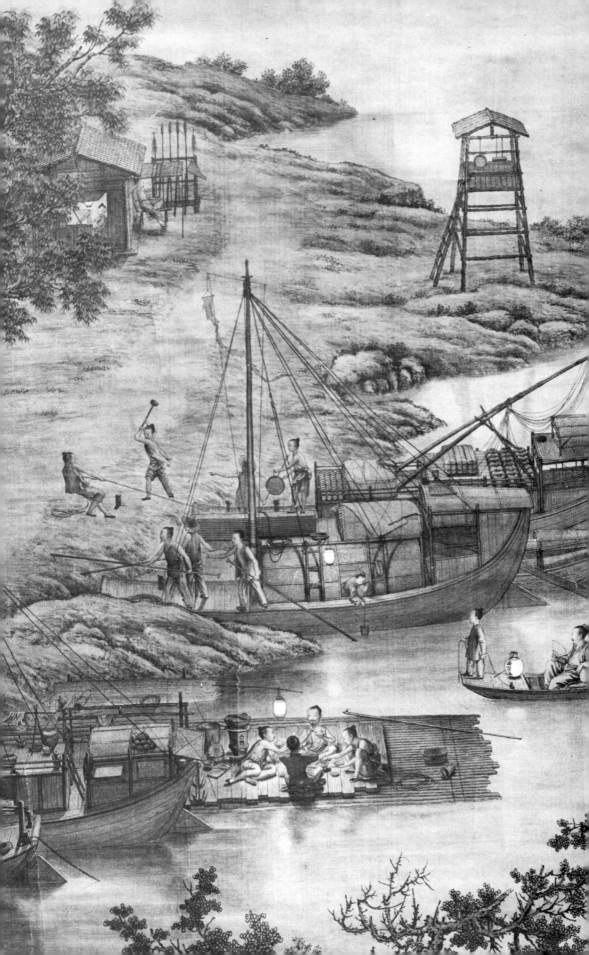

China and European Art, 1600–1800

The Seventeenth Century

The Jesuits formed the spearhead of European cultural penetration of China, as they did of Japan. Their pictures, prints and books produced the first signs of European influence in Chinese painting, and their writings in turn brought seventeenth-century Europe the first detailed account of the arts of China. But long before the Jesuits appeared on the scene, foreign travellers had gazed in admiring incomprehension at Chinese paintings. An Arab merchant who visited China in the ninth century had reported that 'the Chinese may be counted among those of God's creatures to whom He hath granted, in the highest degree, skill of hand in drawing and in the arts of manufacture'.

Marco Polo, in the service of Kublai Khan in the last decades of the thirteenth century, had plenty of opportunities to see Chinese paintings, but he mentions only the gaudy decorations in the imperial palaces. In the palace at Khanbalik (Peking), for instance, 'the walls and chambers are all covered with gold and silver and decorated with pictures of dragons and birds and horsemen and various breeds of beasts and scenes of battle'. He found similar paintings in a hall of the former Sung imperial palace at Hangchow, and, in P'ing-yang-fu in Shansi, he came upon a castle whose hall was decorated 'with admirably painted portraits of all the kings who ruled over this province in former times'. Beyond this he has nothing to say about Chinese art.

Fifty years later Ibn Baṭṭūṭa, 'the Traveller', was much more enthusiastic. 'The people of China of all mankind', he wrote, 'have the greatest skill and taste in the arts. This is a fact generally admitted; it has been remarked in books by many authors and has been much dwelt upon. As regards painting, indeed, no nation, whether of Christians or others, can come up to the Chinese, and their talent for art is something extraordinary'. After this, it is a little disappointing to find that what Ibn Baṭṭūṭa admired so much was not the towering landscapes of the literati, which he obviously never saw and would not have understood in any case, but the skill in catching a likeness shown by those professional painters at frontier stations whose job it was to record the features of strangers entering and travelling about the country.

We hear nothing more of Chinese art until the arrival of the Jesuits. By 1557 they were established in the Portuguese colony of Macao, more open and accessible to foreigners than Deshima, but even more remote from the capital. Soon their influence and that of their Dominican and Franciscan competitors spread to Canton and beyond.

But our story properly begins with the arrival in Macao in 1592 of the great scholar and missionary Matteo Ricci. Born in Ancona in 1552, Ricci entered the Jesuit order in 1571 at the age of nineteen and left Genoa for the Far East six years later. This priest of formidable learning, energy and presence was destined by his scholarship and writings to engage the interest of Chinese intellectuals in European culture, and that of European scholars in Chinese culture, as did no other man in this momentous era of mutual awakening.

Ricci remained in Macao and Kwangtung until 1595, when he headed north. An invitation from an official to come to Peking to work on correcting the official Chinese calendar brought him to the gates of the city, where he waited for two months before returning to Nanking; he did not try again until the spring of 1600. Meantime, he had not been idle. During the years of waiting he had consolidated the missions in Nan-ch'ang, and in Nanking, which during the next fifty years was to become the centre of the one school of Chinese scholarly landscape painting that seems to show unmistakable signs of European influence.

On his way northwards in 1600 Ricci paid his respects to the viceroy of Shantung at Tsining, to whom he showed a painting of the Virgin and Child with St. John the Baptist that he was taking to the emperor. The viceroy's wife liked it so much that Ricci gave her a copy painted by a young man of their mission in Nanking—but who this painter was is a mystery.

Ricci arrived in Peking in midwinter, and on 25 January 1601 was received in audience by the Wan-li emperor.[1] Ricci had only nine more years to live, but in this brief time he laid the foundation for nearly two hundred years of Jesuit

---

1 In fact, Wan-li had long given up receiving foreign visitors, and Ricci was reduced to prostrating himself to an empty throne.

presence at the Chinese court. His reputation seems to have preceded him to Peking, for very soon he numbered among his friends many leading intellectuals, some of whom—men of the calibre of Hsü Kuang-ch'i, Li Chih-tsao and Yang T'ing-yün—became converts. They must have shown him pictures in their collections, for he has a paragraph on Chinese painting in his wonderful account of China, which until recently was known only in Father Trigault's heavily edited Latin version. It is not very complimentary. 'The Chinese use pictures extensively', he wrote, 'even in the crafts, but in the production of these and especially in the making of statuary and cast images they have not at all acquired the skill of Europeans. They know nothing of the art of painting in oil or of the use of perspective in their pictures, with the result that their productions are lacking any vitality'. Evidently the paintings and engravings that Ricci brought with him were already being copied, for he goes on, 'I am of the opinion that the Chinese possess the ingenious trait of preferring that which comes from without to that which they possess themselves, once they realise the superior quality of the foreign product'. Here, for once, he was wrong.

He must have been gratified, though hardly surprised, at the intense interest that his own works of art aroused among the gentry. He had with him engravings of Venice, devotional pictures sent from Rome and the Philippines, and a large altarpiece by Giovanni Niccolò, the painter-priest 'of less than medium intelligence' whose academies at Nagasaki and Arima were the training ground for Japanese icon painters. Of one of these pictures—very probably a copy of the sixth-century *Virgin of St Luke* in the church of Santa Maria Maggiore, Rome—the scholar Chiang Shao-shu wrote in the brief section on Western painting in his *History of Silent Poetry* (*Wu-sheng shih-shih;* 1720): 'Li Ma-tu [Matteo Ricci] brought with him an image of the Lord of Heaven in the manner of the Western countries; it is a woman bearing a child in her arms. The eyebrows and the eyes, the folds of the garments, are as clear as if they were reflected in a mirror, and they seem to move freely. It is of a majesty and elegance which the Chinese painters cannot match'.

The first recorded Chinese copies of European paintings had been made in Peking for the Italian priest Jean de Monte Corvino, who visited China early in the fourteenth century. The next instance occurred three hundred years later, when Ricci presented to the emperor an engraving of souls in purgatory, including the pope, a duke and an emperor, because Wan-li wanted to know how such dignitaries dressed in Europe. Ricci accompanied the engraving with a description, but as the detail was too fine, the emperor had his court artists paint an enlarged version in colour, under Ricci's supervision.

Not until Ricci had been two years in Peking did he have a resident painter of his own attached to the mission. In 1602 Jacopo Niva, son of a Japanese father and a Chinese mother, arrived from Japan, where he had been a pupil of Niccolò. In 1604 Niva made a copy of the *Virgin of St Luke* for the high altar of the church in Peking, and in 1606 was decorating the new church in Macao. In the capital he worked in secret with only two Chinese Christian helpers, because he was afraid that if his skill became known, he would have to spend all his time painting for the emperor and high officials, a fate that did indeed befall the Jesuit artists in Peking a century later. In 1610 Niva was sent to decorate a church in Nan-ch'ang, and in the following year he executed the wall paintings for the Buddhist temple that the emperor had given as a tomb for Ricci. Ricci had noted that the Chinese were amazed at Niva's pictures, which seemed to them more like sculpture than painting. Alas, the churches that he decorated were all rebuilt or destroyed, and not a scrap of his work survives.

The Chinese artist Yü Wen-hui, whom the Portuguese christened Mañoel Pereira, had been sent to study Western painting under Niccolò in Japan. He returned to Peking where, between 1605 and 1607, he completed his novitiate under Ricci and possibly painted his portrait of the great missionary (Colour Plate 3). Yü Wen-hui later went to continue his painting studies under Niccolò, who had fled to Macao in the face of the growing anti-Christian feeling in Japan. Yü's portrait of Ricci eventually found its way to the Jesuit residence in Rome, where it can still be seen today—no masterpiece certainly, but important because it is probably the earliest documented painting by a known Chinese artist working in the European manner.

Among Ricci's presents to the Wan-li emperor was Ortelius's great folio atlas of the world, *Teatrum Orbis Terrarum,* published by the Plantin Press in 1579, which included five large engravings: two of the pope and nobles of the Holy Roman Empire, a view of Daphne in Greece, another of the Vale of Tempe and one of the Escurial. We know that this book must have reached Japan as well, for the figure subjects appear from time to time, cleverly adapted and varied, in *Namban* screens.

Far more richly illustrated was the six-volume work on the cities and towns of the world, Braun and Hogenberg's *Civitates Orbis Terrarum,* published in Cologne between 1572 and 1616, of which several volumes had by this time reached Peking (Figure 29). Ricci had written home of the importance of such books to impress the Chinese officials with the splendours of Western civilisation. When he was staying near Canton ten years before, he had noticed how visitors to the mission were especially attracted by the books on cosmology and architecture. Braun and Hogenberg filled the bill admirably. The Jesuit Father

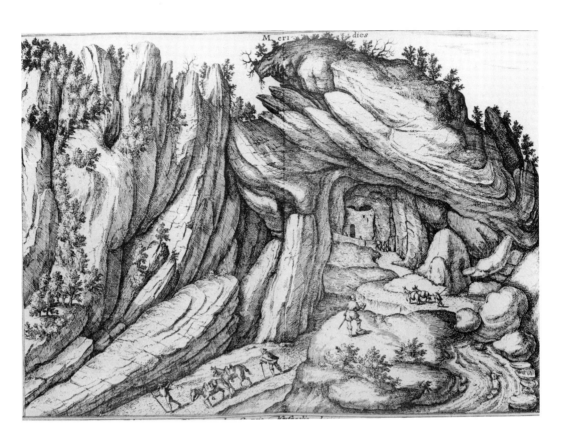

29.

Braun and Hogenberg. Mount St.
Adrian. Engraving from *Civitates Orbis
Terrarum* (Cologne, 1572–1616). The
fantastically distorted rocks in this print
could have stimulated the distortions of
classical landscape styles practised about
1600–1610 by Chinese professional
painters such as Wu Pin.

Longobardi was even more imaginative in his requests; when Father Trigault went on his European tour to gather support and material for the China mission, Longobardi asked him to bring back a bird of paradise, a lion and a rhinoceros.

In view of the curiosity about Western perspective that was later to be shown at the Chinese court, it is interesting to note that the Jesuit library in Peking contained a number of books on architecture published before 1600 that could well have reached the mission in Ricci's day or shortly after. One copy of Palladio was brought back by Trigault in 1616; there were three copies of Vitruvius and one of Giovanni Rusconi's *Della Archittetura,* published in Venice in 1590. Ricci also asked for books on ancient Rome—evidently not in vain, for the library also contained a copy of Théodore de Bry's *Topographia Urbis Romae* (Frankfurt, 1597) in three volumes, illustrated with engravings of the city from its beginnings, showing streets, public baths, monuments, sarcophagi and inscriptions.

We may well wonder what possible value such books had in late Ming China or in forwarding the spiritual aims of the mission. But from the start the Jesuits had visions of building new Renaissance cities in China, such as they were creating in Mexico, South America and the Philippines. Indeed, flushed with their first extraordinary success in Peking, they could look forward to the time, not too many decades hence, when China would be a Christian country, its emperor himself a convert and its cities crowned with magnificent Baroque churches decorated by Chinese followers of Rubens and Bernini.

While the oil paintings brought by the Jesuits were greatly admired, the illustrated books and engravings were probably more influential in the long run, for they were more widely circulated and could much more easily be copied or adapted by Chinese wood-engravers. In 1598 Father Longobardi had written to Rome for devotional books by Father Nadal. 'Particularly to help illiterates', he added, 'it would be especially valuable if you could send me some books which represent the figures of the faith, the commandments, the mortal sins, the sacraments and so on. Here all such books are considered very artistic and subtle because they make use of shadows, which do not exist in Chinese painting'.

In 1605 there arrived in Nanking a copy of Nadal's life of Christ, *Evangelicae Historiae Imagines,* published by Plantin in Antwerp in 1593 with 153 engravings, chiefly by the Wierix brothers and Adrien Collaert, after paintings by Bernardino Passeri and Martin de Vos (Figure 30). Ricci at once wrote for a copy for the Peking mission. These exquisite engravings, in which successive events in the life of Christ are illustrated in detail with masterly perspective and a dramatic

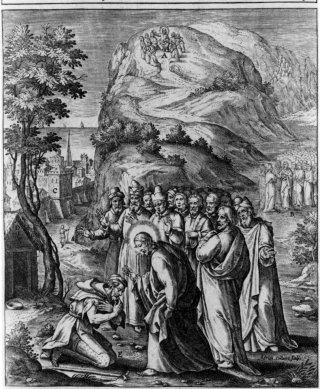

DOMINICA III. POST EPIPHANIAM.
Mundatur Leprosus. 26
Matth. viij. Marc. i. Luc. v. Anno xxxi. xij

A. *Thabor mons, vbi Christus Apostolos docuerat.*
B. *Locus campestris ad montis radicem.*
C. *Capharnaum, quo iter habebat IESVS.*
D. *Domuncula leprosi extra Capharnaum.*
E. *Leprosus adorans Christum sanatur.*
F. *Leprosus Hierosolymam iussus proficiscitur.*

30.
Adrien Collaert. *Mundatur Leprosus* (Healing the Leper). Engraving from Nadal's life of Christ, *Evangelicae Historiae Imagines* (1593). Bodleian Library, Oxford. Chinese artists were impressed by the drama and chiaroscuro of these biblical engravings, and several landscape painters, including Chang Hung, borrowed the device of the hill with a path winding up to a group of figures seated on the summit.

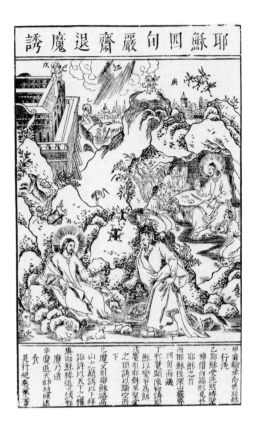

31.
A Page from the *T'ien-chu chiang-sheng yen-hsing chi-hsiang,* Showing Three Scenes from the Temptations in the Wilderness. Wood engraving, published in Foochow in 1635–37. Bodleian Library, Oxford. The scene upper right is adapted from the plate in Nadal (Figure 32).

use of chiaroscuro, must have made a profound impression (Figures 31 and 32). The simpler European paintings too aroused admiration, even at second hand, and Ricci tells of presenting to a mandarin a copy of Aesop's *Fables,* probably engraved in Japan by students of Niccolò, which the gentleman treasured 'as if it were a masterpiece of Flemish printing'.

The big volumes in which the cities and landscape of Europe are spread across a double folio page, such as Braun and Hogenberg's *Civitates Orbis Terrarum,* achieved another effect that Ricci does not mention and certainly would not have thought important. There are features in the style of some seventeenth-century Chinese landscape painters that can be explained only by supposing that they had seen some of these engravings. I will have more to say about this later.

Only in two or three cases can we be sure that the painter actually knew the Jesuits personally. In 1597 the landscapist and critic Li Jih-hua (1565–1635) wrote a rather extravagant ode to Ricci; ten years later in Peking the painter

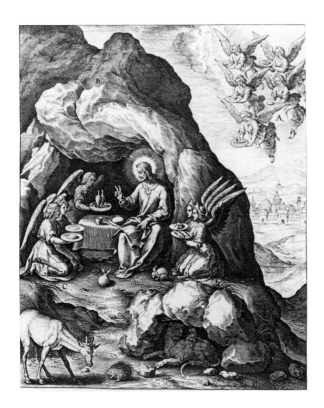

32.
Nadal. *Evangelicae Historiae Imagines* (1593). The engraving that is included in the Chinese woodcut in Figure 31. Bodleian Library, Oxford. The Chinese life of Christ in many instances combines several plates from Nadal in a single illustration, no doubt in the interests of economy.

Chang Jui-t'u was one of a stream of gentlemen who called on the great Jesuit. Ricci gave him a Chinese translation of his essay on friendship, *De Amicitia*. Did Ricci know the great landscape painter and theorist Tung Ch'i-ch'ang? Arthur Waley thought he had found a connection between them, which has not been substantiated, and a set of very bad paintings of Christian subjects that Berthold Laufer found many years ago in Sian bear Tung's most improbable signature. If they ever did meet, it would have been through Tung's associates in the Tung-lin Society, a movement dedicated to the reform of the Ming administration. Several of its most prominent members were Christians and close to Ricci. Such an encounter between the great Jesuit and the most formidable scholar, painter and critic of his day, if in fact it ever took place, would have been a summit meeting indeed.

Some of the topographical landscapes by Chang Hung (1557–after 1652), a Soochow painter famous in his day but about whose career very little is

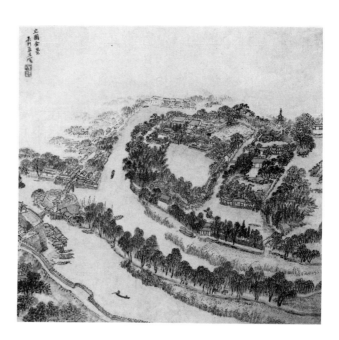

33.
Chang Hung (1577–after 1652). Whole
View of the Chih Garden. Album leaf.
Ink and slight colour on paper. Dr.
Franco Vannotti Collection, Lugano.
How Chang Hung came to see books
such as Braun and Hogenberg, who illus-
trate a strikingly similar aerial view of
Frankfurt, has not been established, but
that he did see it, or something very
similar, seems beyond question.

known, contain elements clearly derived from the study of Western landscapes.
Most notable in this respect are his *Night Ascent of Hua Tzu Hill,* a handscroll of
1625, dominated by a long path winding up the flat slope of the hill on which
three men are standing—a device borrowed from a plate in Nadal's *Evangelicae
Historiae Imagines*—while his *Whole View of the Chih Garden* (Figure 33), an astonishing aerial perspective, would have been impossible for a Chinese artist
who had not seen an engraving such as Braun and Hogenberg's bird's-eye view
of Frankfurt (Figure 34).

There is no evidence that Chang Hung was in direct touch with the Jesuits,
but that he must have seen some of their books seems undeniable. In another
album that uses similar devices, Chang Hung says he is 'relying on my eyes' and
'depicting what I saw', suggesting that he is not taking the conventional Chinese
approach. It is indeed in topographical views of famous scenic spots such as
those done for the tourist that Western techniques would have come in most
handy.

Towards the end of 1605 the scholar and bibliophile Ch'eng Ta-yü came to
Peking from Anhui with a letter of introduction to Ricci from the viceroy of
Nanking, especially to ask him for some specimens of writing to include in a

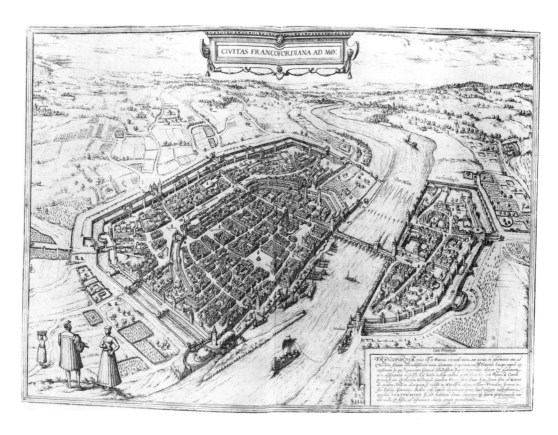

34.
Anonymous. View of Frankfurt. Engraving from Braun and Hogenberg, *Civitates Orbis Terrarum* (Cologne, 1572–1616).
This volume was already in China in 1608.

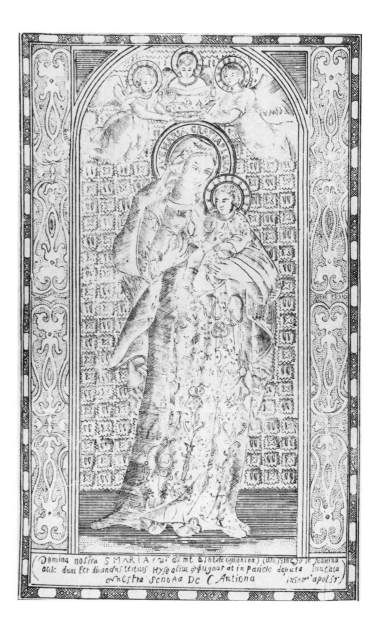

35.

Anonymous. *Nuestra Señora de l'Antigua.*
Chinese woodcut copy after a Japanese
engraving based on a print by Wierix of
the painting in the Cathedral of Seville.
Percival David Foundation, London. The
engraving was given by Matteo Ricci to
Ch'eng Ta-yü, who included it in his collection of designs for ink cakes, *Ch'eng-
shih mo-yüan* (1606).

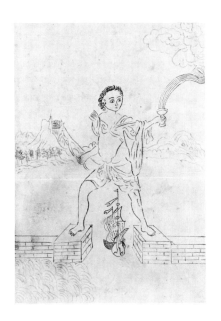

36.
Unknown Chinese artist. *The Colossus of Rhodes*. Brush drawing. Early seventeenth century. Library of Congress, Washington, D.C. Heemskerck's engravings of the Seven Wonders of the World were copied in many Chinese and Japanese works, including Father Aleni's *K'un-yü t'u-shuo,* from which the Chinese artist probably made this sketch.

miscellany he was compiling. Ricci obliged, giving him, among other things, four engravings; these included one of the destruction of Sodom by Crispin van de Passe, one of Christ on the way to Emmaus from Nadal and—an intriguing instance of the peregrinations of a masterpiece—an engraving made in 1597 in Niccolò's academy in Arima after a plate by Jan Wierix, taken from the painting of Nuestra Señora de l'Antigua in Seville. These all appear, somewhat transformed, in *Mr. Ch'eng's Ink Remains* (*Ch'eng-shih mo-yüan*) of 1606, which has the added distinction of being one of the first books ever produced with woodblock illustrations—although not the biblical ones—in full colour (Figure 35).

By now interest in the value of European art in Christian propaganda was lively enough for Father Sambiaso to publish, in 1649, a little monograph in Chinese, *Hua ta* (literally, Answers about Painting, known by its title in French as *Réponses sur la peinture allégorique*), with a preface by Ricci's friend and collaborator Li Chih-tsao. When in about 1672 Father Verbiest brought out a large map of the world, Father Aleni accompanied it with a two-volume work of cosmography, *K'un-yü t'u-shuo,* which contained engravings of animals real and imaginary and of the Seven Wonders of the World and the Colosseum, the latter derived from the plates engraved by Heemskerck in about 1580. The Seven Wonders were to appear again and again in Chinese illustrated books (Figure 36) and eventually found their way, as did some of the Wierix engravings, into the decoration of early Ch'ing porcelain.

The idea of plasticity, of the rendering of three-dimensional objects as solid forms occupying space—rather than the rendering of space itself—was always foreign to Chinese art. Arbitrary shading and 'painting in relief' as the Chinese critics called it, had been introduced with Buddhist art a thousand years earlier and had been admired and imitated in some quarters, but these were always looked on as foreign techniques, appropriate to foreign subjects, and faded away as Buddhism lost its hold. Now perspective and chiaroscuro aroused the same curiosity. In 1729 Nien Hsi-yao, commissioner of customs and an expert on Western mathematics, enlisted the help of the Italian Jesuit missionary Giuseppe Castiglione (of whom more later) to produce a volume of plates with commentary adapted from the *Perspectiva Pictorum et Architectorum* of Andrea Pozzo, the Jesuit painter whose most spectacular achievement had been the decoration of the ceiling of the church of St Ignazio in Rome with a vast allegory of Jesuit work in the four continents (Figures 37 and 38).

In the meantime, Father Buglio instructed court painters in the art. Du Halde records that 'he exhibited copies of these drawings in the Jesuits' garden in Peking. Driven by curiosity, the Mandarins came to see them, and were amazed. They could not imagine how one could, on a single sheet, represent the halls, galleries, gateways, roads and alleyways so convincingly that at first glance the eye was deceived' into thinking them real. So fascinated was the emperor K'ang-hsi by this new art that he asked the Jesuits to send out, with enamellers (another foreign technique for which he had a passion), an expert in perspective.

The mission chose Giovanni Gherardini, a native of Bologna who had worked there and in Modena before he was summoned in 1684 to Nevers, where he decorated the Jesuit church of St Pierre. He then moved on to Paris where he painted frescoes—strong in perspective, it was said, but weak in colour—for the library of the Jesuit headquarters (now the Lycée Charlemagne). In March 1698 he set sail for China with Father Bouvet and seven other Jesuits on the famous voyage of the *Amphitrite* (see page 99). Arriving in Peking in February 1700, he decorated the new Jesuit church with illusionistic frescoes, including a 'dome' on the ceiling, which amazed Chinese visitors, and gave instruction in perspective and oil painting to students in the palace. Eleven years later Father Ripa met seven or eight of Gherardini's pupils and watched them painting Chinese landscapes, in oils, on tough Korean paper. Gherardini, a layman, had evidently found the Jesuit discipline too much for him. By 1704 he was back in Europe, and the sole relic of his journey is his frivolous and highly implausible *Relation du voyage fait à la Chine,* which the connoisseur and engraver Mariette dismissed, in his *Abécédario,* as 'un badinage continuel'.

In an appendix to his biography of the academic painter Chiao Ping-chen in the *History of Silent Poetry,* Chiang Shao-shu puts into the mouth of Ricci a little lecture on Western art, emphasising its effects of relief and chiaroscuro. Chiang

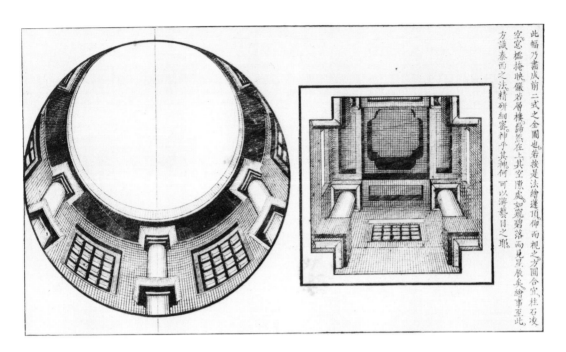

37.
Anonymous. How to Set Out a Cupola
from Below. An illustration from Nien
Hsi-yao (d. 1738), *Shih-hsüeh* (revised
edition, 1735), prepared with the help
of Giuseppe Castiglione (1688–1766).
Bodleian Library, Oxford.

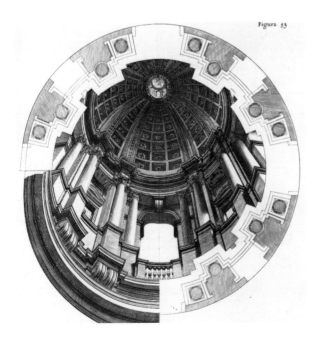

Figura 53

38.
Andrea Pozzo (1642–1709). How to Set
Out a Cupola from Below. From the *Perspectiva Pictorum et Architectorum* (1693
edition). Bodleian Library, Oxford. In
his manual for Chinese artists, Nien Hsi-
yao adapts and simplifies Pozzo's elabo-
rate plates. Yet even with the explanation
in the commentary, it is doubtful how
well the science of perspective could be
understood from Nien's engravings.

says that Chiao Ping-chen grasped the idea and modified it somewhat, but that 'it did not correspond to scholarly taste, and consequently connoisseurs have not adopted it'. Chiao Ping-chen, who probably learned perspective from Father Verbiest in the Imperial Observatory, where he was employed, put his skill to good use in the well-known series of forty-eight paintings that he made for the *Keng-chih t'u* (Illustrations of Rice and Silk Cultivation), executed for the emperor in 1696 and soon after engraved on wood and widely circulated. Much less well known are his scroll paintings. The country scene illustrated here (Figure 39) combines with immense charm and delicacy a traditional composition, an almost Dutch feeling for genre and a sound, if somewhat timid, use of Western perspective.

The landscape painter Wu Li (1632–1718) is the best known among all the Chinese artists who came in contact with European culture. A native of Chekiang, he grew up in scholarly circles in Ch'ang-shu, where the French Jesuits had a mission. He got to know them well, and in 1676 painted a landscape, *Spring Colours in Lake and Sky,* for Father Louis de Rougemont, a protégé of the pious Candide Hsü. In 1681 he was baptised and, in the same year, set off for Macao en route to Rome. Afraid, it has been suggested, of a long sea voyage (though there may have been some other reason for his decision), he chose to stay in Macao and began his training there as a novice in the following year. After his ordination as Père Acuñha in 1688, Wu Li returned to Kiangsu to spend the rest of his life, chiefly in the Shanghai area, in the service of the church, to which he gave himself humbly and completely.

We know practically nothing of Wu Li's later years. For a time he seems to have lost touch with many of his former friends and associates. Louis Pfister, quoting an unnamed nineteenth-century biography of Wu Li, says that he repented of his pagan youth and called in and destroyed as many of his old pictures and poems as he could lay hands on, because they contained 'superstitious matter', and that he now composed, instead of poems to his friends, sacred songs to God, the Virgin and the angels. But another Chinese writer says that the later paintings became even freer and more original. It seems that he did stop painting for a considerable time, returning to it, and to some of his old friendships, only after about 1680. None of his work shows any obvious Western influence, although the negative effects of his isolation from his scholarly friends may perhaps be discerned in a certain hardening of his brushwork in paintings having dates in the 1680s and 1690s. One of his later poems suggests that he never had practised Western techniques. A quatrain that he wrote on a painting for a parting friend in 1704 ends with these lines:

> In my old bag [that is, my repertoire] are no Western things at all,
> So I paint a plum branch and present it to you.

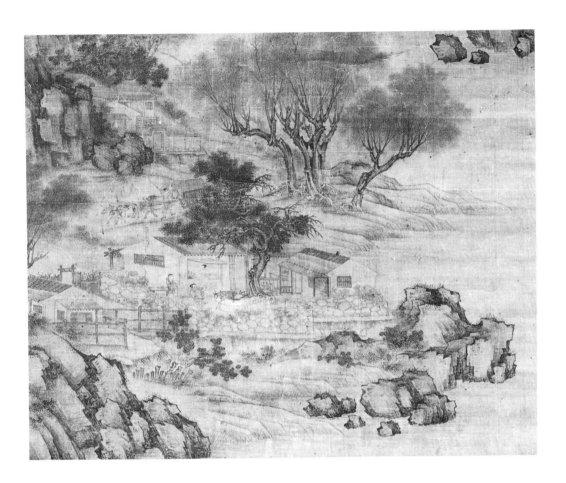

39.
Chiao Ping-chen (active c. 1680–1720).
Landscape with Cottages. Ink and colour
on silk. Private collection, Atherton,
California. This detail shows how skillfully the artist integrates Western perspective with a traditional landscape. A
Chinese eighteenth-century critic, however, wrote that Chiao's synthesis 'is not
worthy of refined appreciation, and lovers
of antiquity will not adopt it'.

Nevertheless, Wu Li must certainly have seen a great deal of Western painting and engraving in the Jesuit mission churches and libraries, for he wrote a
brief and sensible account of the differences between Chinese and Western art
that is worth quoting. After speaking of customs, he goes on:

> In writing and painting, the differences are just as striking: our characters are made
> by gathering dots and strokes, and the sound comes afterwards; they begin with
> phonetics, then words, making lines by scattering hooks and strokes in a horizontal
> row. Our painting does not seek physical likeness [hsing-ssu], and does not depend
> on fixed patterns; we call it 'divine' and 'untrammelled'. Theirs concentrates entirely
> on the problems of dark and light, front and back, and the fixed patterns of physical
> likeness. Even in writing inscriptions, we write on the top of a painting, and they
> sign at the bottom of it. Their use of the brush is also completely different. It is this
> way with everything, and I cannot describe it all.

None of the Chinese seventeenth-century landscapes that seem to hint at the
possibility of Western influence are direct copies of European works. Rather
what emerges, here and there, is a new approach to the rendering of form in
nature and a little widening of the range of subject matter that can be depicted.
In painting mountains, rocks and terrain generally, there is sometimes a sharper
edge and a more calculated grading of tone to render form more objectively; the
continuously receding ground is made more explicit; the transitions from light
to dark produce a more telling and illusionistic chiaroscuro; shading is used to
suggest a single light source; and most important, the free, calligraphic brushstroke is replaced by an even, close-knit texture of dots and strokes that sometimes suggests engraving, and in the process the ink wash inevitably loses some
of its transparency.

Many of these qualities can be found in the landscapes painted by the professional artist Wu Pin in about 1605, and by the Kiangsu painter Chao Tso, active
in about 1600–30, when the first little wave of Western influence was at its
height. That morose eccentric Kung Hsien (c. 1640–89), the greatest of the
Nanking painters, achieved a powerful chiaroscuro by stippling. For the 'un-
calligraphic' ink blob there is the august precedent of the Sung master Mi Fu,
but Mi Fu's ink was, we assume, wet, luminous and transparent, while Kung
Hsien's dry, opaque surfaces produce a deadening effect, giving his landscapes an
un-Chinese coldness and stillness. Such movement as they possess is expressed
in the contorted shapes of rocks and hills rather than in the brushstroke itself
(Figure 40). It is hard to believe that Kung Hsien had not seen, possibly at the
Jesuit mission in Nanking, engravings such as those in Braun and Hogenberg's
Civitates Orbis Terrarum.

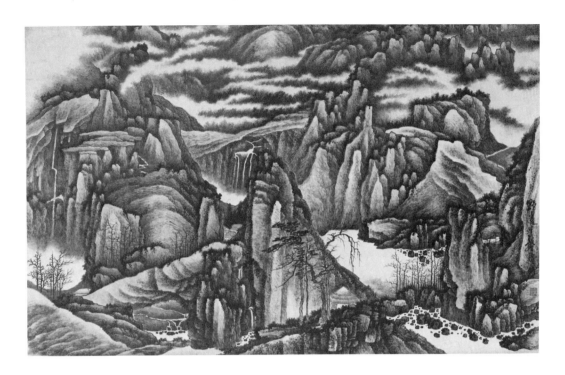

40.
Kung Hsien (c. 1617–89). *A Thousand Peaks and Myriad Ravines*. Ink on paper. Drenowatz Collection, Rietberg Museum, Zürich. There is no evidence that Kung Hsien had firsthand knowledge of Western art, but the stillness, the lack of calligraphic brushwork and the strong chiaroscuro here and in some of his other paintings raise the question of whether he might have seen some European engravings.

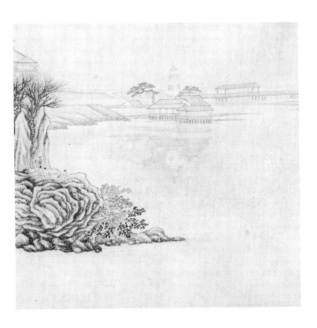

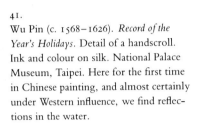

41.
Wu Pin (c. 1568–1626). *Record of the
Year's Holidays*. Detail of a handscroll.
Ink and colour on silk. National Palace
Museum, Taipei. Here for the first time
in Chinese painting, and almost certainly
under Western influence, we find reflec-
tions in the water.

Occasionally a subject seems to be borrowed straight from Western art: for
instance, the motif of a group of men on a flattened hilltop approached by a path
winding up the spine of the hill, which occurs several times in Nadal, is repeated
in Wu Pin's handscroll *Occupations of the Months* (National Palace Museum, Taipei) and in a woodcut view of the scenery near Nanking in the 1608 edition of
the Ming pictorial encyclopedia *San-ts'ai t'u-hui*. Both these motifs, however,
appear also in Sung dynasty painting.

But these new elements emerge in Chinese seventeenth-century landscape
painting chiefly in details rather than in composition or general theme: a building carefully mirrored in the water (Wu Pin; Figure 41); a sunset (itself a rare
subject outside early Buddhist painting) reddening the sky and reflected in the
water or shooting out its rays in radiating lines (Wu Pin again); smoke curling
up from a cottage chimney (Wu Pin; Figure 42); a continuously receding ground
line (Fan Ch'i); the horizon at sea shown by a sharp straight line across the picture with islands sitting on it, rather than being indicated only by the islands and
land-spits (Fan Ch'i; Figure 43); objects and features shaded to suggest volume

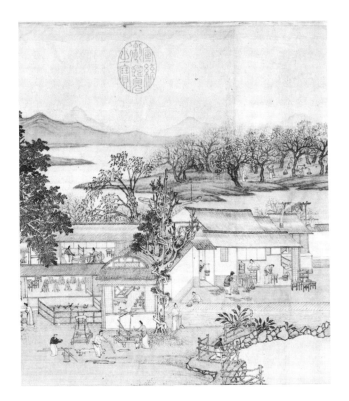

42.
Wu Pin (c. 1568–1626). *Record of the Year's Holidays*. Detail of a handscroll. Ink and colour on silk. National Palace Museum, Taipei. The smoke coming from the chimney to the right is another realistic touch that appeared, very rarely, only after the arrival of European engravings.

43.
Fan Ch'i (1616–c. 1694). Landscape on the Yangtse River. Handscroll. Ink and colour on silk. Staatliche Museen für Ostasiatische Kunst, Berlin. In a purely Chinese landscape the foot of the distant hills and island would be lost in mist. Here, they and the sailing boats sit firmly on a horizon line drawn in the Western manner.

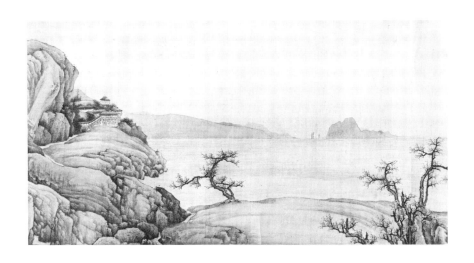

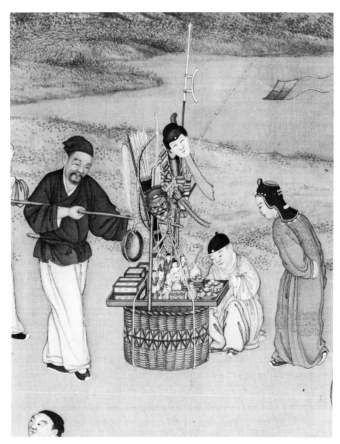

44.
Ting Kuan-p'eng (active c. 1714–60).
Toy Seller at New Year. Detail of a handscroll. Ink and colour on silk. National
Palace Museum, Taipei. Chinese artists,
if they used shading at all, used it very
sparingly to make an object look more
solid, while avoiding cast shadows and
a single light source.

(Ting Kuan-p'eng; Figure 44); and accurate perspective and foreshortening
(Chiao Ping-chen). Most inexplicable except in terms of direct Western influence is a new boldness and realism in the use of colour, which appears for the
first time after 1600 in the work of artists such as Lan Ying and Hsiang Sheng-
mou. A leaf from an album of 1649 by the latter artist depicts with thoroughly
un-Chinese realism a bare tree against a blue mountain, the sky behind reddened
by the setting sun (Colour Plate 4). Such colouristic effects must have seemed
much too obvious for cultivated Chinese taste, for they were not repeated in the
painting of the literati.

Some of these effects—foreshortening, shading and the receding ground
line, for example—appear in that remarkable monument of late Northern Sung
realism, the handscroll *Going Up River at Ch'ing-ming Festival Time* (see Figure

168), by Chang Tse-tuan. But now, after a lapse of five hundred years, they appear again in company with others that are entirely new. It seems that the revival, or perhaps the rediscovery, of some elements of realism and the first appearance of others can be explained only by the stimulus of European art. Every one of these effects that does not involve the use of colour could be accounted for by supposing that the artists had seen engravings like those in Nadal.

Not far from Nanking lies Yangchow, the prosperous city at the junction of the Yangtse and the Grand Canal, which by the end of the seventeenth century had become a centre of liberal patronage and eccentric painting. Perhaps in the work of the Yangchow artists Yüan Chiang and Li Yin we see a hint of Western influence, grafted on to their very original interpretation of the landscape style of Northern Sung masters such as Fan K'uan and Kuo Hsi—as, for instance, in Yüan Chiang's *Carts on a Winding Mountain Road* (Figure 45), in which the view from above of the foreshortened carts could well have been lifted out of the engraving of Aquapendente and Tarvisi in Braun and Hogenberg (Figure 46). In fact, the marriage is not an unnatural one, for Northern Sung painting was—on its own terms—realistic, and these later painters may have found that the study of European engravings helped them to obtain a monumental antique effect, although the direct evidence for this is lacking. Yüan Chiang was summoned, some time after 1723, to the palace, where for nearly twenty years he worked alongside the Jesuit painters and craftsmen under conditions bordering on slavery. But the style that suggests that he knew something of Western art was formed long before then, and the datable landscapes of his later years seem to be far less 'European' than those he had painted in Yangchow.

One area in which we might expect to find Western influence is that of portrait painting, for the traditional Chinese portrait is seldom a physical likeness of the subject. It is rather an attempt to capture the subject's 'spirit', or role as emperor, official, scholar or poet; the features, unless the subject has striking peculiarities, are of little importance. Chinese connoisseurs found in Western portraits a new kind of realism. Writing of the portraits by the Fukienese artist Tseng Ch'ing, who died in Nanking in 1650, the author of the *History of Silent Poetry* describes how 'their eyes seem to move and follow you like the eyes of living people' and notes that Tseng Ch'ing used several layers of colours in painting the faces. His surviving portraits, and those by his followers in Nanking, are all in ink with slight colour, but most of them look straight out of the picture, and the faces are modelled in light and shade. In their directness and realism they have—although the modelling is generally much subtler—something in common with Ming ancestral portraits, done by craftsmen who so far as we know had no contact whatever with Western art and who achieved likenesses by assembling eyes, ears, noses and mouths out of a pattern book. Yet Western

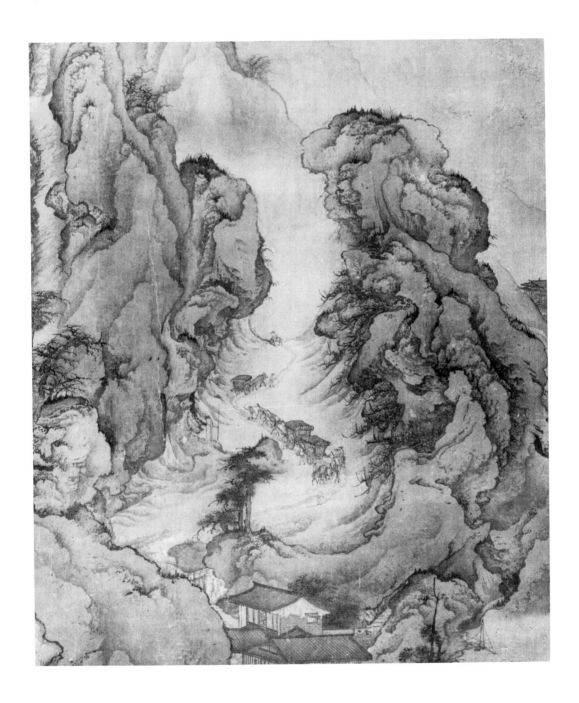

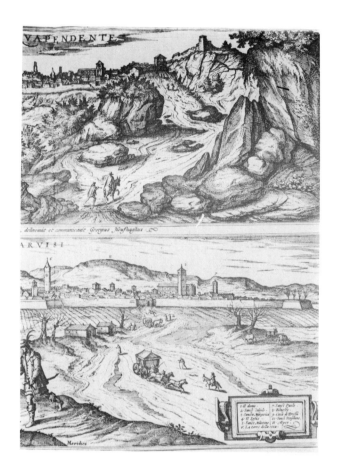

45 (facing page).
Yüan Chiang (active c. 1690–1724).
Carts on a Winding Mountain Road, in
the Manner of Kuo Hsi. Detail of a hanging scroll. Ink and slight colour on silk.
1694. Nelson Gallery–Atkins Museum,
Kansas City, Missouri. A striking example of the coming together of European and Northern Sung art; the foreshortened treatment of the bullock cart
can be found both in surviving Sung
works and in Western engravings of the
early seventeenth century.

46.
Georg Hoefnagel. Aquapendente and
Tarvisi. Engraving from Braun and
Hogenberg, *Civitates Orbis Terrarum*
(1572–1616). By 1608 this splendid set of
six volumes of views of European cities
and landscapes had reached the Jesuit
mission in Nanchang, where it could
have been studied by artists in touch
with the missionaries.

66

47.
Anonymous. Portrait of Kuan T'ien-p'ei (1780–1841). Detail. Ink and colour on paper. About 1835–40. Nanking Museum. This detail from an almost life-size portrait of the commander-in-chief of the southern Chinese navy in the first Opium War, who was killed in action against the British outside Canton, is a striking example of how successfully Chinese artists could adapt Western realism to their own tradition of formal portraiture.

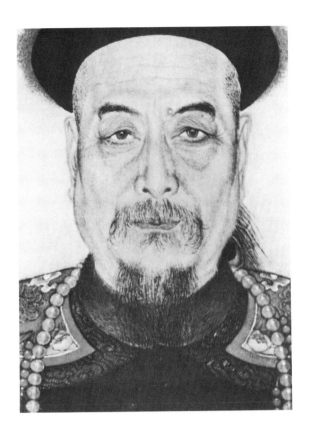

48.
Lu Wei (active c. 1700). Landscape. Detail of a handscroll. Ink and slight colour on paper. Dated 1697. National Museum, Tōkyō. Lu Wei's use of graded washes and subtle chiaroscuro to indicate a continuous ground surface is unlike that of other early Ch'ing artists and may possibly reflect a knowledge of European landscape techniques.

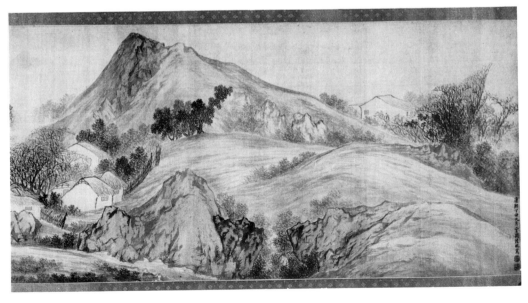

influence is often present, an example from the first half of the nineteenth century being the portrait of the heroic admiral Kuan T'ien-p'ei, of which the arresting head is illustrated in Figure 47.

Certain eighteenth-century court painters, notably Leng Mei, Tsou I-kuei and Shen Yüan, show unmistakable signs of Western influence in their work. There were other seventeenth-century painters, such as Shang-kuan Chou, Lu Wei and possibly the curious Fa Jo-ch'en, in whom Western influence is less obvious but still discernable. In the handscroll by Lu Wei in the Tōkyō National Museum (Figure 48), the definition of continuous ground surfaces by means of gradations of shading is something quite new in Chinese landscape painting that must have been stimulated by contact with Western art. Such borrowings are elusive and difficult to substantiate; they need to be further investigated.

The Eighteenth Century

With the arrival in Peking, in December 1715, of Giuseppe Castiglione, a young Milanese Jesuit trained in Genoa, the court at last acquired a European painter of some quality—a man who was destined to have a considerable impact on Chinese court taste for over half a century. En route, he had spent four years in Portugal, where he had decorated the chapel of the Jesuit novitiate in Coimbra with frescoes of the life of St Ignatius Loyola. But if he imagined that his career in China would likewise be dedicated to the decoration of Christian churches, he was in for a cruel shock.

Within a short time of his arrival in Peking, Castiglione, now bearing the Chinese name Lang Shih-ning, found himself at the workbenches in the dismal atelier that occupied one corner of K'ang-hsi's huge, rambling country palace, the Yüan-ming-yüan. In these crowded, malodorous workshops, 'full of corrupt persons', as one of the Jesuits put it, Lang Shih-ning and Father Matteo Ripa, another recent arrival, slaved away at enamelling on porcelain. The Jesuits were prepared to do almost anything to further the aims of the mission—'tout pour l'amour de Dieu'—but this was too much. They petitioned to be excused, and succeeded only by painting so clumsily that the emperor reluctantly released them, though not to the kind of freedom that they had hoped for.

Jean-Denis Attiret, who joined Lang Shih-ning in 1738, complained bitterly that they were forced always to work in the Chinese medium and never had the time or the energy for the devotional pictures they longed to paint. Though loaded with honours, Lang Shih-ning and Attiret found no relief from unremitting labour. In 1754, when he had been working night and day for several weeks in Jehol, painting portraits and commemorative pictures for the emperor, Attiret wrote to Father Amiot in Peking, 'Will this farce never come to an end? So far from the house of God, deprived of all spiritual sustenance, I find it hard to persuade myself that all this is to the glory of God'.

Lang Shih-ning spent the rest of his life in the service of three emperors, K'ang-hsi, Yung-cheng and Ch'ien-lung, gradually perfecting a synthetic style in which, with taste, skill and the utmost discretion, Western perspective and shading, with even on occasion a hint of chiaroscuro, were blended to give an added touch of realism to paintings otherwise entirely in the Chinese manner.

In April 1723, Father Amiot reported:

> Our most dear Castiglione has been daily occupied in the Palace, with his art . . . which has been thoroughly investigated by the Emperor [Yung-cheng], first in enamel painting, then in the usual technique, whether in oil or in water-colour. By imperial order he had to send the ruler whatever he did. It can be said that his works have succeeded in winning the Emperor's favour, for he has on various occasions benignly praised the artist, and sent him gifts even to a greater degree than his deceased parent. Frequently, . . . dishes were sent from the Imperial table; again, the Emperor rewarded him with twelve rolls of the best silk, accompanied by a precious stone, carved in the shape of a seal, with the effigy of Christ our Saviour, on a cross. Latterly, he was presented with a summer hat, which gift denotes great honour.

The Ch'ien-lung emperor (1736–96) was as lavish in his praise of Lang Shih-ning as his father and grandfather had been before him—and was as exacting in his demands. Before long the Jesuit found himself appointed chief architect for the new complex of buildings in the northeast corner of the Yüan-ming-yüan, Ch'ien-lung's 'Garden of Everlasting Spring' (its earlier name having been Ch'ang-ch'un-yüan). There Lang Shih-ning designed a series of palaces, pavilions and terraces in an ornate pseudo-Rococo style that delighted the emperor (Figure 49). These structures—the product of the Jesuit's fertile imagination, lack of professional training and remoteness from any possible critics—must have given him enormous pleasure too, for this seems to be the one occasion in his career at court when he was able to do exactly what he pleased. Between his pavilions stood huge fountains worked by machinery designed by Father Benoist that were Ch'ien-lung's special pride.

Ch'ien-lung filled these remarkable buildings with furniture, clocks, pictures and mechanical toys that had been sent as gifts to the court by Louis XIV and Louis XV. On the walls he hung tapestries designed by Boucher, the *Teintures Chinoises,* which were said to have been based on sketches made in the Forbidden City by Lang Shih-ning's young Jesuit colleague, Attiret, though this seems rather unlikely. Could Ch'ien-lung have imagined that these charming chinoiseries were meant to depict his own court? Perhaps he thought they represented Versailles. Another pavilion was built to accommodate the set of Gobelins tapestries sent out by Louis XV in 1767.

Just as it amused Louis XV to attire his court on occasion in Chinese dress, so, in reverse, with Ch'ien-lung. He had himself and his lovely Mongolian consort, Hsiang Fei, painted dressed up in European armour and helmet, and there exists a charming portrait of the 'Fragrant Concubine', as she was called, dressed *en paysanne,* with a shepherd's crook and basket of flowers—a figure straight out of Boucher, possibly painted by Attiret or one of his pupils (Figure 50).

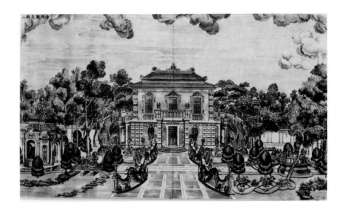

49.
Anonymous follower of Lang Shih-ning (Giuseppe Castiglione; 1688–1766). *The Belvedere (Fang-wai kuan), in the Yüan-ming-yüan.* Engraving. 1793. Bibliothèque Nationale, Paris. By the time these engravings were made, Castiglione's Chinese pupils had begun to forget some of what he had taught them, particularly in drawing trees; perhaps also they found the European idea of the formal garden unnatural, even ridiculous.

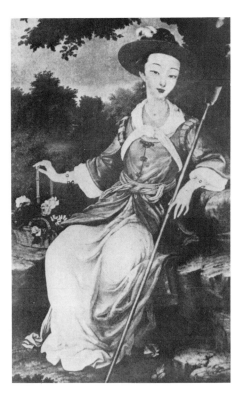

50.
Anonymous follower of Lang Shih-ning. *Portrait of Hsiang Fei, the 'Fragrant Concubine'.* Eighteenth century. Palace Museum, Peking. This charming figure, possibly inspired by Boucher, was popular in China where it was copied in carved and painted ivory.

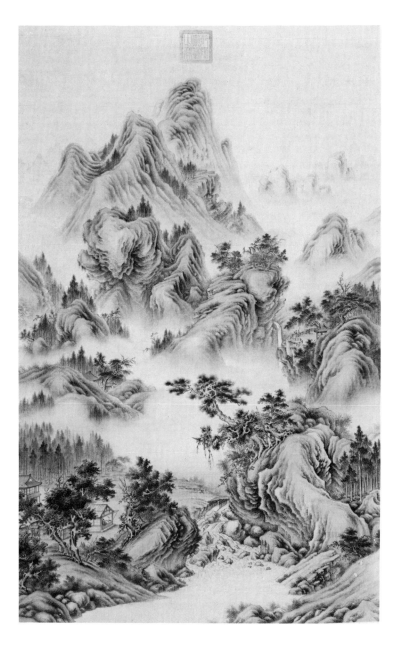

51.
Lang Shih-ning (Giuseppe Castiglione;
1688–1766). *Landscape*. Ink and slight
colour on silk. National Palace Museum,
Taipei. A brilliant exercise in the academic manner of Wang Hui (1632–1717).

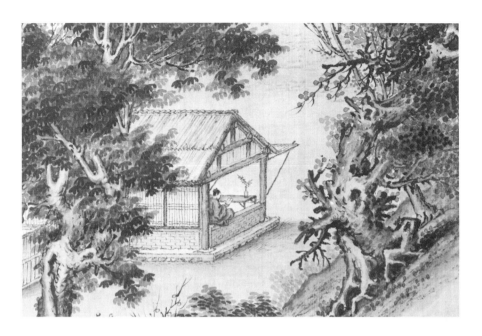

52.

Detail of Figure 51. Lang Shih-ning shows his Western training only in the drawing of the little thatched pavilion and of the young gentleman reclining in the window.

When not employed in painting portraits of the emperor or of historical events in his reign or decorating the walls of the Yüan-ming-yüan, Lang Shih-ning devoted himself to painting scrolls depicting the emperor's favourite pets, horses and auspicious plants. Occasionally, he painted landscapes, and his tall landscape in the National Palace Museum, Taipei, is, except in some details, a clever pastiche of the manner of the seventeenth-century orthodox master Wang Hui (Figures 51 and 52). Perhaps his most successful blending of Chinese and Western methods was achieved in the long handscroll, *A Hundred Horses in a Landscape,* which he painted for Yung-cheng in 1728 (Colour Plate 5). The continuous perspective, required by the handscroll format, is of course Chinese, but the depth achieved by means of a continuous ground plane is Western, as are the reflections and shadows. But the extreme restraint with which they are used is a concession to Chinese taste, while Chinese conventions for mountains, rocks and trees are transformed by a quite Western realism in the drawing. In all, this is a brilliant synthesis, cleverly calculated to give the emperor enough of Western realism to delight him, but not enough to disconcert.

The large panel on silk from a private collection in London seems to belong to this group of courtly portraits painted by the Jesuits and their pupils (Colour Plate 6). An elegant young lady sits in a foreign chair, wrapped in velvet, with a fur-trimmed muff, looking tranquilly down at the little servant girl warming her hands at the charcoal brazier, while another brings what looks like a Dutch coffee pot, jug and teapot on a tray of mother-of-pearl. The setting is subdued Rococo; the painting of many details—such as the glass bulb-bowl, the landscape over the door, the furniture and brackets, and above all the lively, delicate treatment of the lady's face, with its deft highlights and shadows—proclaims the hand of a European, possibly working with Chinese assistants.

Who this European was is not known. The peculiar charm of the figures is French rather than Italian. In a letter of November 1743 Attiret wrote that he painted chiefly in watercolours on silk, or in oil on glass, and seldom in the European manner, except for his portraits of 'the brothers of the Emperor, his wife and several other princes and princesses of the blood, and certain favourites and other seigneurs'. Not only is the central figure disproportionately large, but her face is painted with a care and realism not devoted to the others. This suggests that it is a portrait, and not merely a decorative composition, though whether it is indeed by Attiret, we cannot of course be certain.

In his large compositions Lang Shih-ning sometimes cooperated with a Chinese court painter, the Jesuit putting in the figures, the Chinese the landscape. Among Lang Shih-ning's known collaborators were Ting Kuan-p'eng, Ch'in K'un and T'ang-tai. There was formerly in the Imperial Palace collection an album of illustrations to a section of the ancient *Book of Odes,* in which the landscapes are by T'ang-tai, the buildings by Lang Shih-ning and the figures and animals by Shen Yüan, one of the artists who produced a series of forty views of the Yüan-ming-yüan.

Perhaps it is the hand of T'ang-tai, collaborating with Lang Shih-ning, that we see in a huge and remarkable painting now hanging in the Stanford Museum, known as *Night Market at Yang-ch'eng* (Figure 53). The picture is signed with

53.
Attributed to Lang Shih-ning. *Night Market at Yang-ch'eng.* Detail. Hanging scroll on silk. Dated 1736. Stanford University Art Museum, Stanford. Although the landscape in the background of this fascinating picture may be by a Chinese artist, the drawing of the buildings and figures and the handling of light and shade show the unmistakable hand of a European.

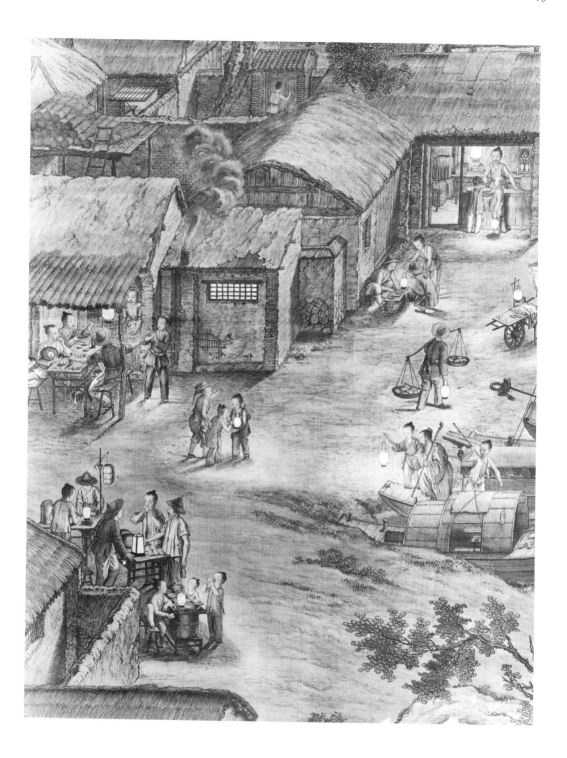

Lang Shih-ning's name and the date 1736, but this may have been added later. The *Night Market* depicts with a wealth of fascinating detail the life along a river-bank outside a city wall on a summer night. There are pedlars and boatmen, wine shops and roadside stalls, drawn in the Chinese medium yet obviously by a European who had exchanged his pen for a Chinese brush. His handling of light and shadow, of human anatomy and the very texture of walls and roofs could not have been learnt in Peking, and there are details, such as the gentleman step-ping ashore from a sampan and a girl in a boat drawing water from the river, which look very French, as though the painter had studied engravings after Watteau and Boucher. In the distance, however, there rises a mountain land-scape bathed in moonlight, executed, unlike those in the *Hundred Horses* scroll, by an unmistakably Chinese hand. It may be that the *Night Market* represents no actual place, but was painted to give Ch'ien-lung an idea of how his subjects might spend a hot summer night. The origin and history of this painting before the twentieth century are a mystery. It bears no imperial seals, and, like many of the works of the court painters, may have been painted simply as a wall decora-tion for one of the pavilions of the Yüan-ming-yüan. If so, it must have been taken down long before that great, rambling complex of buildings and gardens began to decay, for it is still in very good condition.

In 1762 Ch'ien-lung completed the conquest of Turkestan, and his generals returned in triumph to Peking. The Jesuits had shown him engravings after the panoramic battle pictures of Georges Philippe Rugendas of Augsburg (1666–1743) and possibly also others after Jacques Courtas, le Bourguignon (1621–76), and these seem to have inspired the emperor to celebrate his own victories in a similar fashion. Sixteen pictures were executed under the direction of the Jesuits, who presumably made the preliminary drawings and supervised the making of the enlarged colour versions. In addition to Lang Shih-ning and Attiret, the work was directed by Ignace Sichelbarth (1708–80), who had arrived in 1745 (a few of whose wretched Castiglionesque paintings survive in the National Palace Museum), and by Jean-Damascène Sallusti, an Augustinian father who became bishop of Peking after the suppression of the Jesuit order in 1773. The sixteen huge battle paintings were hung in the Tzu-kuang-ko, a hall in the western part of the Forbidden City where foreign ambassadors were received. Above them were arranged the portraits of fifty victorious generals, mostly painted by Attiret.

In July 1765 the emperor ordered the Jesuits to make ink copies of the battle pictures to be sent to Europe to be engraved. Lang Shih-ning intended them for Rome, but when the first batch of four reached Canton, the French mission there intercepted them and persuaded the viceroy to direct them to France,

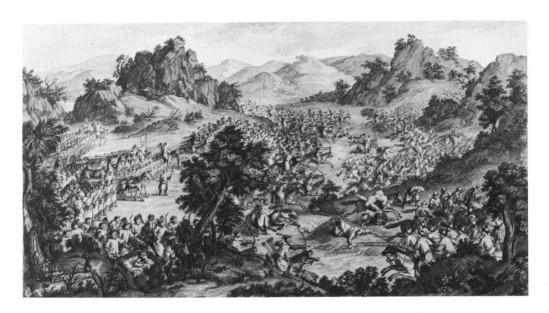

54.
Anonymous. *Ch'ien-lung's Conquest of Turkestan*. British Museum, London. One of a set of sixteen engravings made in Paris between 1767 and 1774 after paintings by Jean-Damascène Sallusti and other missionary artists in Peking.

whose engravers, they said, were the best in Europe. The drawings arrived in Paris in the autumn of 1766. Bertin, minister to Louis XV, saw that they were put into the hands of the director of the Royal Academy, the Duc de Marigny, who, on seeing them, wrote to Attiret that his drawing was very much in the Chinese manner. This must have pleased the Jesuit, for he had said of himself that his own taste, since he had been in China, had become 'a little Chinese'.

The remaining twelve drawings reached Paris by 1772 and the set of sixteen magnificent plates, meticulously engraved by Le Bas, Saint-Aubin and others under the direction of Cochin, was completed two years later. By this time the style had, apart from a vaguely exotic treatment of the mountains, lost all its Chinese flavour (Figure 54). With the exception of a few sets kept in Paris, the whole edition of two hundred impressions, with the original drawings and the plates, was, at the express order of Ch'ien-lung, sent back to Peking in December 1774.

The emperor presented sets to imperial relatives and deserving subjects, and they were immensely admired. He then set out to show that his own engravers could do just as well. He can hardly have been aware of how little developed the

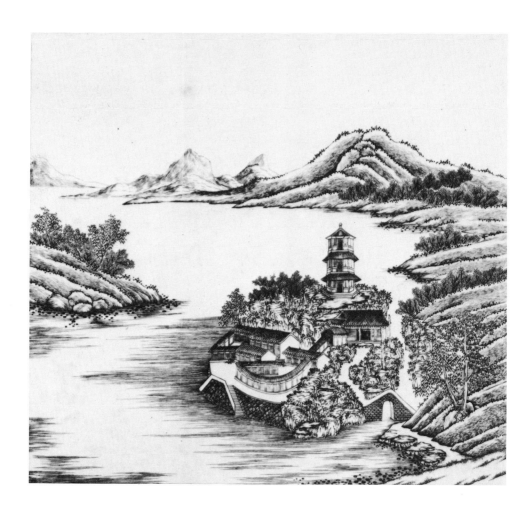

55.
Matteo Ripa (1682–1765). One of the
*Thirty-six Views of the Summer Palace (Pi-
shu shan-chuang) at Jehol.* Copperplate engraving. 1712–14. Here, by contrast, the
European artist is trying to make his engraving look like a Chinese painting,
even to the extent of distorting the perspective and imitating the *tien* (dots)
along the edges of the hills. These were
the engravings that Ripa showed to Lord
Burlington in 1724.

art of copperplate engraving was in China. Very shortly after arriving in Peking in 1711, Father Matteo Ripa had been obliged by K'ang-hsi to execute some Chinese landscapes in oils, for which he was ill-fitted. 'I recommended my efforts to the direction of God', he wrote, 'and began to do what I had never before undertaken'. The emperor was satisfied. 'Thus I continued to paint till the month of April, when His Majesty was pleased to command that I betake myself to engraving'. Of this latter art Ripa knew even less. When called upon to engrave the huge maps prepared by the Jesuit fathers, he had to build his own press and make his own ink. K'ang-hsi was so pleased with the result that he ordered Ripa to make thirty-six engravings, after paintings by court artists, of the summer palace at Jehol (Figure 55). In these, the first copperplates (apart from the maps) engraved in China, Ripa with naive and cunning charm manages to convey something of the quality of the Chinese brush technique. When these engravings later appeared in England, they, and Ripa's descriptions, exerted a major influence on the revolution of English garden design initiated by William Kent.

Ripa left for Europe in 1723, but Lang Shih-ning kept the craft going in the Imperial Printing Office (Ts'ao-pan ch'u) and supervised the delightful set of plates of his fantastic Sino-Rococo pavilions in the Yüan-ming-yüan, engraved in 1786. In Ch'ien-lung's lifetime five more sets of campaign engravings were produced by his Chinese craftsmen. One set, cut between 1798 and 1803 after paintings by Feng Ning, depicts the ruthless campaign to exterminate the rebellious Miao aborigines (Figure 56). These later plates, by many hands, are varied in style and sometimes awkwardly composed, but they show a determined attempt to follow the model of the original Conquest series, even using the same landscape elements over and over again. Interesting as they are, however, they represent a stream in eighteenth-century court art that had little influence outside the palace and soon dried up altogether.

The halcyon days of the Yüan-ming-yüan ended with the abdication of Ch'ien-lung in 1796. By then Father Benoist had long been dead, and his defunct mechanical fountains were being supplied, on special occasions only, by chains of men with buckets. Ch'ien-lung's successors continued to use the royal apartments of the Yüan-ming-yüan, but Chia-ch'ing (r. 1796–1820), weighed down with debts, was rigidly economical, and there were no more extravagances. Already the Yüan-ming-yüan was becoming a place of ghosts and memories, while neglect and pilfering were beginning to take their toll.

When Lord Elgin's punitive force put it to the torch in October 1860, only the royal apartments were in decent order. In fact, contrary to popular belief, the British and French managed to destroy only a small part of this vast complex of

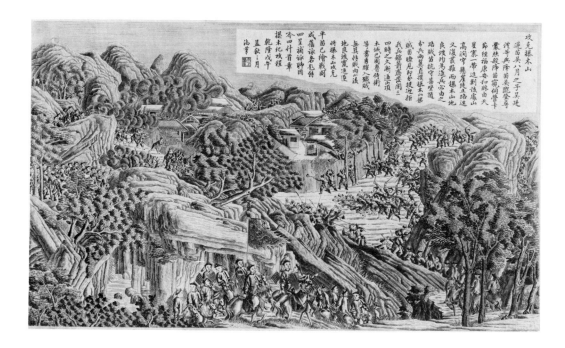

56.
Anonymous. *The Subjugation of the Miao Aborigines in 1795.* One of a set of sixteen engravings made by Chinese artists in Peking between 1798 and 1803 after paintings by the court artist Feng Ning. Formerly Richard B. Arkway, Inc., New York. A comparison between this engraving and that in Figure 55 shows how much, by the end of the eighteenth century, Chinese engravers had modified, stiffened and formalised the European style, while still keeping some Western flavour in the figures and the shading.

over two hundred buildings. In spite of the looting that went on for years afterwards, there was enough still standing for the empress dowager to embark in the early 1870s on a costly restoration. But in the face of popular protests this was abandoned in 1874, and the dismantling was resumed; even the wooden piles were dug up and sold for fuel. Today Ch'ien-lung's great fairy palace, in which, long ago, the Jesuits had staged an Italian light opera and Hsiang Fei had dressed up as a French peasant girl, has almost disappeared. Only the ruins of the marble buildings survive.

In 1772 Father Giuseppe Panzi arrived from Paris as a replacement for Attiret. Though his patron dismissed him as obsequious, he sounds from his letters a delightful man, charitable, modest and gay. 'Tout pour l'amour de Dieu!', he wrote home. 'Je suis le peintre, ou mieux le serviteur de la mission pour l'amour de Dieu'. He painted a portrait of the emperor soon after his arrival and other portraits of high officials and Jesuit missionaries, but little is known about his work, and it is doubtful whether, with Ch'ien-lung old and tired and his successor, Chia-ch'ing, immersed in his inherited problems, Panzi was able to sustain his enthusiasm. He died, very old and obscure, in Peking in about 1812 or a little earlier. We hear of two more European painters in the service of the Chinese court before the curtain descends: Joseph Paris, a mechanic, clockmaker and painter of sorts sent out by the Lazarists in 1784, who worked in Peking for twenty years; and Father de Poirot, who lingered on till 1814.

This is a good moment to ask ourselves what the missionary artists accomplished during their two hundred years of dedicated work in China. When we think of the intense interest that they aroused in the seventeenth century, we cannot help being surprised that their ultimate achievement was so meagre. Although in the eighteenth century they painted only for the emperors, many scholars and officials at court must have seen their work. Yet hardly one thought it worth mentioning. The influence of Western art, if it did not peter out altogether, trickled like sand to the lower levels of the professional and the craftsman painters, where it stayed till modern times.

The explanation is not far to seek. In the late Ming period some enlightened intellectuals—as in Japan a century later—looked to the Jesuits for leadership or support, and Western culture was eagerly studied. This was the only time that the literati took Western art seriously. But with the reestablishment of stable authority under the Manchus they no longer needed, or perhaps no longer dared, to associate too closely with the foreigners. From the time of K'ang-hsi until the Opium War, China felt it could afford to ignore European culture. As Ch'ien-lung made plain in his celebrated letter to George III, China needed nothing from the 'Outer Barbarians'. Western thought was almost unknown, Christianity was kept very firmly in its place, and Western technology and the Western arts were confined to serving Ch'ien-lung's own domestic and courtly needs. Besides, Western painting had one fatal flaw, which the court artist Tsou I-kuei summed up in these words:

> The Westerners are skilled in geometry, and consequently there is not the slightest mistake in their way of rendering light and shade [*yang-yin*] and distance (near and far). In their paintings all the figures, buildings, and trees cast shadows, and their brush and colours are entirely different from those of Chinese painters. Their views (scenery) stretch out from broad (in the foreground) to narrow (in the background) and are defined (mathematically measured). When they paint houses on a wall people are tempted to walk into them. Students of painting may well take over one or two points from them to make their own paintings more attractive to the eye. But these painters have no brush-manner whatsoever; although they possess skill, they are simply artisans [*chiang*] and cannot consequently be classified as painters.

'No brush-manner whatsoever'—there is the key. To the Chinese gentleman-painter who aimed at a triple synthesis of painting, poetry and calligraphy, what had the laborious realism of Western oil painting to do with fine art?

Early Nineteenth-Century Contacts in South China

While the foreigners and foreign art were slowly but surely losing their foothold at court, they were beginning to make a very different kind of impact on the South China coast. Macao, larger and much more accessible than Deshima, had been the centre of Portuguese influence in South China since early in the sixteenth century. In the eighteenth century foreign ships were trading directly with Canton. The Cantonese craftsmen were immensely skilled in imitating and adapting European styles and techniques to textiles, screens, furniture, porcelain and a dozen other products made for the European market. This export art, however, which has been exhaustively studied, made almost no impact on what we may call 'fine art' in South China. The gentleman-amateurs continued to paint in the traditional style, being if anything less curious about Western painting than had been some of the seventeenth-century literati who had consorted with the Jesuits. A good deal of semiforeign painting, however, was produced in Canton from about 1750 onwards, some of it of great charm and delicacy (Figure 57) and much of it wrongly attributed by dealers to Lang Shih-ning and his pupils.

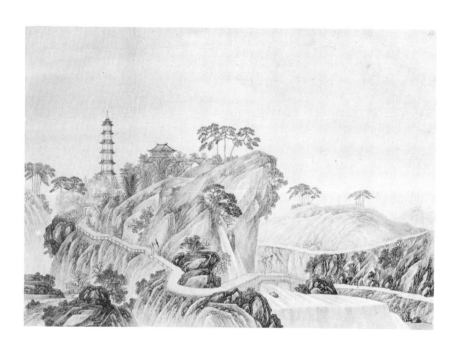

57.
Anonymous. Page from a Set of Albums
of Chinese Landscapes. Made in 1794 for
A. E. von Braam Houckgeest, Dutch
ambassador to the court of Ch'ien-lung.
British Museum, London. Many Chinese
professional artists working on commission for the foreigners successfully combined a Chinese flavour with a touch of
Western realism.

The reason for the lack of European influence in South China at a higher level was that the foreigners were for the most part merchants who had little interest in art and formed few contacts with educated Chinese, or none at all. As for the missionaries, there were no Catholic painters to replace the Jesuits, and fine art withered in the evangelical fire of the Protestant pioneers. From this time forward such influence as the Christian missions had on Chinese painting was wholly bad.

In the century between 1750 and 1850 a number of Western painters travelled in China or settled on the coast, and sometimes their activities were noted, if not always correctly. A Chinese historian of Ch'ing painting records that 'an envoy from England came bringing tribute during the years of Ch'ien-lung and Chia-ch'ing. As he travelled through the country he beheld the scenery of lakes and mountains. Thereupon he made some drawings which he took away with him. His figures and houses clearly demonstrate the principles of chiaroscuro and perspective. The method is like *chieh-hua* ['boundary painting', that is, architectural painting done with a ruler] in Chinese painting, and even more refined'. This writer is probably fusing, or confusing, two or more of four artists: the English watercolourists Alexander and Hickey, who accompanied Lord Macartney's mission to Peking in 1792, and Abbott and Fielding, who were with the abortive Amherst mission in 1816.

Macartney's secretary, John Barrow, has much to say about Chinese painting in his popular account of the mission, *Travels in China*. He relates how in the Yüan-ming-yüan he saw two very large landscapes in a Sino-European style, and some albums of the ever-popular trades and occupations, all bearing the Chinese signature of Castiglione. When he pointed out to his Chinese guide, who admired them exceedingly, that they were painted by a foreigner, the eunuch was very annoyed and refused to show him any more. Barrow thought that the Cantonese painters were better than those in Peking, for they painted flowers with painstaking accuracy for their foreign clients, and they 'will even count the number of scales on a fish, and mark them out in their representation', while they copied exactly, even to the blemishes, the coloured prints sent out from Europe. Like most foreign observers, Barrow thought Chinese painting was better the less Chinese it was.

Other European painters visited China from time to time. John Webber was the official artist on Captain Cook's third voyage, which touched at Macao early in 1777. Thomas Daniell and his nephew William were in India—and, more briefly, in South China—between 1784 and 1794. James Wathen, a retired glover from Shrewsbury, painted charming watercolours in Macao in 1812. A more considerable artist was Auguste Borget (1808–77), an intimate friend of Balzac;

he was in Macao for a few months in 1830. If any of these men had Chinese pupils, there is no record of them.

By far the best of the China coast artists was George Chinnery. Born in London in 1774, he had studied with Turner and Girtin under Sir Joshua Reynolds at the Royal Academy School, and in 1795 moved to Dublin, where he set up as a fashionable portrait painter and married Harriet Vigne, who was to plague him for the rest of his life. In 1802 they returned to England, and Chinnery immediately set off, alone, to India, where he remained for seventeen years. At length his wife joined him. He ran up heavy debts, and to escape both debts and wife he took ship to Macao, where he landed on 30 September 1830. There he remained for the rest of his life, paying, when he feared his wife might be coming on a convoy from India, a few visits to Canton, finally settling in Hong Kong after the Opium War.

Chinnery was an able portrait painter, but it is in his small landscapes in oils and above all in his drawings that his talent shows best. He was immensely prolific, going out at dawn to make those studies and watercolours that show him to be a worthy follower of Canaletto. He was a teetotaler, a heavy eater, an entertaining conversationalist and very likely had a Chinese mistress. He gave painting and drawing lessons, chiefly to foreign ladies in Macao, and had a number of skilful Chinese imitators, one of whom painted the charming lady in Figure 58. Was the Cantonese oil painter Lamqua (Figure 59), the 'Chinese Chinnery', one of his pupils? Chinnery always denied it, but Toogood Downing, writing in about 1835, tells us that he was, and that he received from Chinnery 'instruction sufficient to enable him to paint in a tolerable manner after the European fashion'. Lamqua must have made good progress, for ten years later he exhibited at the Royal Academy in London a portrait of Captain W. H. Hall, R.N., probably the first painting by a Chinese artist to appear in a European salon.

Whether or not Chinnery gave Lamqua lessons, there is no doubt that the latter was a close student of his work and copied some of his portraits. A pair of riverside scenes in the Alexander Griswold collection (Maryland) signed by Lamqua are almost exact copies of a pair of Chinnery paintings formerly in the Chater Collection, the only difference being that Lamqua has replaced some of Chinnery's figures with top-hatted Europeans, perhaps in the hope that one of the Barbarians would buy them as souvenirs of his years in the East (Figure 60).

Downing gives a fascinating description of Lamqua's studio in China Street. On the lower floor were craftsmen making figure and ship paintings on rice-straw paper or copying European engravings, of which Lamqua had a collection. Some of his assistants, on the other hand, 'confine themselves merely to

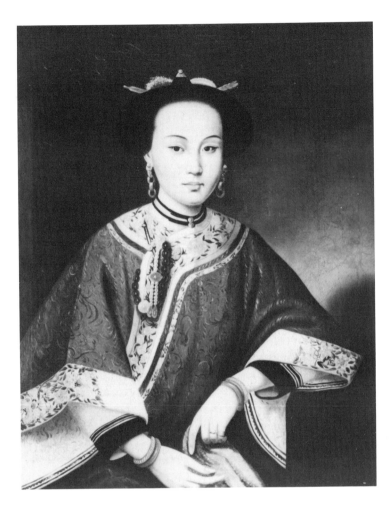

58.
Anonymous. *Portrait of a Chinese Girl*.
Oil. Early nineteenth century. Hong
Kong Museum of Art, Hong Kong.
Often wrongly attributed to George
Chinnery (1774–1852), this work by an
artist probably in Canton or Macao be-
trays its Chinese origin chiefly in the
drawing of the hands and the modelling
of the face.

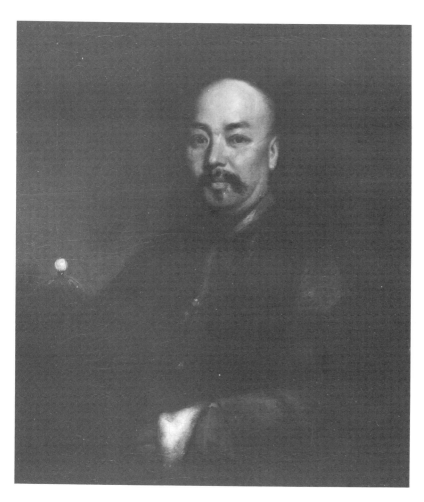

59.
Lamqua (first half of nineteenth century).
Self-portrait. Oil. About 1854. Hong
Kong Museum of Art, Hong Kong.
Lamqua was so well regarded in his day
that two of his portraits were exhibited
in the Royal Academy, London.

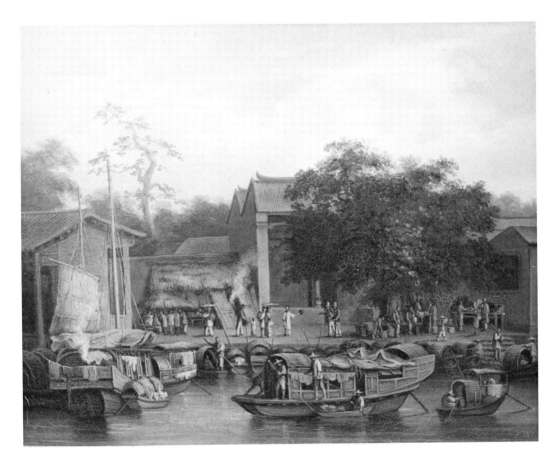

60.
Lamqua (first half of nineteenth century). *Riverside at Canton*. One of a pair of landscapes. Oil. About 1830. A. B. Griswold Collection, Monkton, Maryland. In adopting a Western technique, Lamqua also adopts a Western vision, including accurately observed details that in a Chinesestyle painting would be treated in a generalised way. It is interesting to compare this picture with *Night Market at Yangch'eng* (Figure 53).

that style of drawing which belongs exclusively to the Chinese'. Round the corner, at 34 Old Street, was Youqua, whose stamp appears on the back of some flower and plant drawings in the Bibliothèque Nationale in Paris. On the top floor of Lamqua's establishment was the master himself, constantly occupied with painting portraits in oils, yet unfailingly courteous to the stream of visitors who crowded into his small studio, the walls of which were lined with finished and unfinished portraits of Europeans and Parsees, merchants and sea captains (many of them engaged in the opium trade), 'while here and there may be distinguished the unassuming head of a Chinaman'. But perhaps Lamqua, no more than Chinnery, owed his success to flattering his sitters, if he did indeed make the remark credited to him by Soame Jenyns, 'How can handsome face make, when handsome face no got?'.

Perhaps the most interesting passage in Downing's chapter on painting in Canton concerns the free, spontaneous ink paintings of the literati, which he says are very rare. He writes:

> There are some sketchy kinds of landscapes in high repute among the natives of Canton, who consider them quite masterpieces. They are very scarce, and consist of rough outlines of trees, rocks, waterfalls, etc., painted with a brush dipped in a single pot of colour. Although to our eye these performances have no merit whatever, except perhaps in their freedom, the Chinese reverence them somewhat in the same way as we do the rough sketches in pencil or chalk done by Raphael, Da Vinci, and others of the old masters, and tell you with a chuckle that they are 'wery, wery, olo'.

Downing, as we would expect, remarks that these very, very old landscapes are also very defective by reason of their total lack of perspective, shading and chiaroscuro. But he does notice them, and even comments on their freedom, and on the high regard in which they were held by the Chinese themselves. This must be the first time in the confrontation between Chinese and Western art that any European even mentioned the only kind of painting that the Chinese intelligentsia took seriously.

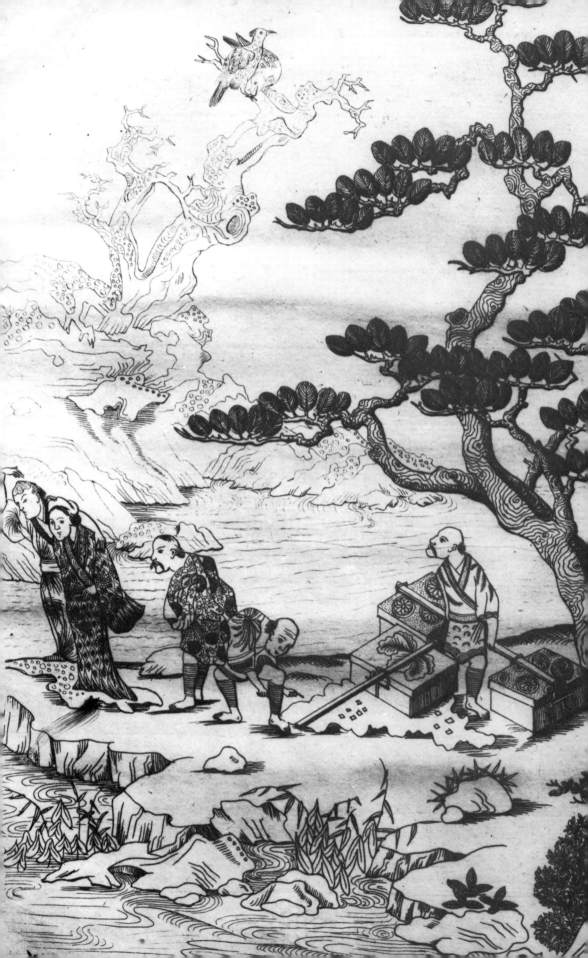

3

Europe and Chinese Art, 1600–1900

The Seventeenth and Eighteenth Centuries

For twenty years, from 1275 to 1295, Marco Polo was in the service of Kublai Khan. In Peking he consorted with Chinese ministers on equal and intimate terms. He must have known the great savant, calligrapher and landscape painter Chao Meng-fu, prime minister and secretary to the Hanlin Academy, and may even have heard of his wife, Kuan Tao-sheng, the foremost woman painter in Chinese history. Yet, as we saw in the previous chapter, never once in his account of Cathay did Marco Polo mention the landscape painting of these scholarly amateurs, although he admired the historical wall paintings that he saw in the palace and in the mansions of the rich merchants. The sole artistic relic of his years in China—symbolic of the craze that three centuries later was to sweep over Europe—is the small vase of white porcelain in the Treasury of St Mark's in Venice, believed on uncertain authority to have been brought back by him.

For a mediaeval merchant-adventurer to have ignored Chinese landscape painting, while being enormously impressed by Chinese architecture and handicrafts, is hardly surprising. The indifference to it on the part of men of taste in the seventeenth and eighteenth centuries is rather harder to understand. On the whole, China was far more receptive to the painting of Europe than were the 'Outer Barbarians', as they were justifiably called, to China's. Europe's enthusiasm for things Chinese was confined almost entirely to the crafts and decorative painting. We are not concerned in this chapter with chinoiserie as such. It is only marginal to our theme, which is not the history of European taste, but an

89

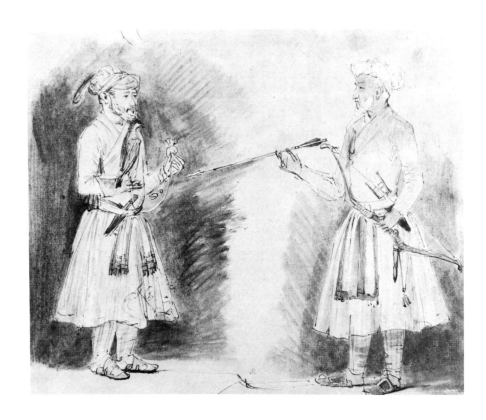

61.

Rembrandt van Rijn (1606–69). *Mughal Noblemen: Man with a Falcon and Abd al-Rahim Khan with Bow and Arrow.* Pencil and ink with touches of chalk gouache on Japanese paper. c. 1654–56. Pierpont Morgan Library, New York. Rembrandt's careful copies of Indian miniatures suggest that had he ever seen Chinese or Japanese brush paintings, he might have copied them also. But there is no evidence that he did.

enquiry into how Europe got to know about Chinese art, what she thought of it, and what influence it had, or failed to have, on her own painting. But first we should mark at least some of the steps by which Europe became aware of Chinese art.

Not long after the Portuguese arrived in the Far East—they were in Malacca in 1509 and in Macao in 1516—there began a trickle of Chinese ceramics westward that was later to swell into a flood. Among the earliest pieces to arrive in Europe must be the two porcelain vessels that feature in a drawing made by Dürer in 1515, now in the British Museum. This drawing shows two fantastic pillars incorporating Chinese vases—one obviously blue and white, the other, from its tall, slender shape, probably a specimen of the ivory-white Ming ware called by collectors 'Kiangnan Ting'. This seems to be the first instance of a European painter of any stature showing interest in any product of Chinese art.

The Portuguese monopoly trade in Chinese ceramics was broken by the Dutch, whose capture of two Portuguese carracks laden with porcelain, in 1600 and 1602, and its subsequent sale in Amsterdam, mark the real beginning of the taste for things Chinese in Europe. In 1596 and 1598 some Chinese portraits appeared in Holland. By the 1630s Chinese porcelain, chiefly blue and white, was appearing in Dutch still-life painting. The inventory of Rembrandt's large and heterogeneous collection of objets d'art and bric-à-brac sold at his bankruptcy in 1660 includes Chinese porcelain bowls and figurines. At one time he owned several Mughal miniatures, of which his copies survive (Figure 61), remarkable for the degree to which he has surpressed his own dynamic calligraphy in order to capture as faithfully as he could the thin, sensitive line of the originals. These copies are on Japanese paper, imported no doubt by the Dutch East India Company from Nagasaki.

It is tempting to believe that Rembrandt might have owned, or seen, Chinese or Japanese paintings. But there is no evidence for this at all. Yet when we look at some of his drawings, notably those sketched freely in ink or ink wash (Figure 62), we find a combination of formal clarity and calligraphic vitality in the movement of pen or brush that is closer to Chinese painting in technique and feeling than to anything in European art before the twentieth century. This, in the absence of evidence to the contrary, we must attribute to coincidence and to Rembrandt's unique gifts as a draughtsman. Moreover, if he ever did set his eyes on Chinese paintings, it is unlikely that these would have been the spontaneous ink sketches of the literati and eccentrics, which most resemble his own, for what Europe admired in Far Eastern art was its exquisite, fanciful craftsmanship, and it is highly improbable that any Dutch factor in Deshima would have acquired the sort of sketches that would have struck a responsive chord in Rembrandt.

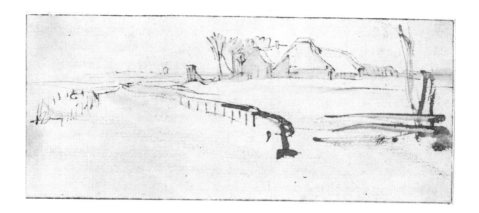

62.

Rembrandt van Rijn (1606–69). *Winter Landscape*. Reed pen and bistre ink with added wash. c. 1647. Bequest of Charles Alexander Loeser, Fogg Art Museum, Cambridge. This wonderful sketch is, in its economy of means and expressive power of the line, the most 'Chinese' of Rembrandt's landscape drawings, but the resemblance must be purely accidental.

A number of writers have drawn attention to the strangely Chinese-looking mountain landscapes in the background of certain Renaissance paintings, notably in Sassetta's *Journey of the Magi* and the works of Patinir and Niccolo dell'Abate. The misty crags in Leonardo's *Virgin of the Rocks* and *Mona Lisa* have the same suggestive air and even the same form as some Northern Sung landscapes, particularly those of Kuo Hsi. Although Near Eastern painting seems to have influenced Venetian art in the fifteenth century, I can find no evidence that there were any Chinese landscapes in Europe before the mid-sixteenth century or that Renaissance painters were influenced by them. The explanation of Leonardo's and Patinir's very 'Chinese' mountains may be that they are not real mountains in nature so much as 'mountains of the mind', the ideal shapes and awe-inspiring crags that we picture when we think of mountains. They may have grown out of the schematic mountains in mediaeval manuscript illumination, just as Sung mountains derived ultimately from the wavelike conventions in Han art. Patinir, Sassetta and Leonardo were not influenced by Far Eastern art but seem to have arrived, by somewhat the same psychological process, at a similar idea of what a quintessential mountain should look like.

The collecting of antiquities was a popular pastime among wealthy Italian gentlemen, and the museum as we know it, with its collections catalogued, published and often accessible to the public as well, is essentially an Italian invention. Indeed, it seems that Oriental paintings, however little understood, were on display as works of art in Italy long before they were regarded in the rest of Europe as anything more than curiosities.

In 1585 four young Catholic samurai had arrived in Rome, bearing gifts that included a Japanese landscape painting and other objects, which were subsequently presented to the museum in Verona. The Milanese traveller, collector and scientist Manfredo Settala (1600–1680) owned several Oriental paintings, including a large Buddhist one. The Marchese Ferdinando Cospi presented to Bologna in 1677 a collection that included, among other Orientalia, a copy of the first book published at the mission press in Foochow, with engravings after Wierix. Early in the eighteenth century Conte Abate Baldini built up a museum in Piacenza that contained, in addition to very fine Mughal miniatures, two long Chinese handscrolls of figure subjects and 'five pieces of the thinnest silk . . . on them painted two hundred little pictures'—figures and landscapes. Alas, Conte Baldini's heirs did not share his enthusiasm, and his collection was scattered on his death in 1725.

Although Italian scholars first noticed Chinese paintings and Italian museums first exhibited them, Italian artists were, as we would expect, indifferent or contemptuous. To painters schooled in Renaissance ideals of form and structure, the expressive function of the line and of 'empty' space in Oriental art would have had no meaning at all. They would have agreed with the verdict of Giovanni Gherardini, whom we have already encountered decorating the Catholic cathedral in Peking. 'The Chinese', he wrote, 'have as little knowledge of architecture and painting as I of Greek or Hebrew. Yet they are charmed by fine drawing, by a lively and well-managed landscape, a natural perspective, but as for knowing how to set about such things, that is not their affair'. Were all Chinese as convinced as Gherardini claims of the superiority of Western art? We shall return to this question in a little while.

Soon after they were established in the Orient, the Jesuits began to send Chinese books and pictures back to Rome, making the Holy City the first centre of Oriental studies in Europe. In 1635 the German Jesuit scholar Athanasius Kircher was drawn thither by the wealth of Oriental material already to be found there. Thirty years later he published his magnificent *China Illustrata,* compiled from the accounts of Ricci and others. Several of Kircher's engravings are based on Chinese paintings and woodcuts brought back from Peking by Father Jean Gruber. One, showing the principal Confucian and Taoist deities, is a

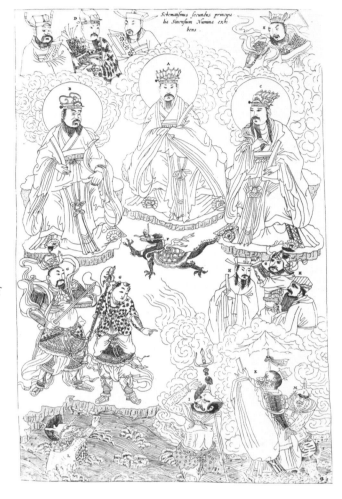

63.
Anonymous. Chinese Deities. Engraving
from Athanasius Kircher, *China Illustrata*
(1665). A careful copy of a drawing of
the Chinese Taoist pantheon, which the
missionary Jean Gruber had sent to
Rome. For decades, Kircher was the chief
authority for Europe on things Chinese.

close copy of a Chinese wood engraving (Figure 63). Another shows a lady
standing by a table with a bird in her hand (Figure 64). The lady herself is certainly taken from a Chinese painting, but to make the scene satisfying to European eyes, the composition is filled out with an invented interior and the Chinese character *yao,* meaning 'very pretty', in a frame above the lady's head. To
heighten the effect of a cultivated Chinese milieu, the engraver shows a landscape scroll draped artistically over the table in a way that would horrify a Chinese connoisseur. This is, so far as I can discover, the earliest representation of a
Chinese landscape painting in European art.

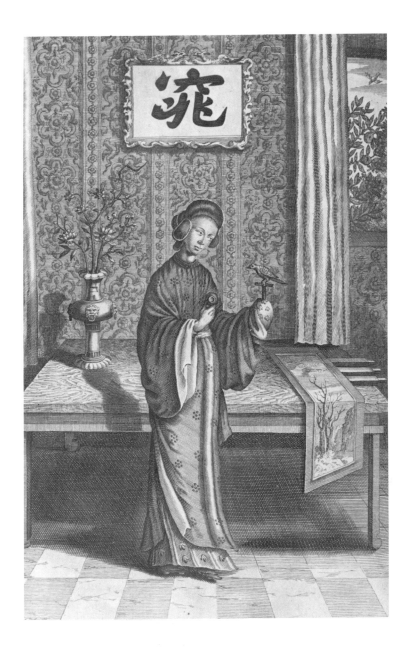

64.

Anonymous. Lady with a Bird. Engraving from Athanasius Kircher, *China Illustrata* (1665). Kircher writes that this is a copy from a Chinese painting sent to him by the Jesuits. He particularly admired the dignity and modesty of the Chinese costume.

Kircher makes no mention of this engraving in the text. Ten years after Kircher's great work appeared, the German art historian Joachim von Sandrart published his *Teutsche Akademie*, which is not only the first Western attempt at a comprehensive study of art but also the first Western book on art to attempt an assessment of Chinese painting. Sandrart echoes the poor view of it expressed by Ricci and by the Jesuit scholar Alvarez de Semedo, who in 1641 had written: 'in Painting, they have more curiositie than perfection. They know not how to make use of either Oyles or Shadowing in the Art. . . . But at present there are some of them, who have been taught by us, that use Oyles, and are come to make perfect pictures'. If Europeans admired Oriental painting at all, it was not on aesthetic grounds. A seventeenth-century German collector shocked Simplicissimus (the writer Hans Jacob Christoffel von Grimmelshausen) by preferring his Chinese scroll to an Ecce Homo, but he explained that this was simply because the Chinese painting was the greater rarity.

Sandrart describes in some detail several Chinese paintings that he says are in his possession, one of which shows a lady nursing a child at her breast—a most improbable subject for a high-class Chinese picture—and another, a lady holding a tame bird in her hand. This sounds so like one of the engravings in Kircher's *China Illustrata,* which Sandrart would certainly have known, that one doubts whether he ever saw any real Chinese paintings at all. Our doubts are reinforced by his remark that 'in their wretched painting the Indian, Higiemondo, known as the Black—although far removed from real art—was considered the best artist'. And he sets before the eyes of 'the noble reader' the likeness reproduced here (Figure 65). The engraving could be a representation of any genial savage, but where Sandrart found the name Higiemondo is a mystery.

This is a warning to examine carefully authors' claims that their engravings are taken directly from Chinese paintings, for by this time the demand for authentic pictures of China was so great and the supply so meagre that illustrators stole from each other openly and used the same figures again and again. In 1684 Father Couplet returned from China, bringing with him a set of portraits of famous men and women painted on silk. Of the engravings that were allegedly made directly from these by Nolin in Paris, only one, a portrait of Candide, niece of Ricci's notable convert Paul Hsü Kuang-ch'i, is actually based on a Chinese painting. The thoroughly transformed portrait of Confucius has a Chinese original somewhere in the background, but the magnificent picture of the king of Tartary bears not the slightest resemblance to a Chinese painting in style or content. In fact all this set, except for the portrait of Candide Hsü, was cribbed from Kircher.

Other sources well known in France were the Dutch engravings in the *Voyages* of von Lindschoten (1656), which included pictures of Chinese life and portraits of Chinese merchants, and de Geyer and de Keyser's account of the Dutch

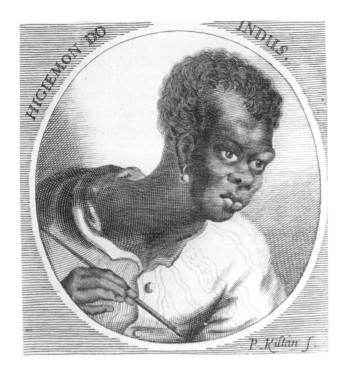

65.
Anonymous. *Higiemondo* (or Higie-
monte). Engraving from Joachim von
Sandrart, *Teutsche Akademie der Bau-,
Bildhauer- und Malerkunst* (1675). The label above the portrait shows that Higiemondo came from the Indies, which at
this time could have meant anywhere
east of the Red Sea; the first part of his
made-up name, Higie-, sounds vaguely
Japanese.

embassies, published in Amsterdam in 1665–75, adorned with 150 plates after
illustrations 'made in China from life' by Jacob de Mieurs. This Dutch engraver
also owned Japanese prints, which he used to illustrate the *Ambassades* of de
Kempen and de Noble (Amsterdam, 1775). These included a seated warrior—
with a dragon amid flames, depicted in a violently Japanese manner—and many
genre scenes.

How far anyone in Europe understood Oriental painting at this time is de-
batable. Even Matteo Ricci's account of it is rather patronising. Yet European
collectors might at least have learned to appreciate Japanese art if they could have
laid their hands on a copy of a remarkable book published in Nagasaki in 1608
by the Portuguese Jesuit missionary João Rodrigues. His monumental *Arte da
Lingoa de Iapam* is far more than a grammar of the Japanese language, for he
includes long and appreciative passages on Japanese painting: not only on Kanō
School decorations in the mansions of Kyōto but on paintings of the *Eight Views
of Hsiao and Hsiang* in the Chinese manner; he describes with real understanding
Zen aesthetics, the garden, the tea ceremony and the Japanese aesthetic ideals of

sabi (the sense of loneliness in this transient world) and *wabi* (rustic yet disciplined simplicity). This book was written for the guidance of missionaries in Japan and was hardly known in Europe. Had it been better known, who can tell what influence it might have had? Perhaps Europe would not have had to wait nearly three centuries before coming to a real understanding of Japanese art.

If Europeans had had to rely on the Italian Jesuits for knowledge of Chinese art, it is doubtful whether they would have learned very much, for the paintings that they sent back from Peking mostly stayed in Italy and became known, if at all, through engravings and the kind of descriptions that I have quoted.

The situation in Paris may have been different. In 1684 Father Couplet brought a young Chinese gentleman, Shen Fu-tsung (called Chin Fo Cum, Michel Chen or Shen Fuzong), to Paris, where he was made a fuss of; he demonstrated the art of eating with chopsticks before the king at Versailles and seemed eager to show a group of savants how to write Chinese characters with a brush. One of them describes a visit to the Jesuit Mission de Saint Louis where Shen Fu-tsung and the fathers showed him a number of Chinese portraits of famous men on silk, brought back by Couplet. Whether they looked at any landscapes or other subjects, he does not say. Later, Couplet and Shen Fu-tsung visited England and dined with Lord Clarendon. Sir Godfrey Kneller painted a portrait of the Chinese convert holding a crucifix, which hangs in the royal collection. Kneller considered it his finest work.

The wave of enthusiasm for things Chinese spread not from Rome but rather from Holland and France. In Holland it dates from the founding of Jan Compagnie in 1602; in France from the time of Cardinal Mazarin, who came to power in 1624 as minister to Louis XIII and remained at the centre of affairs under Louis XIV till his death in 1661. Mazarin was an omnivorous collector and through the agency of one of his servants carried on a brisk trade in antiques on the side. He was also largely responsible for founding the Compagnie des Indes in 1660. There were a number of Oriental objects, including lacquer, porcelain and textiles, in his first sale in 1649. He owned several painted screens, two of which he gave to Louis's queen consort, Anne of Austria, who was Mazarin's confidante and possibly also his mistress. Screens, as we shall see, were to play an important part in introducing Chinese paintings to Europe.

Louis XIV at Versailles and the dauphin at Fontainebleau owned quantities of Oriental objets d'art. The inventory of Versailles for 1667–69 mentions twelve panels from a screen with birds and landscapes on a gold ground, brought from China, and there were many more listed in later inventories, painted with landscapes, figures, birds and flowers, and children's festivals. James II, visiting the dauphin in his apartments at Versailles after his abdication in 1688, speaks with admiration of his Chinese paintings, meaning, presumably, not hanging scrolls but screens and possibly wall panels.

Father Bouvet, author of *l'Estat présent de la Chine en figures,* had brought back from China an urgent request from the K'ang-hsi emperor for men skilled in various arts, including that of perspective, 'in which', he noted, 'the Chinese are most ignorant'. A man of great energy and resource, Bouvet chartered a sloop, the *Amphitrite,* filled it with presents from Louis XIV to the emperor and high officials and set sail for China in March 1698. On board were eight Jesuits, among them Giovanni Gherardini, the expert on perspective whom we have already encountered, and a case of engravings after Poussin and Mignard.

The shrewd Bouvet had the *Amphitrite* registered as a warship to avoid customs duties, but they had trouble with local officials in Canton who wanted their cut, and they were able to preserve the royal presents only with some difficulty. The rest of the European goods were bartered for Chinese arts and crafts at Canton, and in January 1699 the *Amphitrite* left for the return voyage, bearing gifts from K'ang-hsi to Louis XIV. It docked at Port Louis on 3 August 1700, and after the gifts had been dispatched to Versailles, a huge sale was held at Nantes. It included 'des peintures de Chine', thirty-six folding screens, three cases of unmounted screens on paper, and four cases of single-panel screens. So successful was the sale that another expedition was immediately organised. It almost ended in disaster, but the second consignment, which finally reached Nantes in 1703, included no less than forty-five cases of folding screens.

With the screens came hand-printed wallpapers and paintings on paper that could be pasted on a wall. For these, England was as big a customer as France. The *China Letter Book* of the East India Company, for instance, records that between 1699 and 1702 'paper pictures' were ordered in Canton to the value of £200 or £300. In 1742 Lady Cardigan bought eighty-eight 'Indian pictures' and had them pasted all over the walls of her dining room; and a well-known London firm advertised that they fitted up rooms with 'Indian pictures or prints'. A good example of this kind of decoration is the Chinese Room at Milton Hall in Northamptonshire, papered with figure subjects and still-lifes, some dated between 1745 and 1750, and executed in a combination of block printing, freehand brushwork and collage. They have great charm, but if patrons considered such pictures typical of Chinese painting, they may be forgiven for holding so low an opinion of it.

K'ang-hsi's presents to Louis included not only works of art but also books, and the king owned what was, outside Rome, probably the finest Chinese library in Europe. A few volumes had come from Cardinal Mazarin's library; several had been brought back by Father Couplet in 1687; forty-nine books came with Father Bouvet as gifts from K'ang-hsi in 1697. By the time of his death the king's library included no less than 280 volumes of the great illustrated encyclopedia *Ku-chin t'u-shu chi-ch'eng,* completed in 1729, and a book described as *L'Encyclopédie chinoise,* richly illustrated with pictures of scenery, towns and villages, freaks of nature, temples, architecture and an explanation of the arts of drawing and painting, in fourteen volumes. More important still for our purposes was a copy of the *Chieh-tzu-yüan hua chuan* (Painting Manual of the Mustard-seed Garden; 1679), for only this famous book fits the description in Rémusat's *Catalogue:* 'Un traité de l'art du Paysage et de la manière de peindre les fleurs, les oiseaux, les insects, ou comme on dit en présent, *l'Iconographie naturelle*'.

In addition to the Chinese illustrated books in the royal library, others found their way into the collections of the dealers and engravers who played a big part in bringing artists and clients together and in disseminating the fashion for chinoiseries. Jean de Julienne (1686–1766), an intimate friend of Watteau who undertook to engrave and publish as much as possible of his work after his untimely death, owned an enormous collection of pictures also, although these are not mentioned in the sale of his collection in the year after his death. Jacques-Gabriel Huquier (1695–1722), who made many engravings after Watteau and Boucher, possessed several collections of paintings of Chinese flowers of great beauty and rarity. He owned in addition four large volumes of Chinese paintings of plants, destined for the Botanical Gardens. Watteau, Boucher, Fragonard, to say nothing of the decorators who specialized in chinoiseries such as Pillement and Huet, must all have been familiar with the collections of dealers and engravers such as these.

If only we could know what Chinese riches these collections contained! But they are all scattered. Today the Bibliothèque Nationale contains a number of Chinese pictures and albums that arrived in France in the seventeenth and eighteenth centuries and might have been accessible to these artists. Among them are several albums of birds and flowers, and a copy of the *Painting Manual of the Ten Bamboo Hall* (*Shih-chu-chai shu-hua p'u*), a famous collection of colour prints, first published in 1633, which may well have reached Paris before the end of the century. There are also in the collection four exquisite unsigned leaves from an album of landscapes possibly by Yeh Hsin, one of the members of the Nanking School of gentleman-painters who, as I suggested in the previous chapter, may have been in touch with the Jesuits and show signs of European influence in their work.

Watteau painted several pictures in what he claimed to be, and people accepted as, the Chinese manner. Most famous was the series of *Diverses Figures Chinoises et Tartares* (that is, Manchu), which he painted for the Château de la Muette, the royal hunting lodge in the Bois de Boulogne. The château and all but a few of the paintings were destroyed by the middle of the eighteenth century, and today the most famous designs can only be studied in the engravings of Boucher, Aubert and Leaurat (Figure 66). While the style of the figures is very un-Chinese and the settings are purely imaginary, the captions are more or less

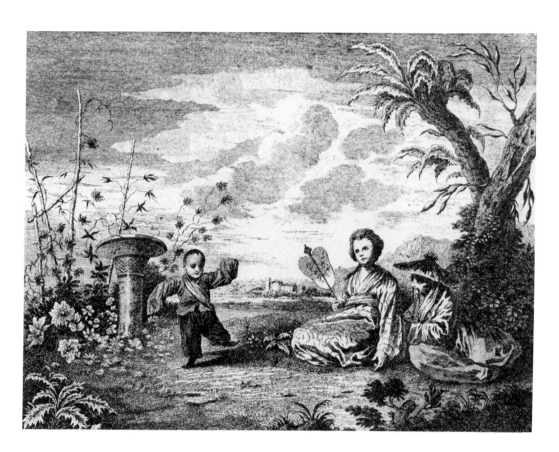

66.
C. Aubert. Panel for the decorations for
the Château de la Muette. Engraving
after a lost painting by Antoine Watteau
(1680–1721). Ashmolean Museum, Oxford. The paintings have all disappeared.
A typical chinoiserie in which only the
dress has a slightly Chinese flavour.

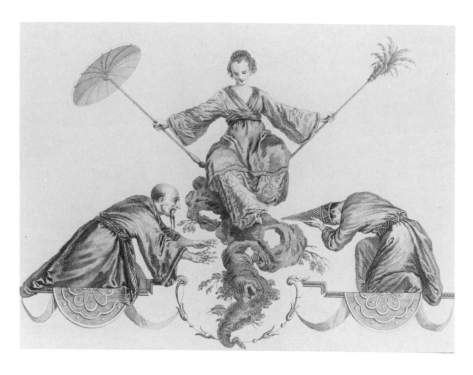

67.
C. Aubert. *La Déesse Ki Mâo Sáo dans le Royaume de Mang au Pays des Laos*. Engraving after a lost painting by Watteau in the Château de la Muette. c. 1719. Ashmolean Museum, Oxford. Compared with Kircher's attempts at accuracy, the Oriental visions of the eighteenth-century artists are simply delightful fantasies.

68.
Antoine Watteau (1680–1721). Chinoiserie. Panel from a harpsichord. Oil. 1708. Collection Besançon de Wagner. The exotic musicians and their instruments are pure invention, but the birds and flowers could have been inspired by Chinese screens, of which Watteau saw many.

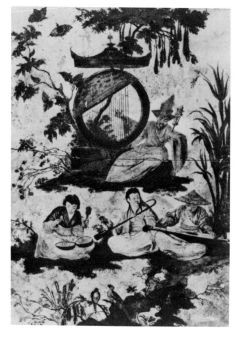

accurate transcriptions of Chinese words. A charming group of an old man and a youth, for instance, is labelled *Lao Gine* [Mandarin: *Lao-jen*] *ou Vieillard, Chao Nien* [*Hsiao-nien*] *ou Jeune Chinois;* a picture of a slave, *Hia-theo* [*Ya-t'ou*]. Watteau must have seen a Chinese illustrated book or album with the captions translated, but in making the pictures he has rejected the Chinese original almost completely.

The same is true of Watteau's famous designs *L'Empereur Chinois* and *La Déesse Ki Mâo Sáo dans le Royaume de Mang au Pays des Laos* (Figure 67). Bélévitch-Stankévitch considered that these two pictures, engraved by Aubert, preserve the Chinese flavour of the originals more closely than do the la Muette panels reproduced by Boucher and Leaurat. But both are pure chinoiseries. There is only one work of Watteau's that seems to preserve a Chinese flavour, and that is a very minor one: a panel from a harpsichord decorated with figures in a garden, in the Besançon de Wagner collection in Paris (Figure 68). The style, if not the technique, of the birds and flowers in the upper left corner is quite Chinese and could have been taken from an imported album, screen or wall hanging.

It is possible that Watteau owned Chinese paintings. He would certainly have known the collection of Jean de Julienne and may possibly have seen some of the albums in the royal collection. He also knew a young Chinese gentleman, a Mr Tsao, and made a superb portrait of him, now in the Albertina, Vienna. Mr Tsao looks a casual, self-confident young man, hardly the sort to be very discriminating or knowledgeable about painting. There were a number of Chinese in Paris at this time, however, and it is conceivable that Watteau may have picked up some hints from them. But this is hardly significant, for there is nothing in any of his surviving work that shows that he knew how to handle the brush in the Chinese manner.

Perhaps the nearest approach to the Chinese brush line is in Pierre Giffart's forty-three plates for *L'Estat présent de la Chine en figures,* published in 1697 (Figure 69). These are based on Chinese paintings brought back in that year by Father Bouvet. Some of Giffart's plates appear again in du Halde's *Description de la Chine* (1735), which met for the eighteenth century the need that Kircher's *China Illustrata* had fulfilled for the seventeenth. In his dedication to the Duc de Bourgogne, Bouvet notes that the emperor, high officials and great ladies whom he presents 'are the masters of an empire celebrated for its antiquity, for the beauty of its government, and for the particular character and spirit of its people'. And he goes on to explain, as had Kircher, that his purpose in these plates is to show the dignity and modesty of Chinese dress. The copy in the Bibliothèque Nationale contains three impressions of each plate, the first of which is uncoloured and shows how skilfully Giffart has preserved the delicately calligraphic line of the original.

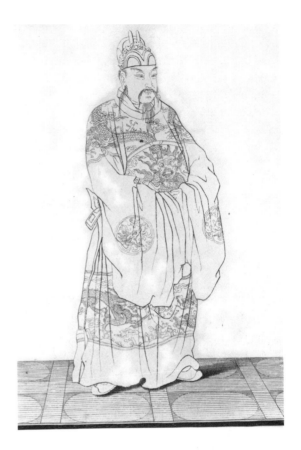

69.
Pierre Giffart (1638–1723). *Empereur Chinois*. Engraving from Joachim Bouvet, *L'Estat présent de la Chine en figures* (1697). A fine illustration of French admiration for the dignity of the Chinese official costume, in which Giffart skillfully suggests the subtle modulation of the Chinese brush line.

Even more remarkable from the technical point of view is a handsome folio volume, *Collection précieuse et enluminée des fleurs les plus belles et les plus curieuses,* containing a hundred engravings of birds, flowers and insects (Figure 70). They are taken directly from Chinese paintings, and the engraver has not merely transmitted the line, as in *L'Estat présent,* but has managed to suggest, with the burin, the tone of Chinese watercolour. Only when we look carefully at these pictures do we realize that they are engraved and not drawn with the brush.

The vogue for things Chinese, or pseudo-Chinese, that swept Europe is obviously discernable only in the minor and decorative arts, in the arabesques and *singeries* of Huet and Pillement, in the exotic furniture, textiles and wallpapers that figure so largely in the Rococo style. It was strong enough to transform what were obviously copies of Japanese prints and Mughal miniatures into chinoiseries, as in the extraordinary *Livre de desseins chinois* [*sic*] *tirés après des originaux de Perse, des Indes, de la Chine, et du Japon,* etched by Fraisse and published

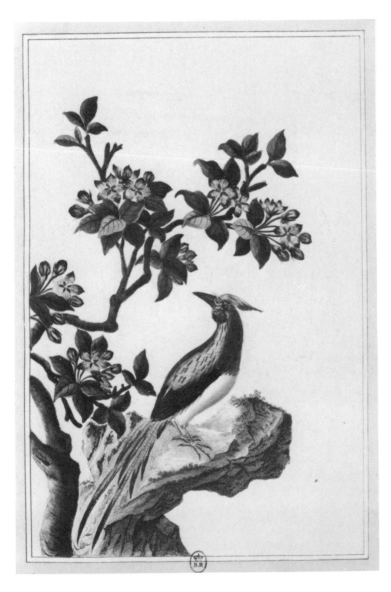

70.
Anonymous. A Page from the *Collection
précieuse et enluminée des fleurs les plus belles
et les plus curieuses*. Hand-coloured engraving. Eighteenth century. Bibliothèque Nationale, Paris. The engraver has
gone to great pains to suggest the quality
and texture of a Chinese bird and flower
painting.

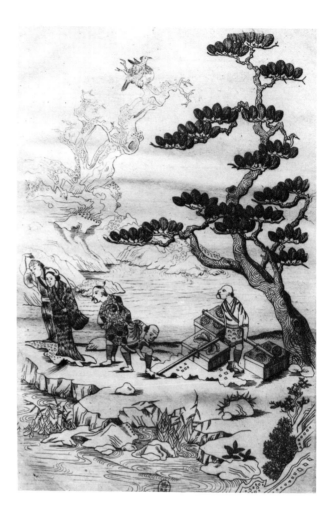

71.
J. A. Fraisse. Etching from the *Livre de desseins chinois tirés après des origineaux de Perse, des Indes, de la Chine, et du Japon.* 1735. Bibliothèque Nationale, Paris. Fraisse calls this series 'Chinese', even when, as in this curious print, they are clearly derived from Japanese originals.

in 1735 (Figure 71). But the effect on high art was negligible. Boucher never, so far as I know—though he must have seen genuine Chinese paintings—consciously attempted a composition in the Chinese manner. Not a line of Watteau's suggests that he had learned the lesson of the Chinese brush.

It is ironic that the only Chinese artist known to have practised in Europe in the eighteenth century had no influence at all: his art was completely Western. In 1769 a Cantonese named Chetqua (Chitqua or Shykinqua), who specialised in small portrait busts and full-length figures modelled in clay and coloured, obtained permission from the Canton authorities to visit Batavia in Java. A staunch anglophile, he instead contrived to sail to London, where he exhibited at the Royal Academy in 1770 and modelled the delightful seated portrait of

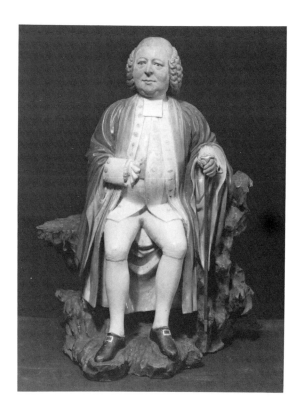

72.
Chetqua (or Chitqua; d. 1796). Portrait
Model of Dr Anthony Askew. Coloured
clay. About 1770–71. Royal College of
Physicians Collection, National Portrait
Gallery, London. *The Gentleman's Maga-*
zine wrote of Chetqua, 'very sensible,
and a great observer. . . . He steals
a likeness, and forms the busts from
memory'.

Dr Anthony Askew, which can still be seen at the Royal College of Physicians
(Figure 72). After nearly drowning in the Thames Estuary on his first attempt to
return to Canton in 1771, the homesick Chetqua eventually reached home, and
died, it was reported in the *Gentlemen's Magazine,* by taking poison in 1796.

It is hardly surprising that China had so little influence on European art
when we consider the attitude towards it expressed by European writers even
while the fashion was at its height. After admitting that the Chinese are good at
painting birds and flowers, a writer in the journal *The World* (25 March 1755)
goes on to say that their figures are ludicrously contorted, 'a high burlesque'.
There is, of course, no perspective: 'false lights, false shadows, false perspective
and proportions, gay colours without that gradation of tints, that mutual variety

of enlightened and darkened objects which relieve and give force to each other, at the same time that they give ease and response to the eye. . . . in short, every incoherent combination of forms in nature . . . are the essentials of Chinese painting'. So long as people held to the view that the accurate rendering of three-dimensional objects, as opposed to three-dimensional space, was funda-mental to good art, so long as they continued to believe that the formal ideals expressed by Claude Lorrain and Poussin were sacrosanct, there was no hope that the aims and methods of Chinese landscape painting would be understood. That even painters who might have shown a purely technical curiosity about Chinese art remained indifferent to it suggests that artists are apt to 'see' in the work of other artists only what they themselves can make use of.

China and the English Garden

Little though China's impact on eighteenth-century European art may have been, there are grounds for thinking that the influence of Chinese aesthetic ideas was eventually felt, in a very indirect and subtle way, in landscape painting. In one sphere, however, that of garden design, its effect was immediate and revolu-tionary. As early as 1683 Sir William Temple, himself an enthusiastic gardener, had described the Chinese garden at length in his essay *Upon Heroick Virtue*. The Chinese, he says, scorn the formal symmetry and straight lines of the Western garden:

> Among us, the beauty of building and planting is placed chiefly in some certain pro-portions, symmetries, or uniformities; our walks and our trees ranged so as to an-swer one another, and at exact distances. The Chinese scorn this way of planting, and say, a boy that can tell a hundred, may plant walks of trees in straight lines, and over-against one another, and to what length and extent he pleases. But their great-est reach of imagination is employed in contriving figures, where the beauty shall be great, and strike the eye, but without any order or disposition of parts that shall be commonly or easily observed: and though we have hardly any notion of this sort of beauty, yet they have a particular word to express it, and, where they find it hit the eye at first sight, they say the sharadge is fine and admirable, or any such expres-sion of esteem. And whoever observes the work upon the best Indian gowns, or the painting upon their best screens or porcelains, will find their beauty is all of this kind (that is) without order.

Temple's praise of irregular beauty was echoed by Addison in his essays, and by Goldsmith, whose Chinese philosopher in London comments:

The English have not yet brought the art of gardening to the same perfection with the Chinese, but have lately begun to imitate them. Nature is now followed with greater assiduity than formerly; the trees are suffered to shoot out with the utmost luxuriance; the streams, no longer forced from their native beds, are permitted to wind along the valleys, spontaneous flowers take the place of the finished parterres, and the enamelled meadows of the shaven green.

But of course the disorder that these early enthusiasts describe is not accidental at all. In fact, as a means of composing a landscape, it is a manifestation of the underlying principles of nature itself, a mode of formal control, as Gustav Ecke so aptly put it in attempting to define Temple's baffling term *sharadge* (or, as it is often written, *sharawadji*) 'in which—this is the deeper meaning of sharawadji—an apparent "disorder" is really rhythm in disguise'. This concept, so new, and so perfectly in tune with developing Rococo taste, dealt a heavy blow to established doctrine that beauty lay in regularity, symmetry and visible order.

In painting his picture of the Chinese garden, Temple was wiser than he knew. Some of his opponents had read du Halde's description of it as small, practical, with more vegetables than flowers, which was certainly true of the majority of domestic gardens. But in this sinophile era people were ready to believe that China excelled in this as in almost every other respect, and when Father Ripa came to the Court of St James's in 1724 and told of the great imperial gardens, or rather garden parks, of the Summer Palace at Jehol, of which he had made engravings with so much pain twelve years before, he was heard with enthusiasm, for here was direct confirmation that the Chinese garden was as Temple had imagined it to be. Further support was provided by du Halde's publication of the Jesuit painter Jean-Denis Attiret's long account of the gardens of Ch'ien-lung's country palace the Yüan-ming-yüan. 'Dans les maisons de plaisance', he had written in 1743, 'on veut que prèsque partout il regne un beau désordre, une anti-symmétrie. Tout roule sur le principe: c'est une compagne rustique et naturel qu'on veut représenter; une solitude, non pas un palais'.

In London, Father Ripa had met Lord Burlington and possibly also William Kent, who was then designing the gardens of Burlington's new villa at Chiswick. Kent, who, in Horace Walpole's famous phrase, 'leaped the fence and saw that all nature was a garden', was chiefly responsible for spreading the taste for a 'judicious wildness', for the imaginative use of rocks and water, for elements of variety and surprise, into the gardens and parks of mid-eighteenth century England. The garden might be studded with classical tempietti, as at Stourhead, or varied with the occasional Gothic folly or Chinese pavilion, as at Painshill, but these were mere ornaments. Sir William Chambers, who by 1749 had visited

Canton twice, if not three times, in the service of the Swedish East India Company and had written extensively on the subject, called the Chinese buildings that he had seen 'toys in architecture'. How much more so were the fragile structures, with their bird-wing roofs and tinkling bells, that adorned the parks and gardens of England, France and Sweden. They, like their Gothic cousins, were not to be taken seriously. What was revolutionary was the concept of the Chinese garden itself and the aesthetic principles that governed it.

Chambers went further than anyone else in his admiration of the Chinese as garden designers, though much of what he said about them was the product of his own imagination. The only important example that conformed to his idea of the Chinese garden, the Yüan-ming-yüan, he never saw, and his contemporaries were justifiably sceptical when he wrote in his *Dissertation on Oriental Gardening* (1720): 'The Chinese rank a perfect work in that art, with the greatest productions of human understanding, and say, that its efficacy in moving the passions, yields to few other arts whatever. Their Gardeners are not only Botanists, but also Painters and Philosophers; having a thorough knowledge of the human mind, and of the arts by which its strongest feelings are excited'. In this respect, he might have added, they were unlike his bête noire, the upstart Capability Brown, whose parks were so natural that a 'stranger is often at a loss to know whether he be walking in a common meadow'.

Chambers maintained, on the basis of what he claimed he had been told by 'Lopqua, a celebrated Chinese painter', that the Chinese distinguished three kinds of garden, which they call the pleasing, the horrid and the enchanted. The scenes of horror, of which he gives a hair-raising description (in the *Gentlemen's Magazine* for 1757), read like something in the more violent paintings of Salvator Rosa. We cannot help wondering what questions he asked the obliging Lopqua, if he existed at all. No wonder Chambers concludes that 'the art of laying out grounds after the *Chinese* manner is exceedingly difficult, and not to be attained by persons of narrow intellects'.

C. C. Hirschfeld, in his *Theorie der Gartenkunst* (1779), rebuked Chambers for serving up his own ideas on garden design in Chinese dress in order to make them more sensational and acceptable. But Chambers, though he exaggerated, was not entirely wrong. There were a few Chinese scholars and painters who laid out irregular gardens on a modest scale, notably in Soochow (Figure 73), though Chambers could hardly have known that an exact contemporary of Temple's was the gentleman-painter and philosopher Shih-t'ao, who designed for his friends in Yangchow gardens that embodied just those principles that both these writers attributed to the Chinese. Moreover, in China as in England, the making of gardens was looked upon as a very proper occupation for a gentleman.

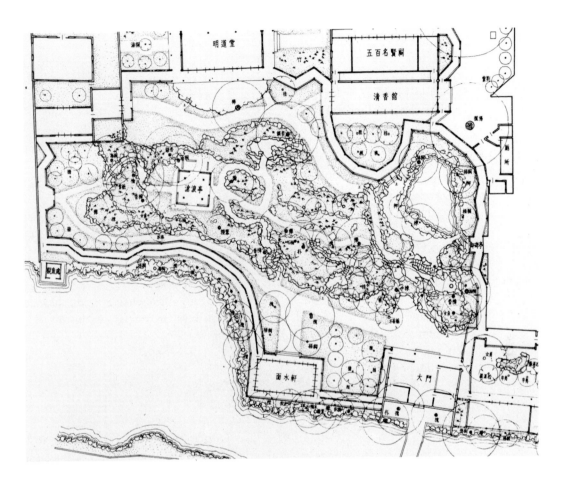

73.
Plan of the Ou-yüan (Double Garden) in
Soochow. Seventeenth century. Although
Matteo Ripa never visited Soochow, his
reports of gardens of this sort were
greatly to influence garden design in
eighteenth-century England.

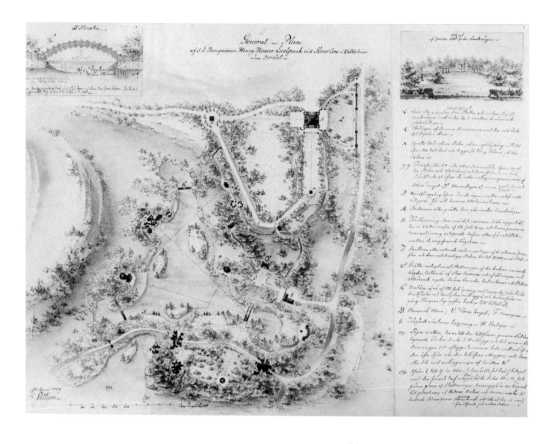

74.
F. M. Piper (1746–1824). Plan of Stour-
head, Wiltshire. From a sketchbook of
1779. Pencil and watercolour. Kunglika
Akademien för de Fria Konsterna, Stock-
holm. Piper, a friend of Sir William
Chambers, included this in his *Description
of the Idea and General Plan of an English
Pleasure Park,* written in 1811–12. He
also made copies of woodcuts of the
Yüan-ming-yüan that had reached
Stockholm.

Henry Hoare and Charles Hamilton studied seventeenth-century landscape paintings, chiefly those of Claude Lorrain, before creating their carefully calculated vistas at Stourhead and Painshill. But if we examine the beautiful plan of Stourhead drawn by the Swedish architect F. M. Piper (Figure 74), we might be looking at the layout of the Yüan-ming-yüan. The winding waterways and artificial islands, the pavilions and tempietti (albeit chiefly classical ones) on little eminences, the sudden twists in the paths to reveal new vistas such as a bridge, a grotto, a rockery—all were as had been described by Ripa and Attiret when writing from Peking. Speaking of Stourhead, Sirén writes: 'The rustic stone material that has been used here is strikingly like that commonly found in China, and it has been exploited with the same endeavour to reproduce something of the picturesque wildness so characteristic of Chinese gardens from the Ming and Ch'ing periods. The resemblance to the Chinese "mountains" is certainly no more a coincidence than were the grottoes at Painshill, but rather a deliberate intention, even if one cannot speak of deliberate imitation'. We may not entirely agree with Sirén in this instance—a Chinese rockery may be hard to distinguish from a ruined Italian grotto—but the consciousness was there.

The Chinese idea of the garden, however, had to compete with the ideals of the Picturesque, for they are subtly different. The Chinese garden is a microcosm; it unfolds in time, like the Chinese landscape handscroll that we slowly unroll as we go on an imaginary journey amid mountains and lakes. The European ideal, embodied in the Picturesque, was precisely what the word implies, a series of carefully composed pictures seen from chosen viewpoints—here a Poussin, there a Claude Lorrain, next a Salvator Rosa. The Chinese concept is organic, and at least apparently natural; the European is static, and its very artificiality a virtue. While the need to pass easily from one picture to the next gave continuity to the Picturesque garden, the experience was still of a series of framed vistas to be looked at from outside—the lowest category in the aesthetics of Chinese landscape painting—rather than of a natural world to be experienced by moving within it.

Nevertheless, Chinese ideals, misunderstood or misapplied though they may have been, did percolate some way towards the centre of eighteenth-century taste and are indirectly reflected even in landscape painting itself. We will look in vain here for so clear an imitation of the Chinese model as Chambers advocated and Kent seems to have applied, for no European artist ever really looked at a Chinese landscape scroll with a discerning or receptive eye. Yet, tentatively in Boucher and Watteau, more wholeheartedly in Hubert Robert and the later Gainsborough (Figure 75), we encounter an apparently spontaneous but in reality highly sophisticated rearranging of nature on the canvas, an assymetry, a

114

75.
Thomas Gainsborough (1722–88).
Mountainous Landscape with a Boat on a Lake. Grey and grey-black washes on buff paper heightened with white. Late 1770s. City Museum and Art Gallery, Birmingham, England. There is no evidence that Gainsborough was interested in Chinese art, although there is a tenuous link through Sir Henry Hoare, the creator of Stourhead, who was one of the first patrons to appreciate, and buy, a landscape by Gainsborough.

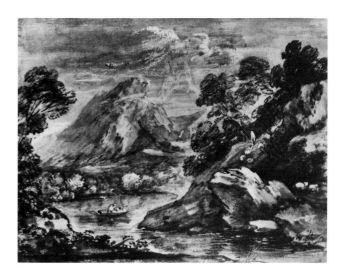

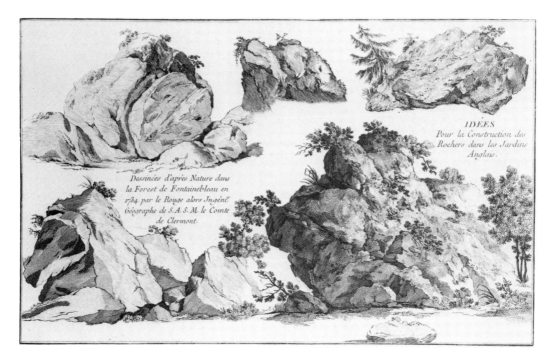

76.
G. L. le Rouge (eighteenth century). Rocks in the Forest of Fontainebleau and Ideas for Rocks in an English Garden. Engraving from *Le Jardin anglo-chinois* (1786). Photo by John R. Freeman and Co. Le Rouge published, between 1774 and 1789, twenty-one volumes of gardens and details from China and Europe.

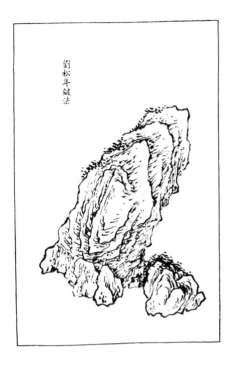

77.
How to Paint a Rock in the Manner of
Liu Sung-nien. Woodcut from the *Painting Manual of the Mustard-seed Garden*
(*Chieh-tzu-yüan hua-chuan*). Modern re-
print from 1679 edition. Although there
is no evidence that the *Chieh-tzu-yüan* influenced English garden design, the Chinese idea of the fancy rock as an element
in the garden certainly played its part.

'controlled disorder', both in composition and brushwork, that owes nothing to
Claude Lorrain. Salvator Rosa's romantic expressionism may have provided the
pictorial techniques, but it is perhaps no exaggeration to claim that in so far as
the new landscape painting had a theoretical foundation, it lay at least partly, if
unwittingly, in Chinese aesthetics.

It is possible that Chinese pictorial art had a more direct influence than can
actually be proved. In the 1780s le Rouge put together two volumes of engravings of gardens and ideas for gardens under the general title *Le Jardin anglo-
chinois*. Some of the plates were copied from Chinese paintings that he had obtained from Stockholm. There are several pages of engravings of rocks (Figure
76), some of which may have been derived from Salvator Rosa; one is taken
from Vernet. But the rest le Rouge says he drew from nature in the Forest of
Fontainebleau. Yet they may have been more or less directly inspired by the rocks
in Chinese painters' manuals such as *The Ten Bamboo Hall* and *The Mustard-seed
Garden* (Figure 77). The slablike faceting, the grouping of big rocks with little
rocks clustered around their feet and the slab in the right foreground of the le
Rouge engraving all conform to the rules for painting rocks set out in these
books, which were also used by Chinese garden designers. The very idea of the
rock as something to be enjoyed for itself, and not merely as a component in a
picturesque landscape, is entirely Chinese in origin.

The Nineteenth Century: The Years of Estrangement

In the early decades of the nineteenth century as chinoiserie became engulfed in the rising tide of austere Neoclassicism, Europe's flirtation with the Orient—for it had been no more than that—came to an end. Japan remained a closed and virtually unknown land. Admiration for things Chinese turned to contempt as the West learned more about the true state of Chinese society. The Jesuits were gone from Peking and there were no European scholars at the Chinese court; diplomatic missions were few—and coldly received if they were received at all. Lord Macartney's embassy of 1792 was the least unsuccessful, but it led to nothing, and now continuous contact was confined to the merchants in Canton and Macao. The Chinese themselves were becoming actively hostile to the West, and the Opium War of 1840–42 was the outcome of fifty years of growing antagonism. Meanwhile, chinoiserie went out in a blaze of glory at the Royal Pavilion in Brighton, completed in 1832 (Figure 78). But that extravagant fantasy was already an anachronism, coming as it did almost half a century after its nearest rivals at Potsdam and Drottningholm, for it appeared, with tremendous éclat, to an empty theatre. The comedy was over, and the audience had gone home.

Though mutual disenchantment was by now complete, decadent chinoiseries still appeared from time to time, and Europe continued to be flooded with Oriental lacquer and garish 'Nankeen' porcelain. For a brief moment at mid-century it seemed that Chinese art was about to become a subject of serious study: P. P. Thoms published *Dissertation on the Ancient Vases of the Shang Dynasty*, prompted by the display at the Great Exhibition of engravings from the Sung dynasty imperial catalogue, *Po-ku t'u-lu,* and in 1858 there appeared Stanislas Julien's scholarly translation of the eighteenth-century monograph on porcelain, *Ching-te-chen t'ao-lu.* These were translations of Chinese texts, however, not books on Chinese art, and they had no influence on current taste. But two years before Julien's work appeared, there occurred, in quite another quarter, the seemingly trivial event that was to open the doors, at last, to a real face-to-face encounter with Oriental art.

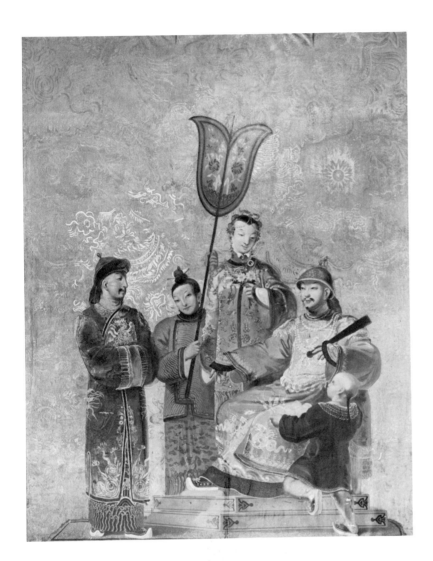

78.
Robert Jones. Chinoiserie Decoration
in the Interior of the Royal Pavilion,
Brighton. 1820–22. The last and most
spectacular example in England of the
taste for pseudo-Chinese style. The decoration was inspired by some Chinese
wallpapers that had been given to the
Prince Regent in 1802.

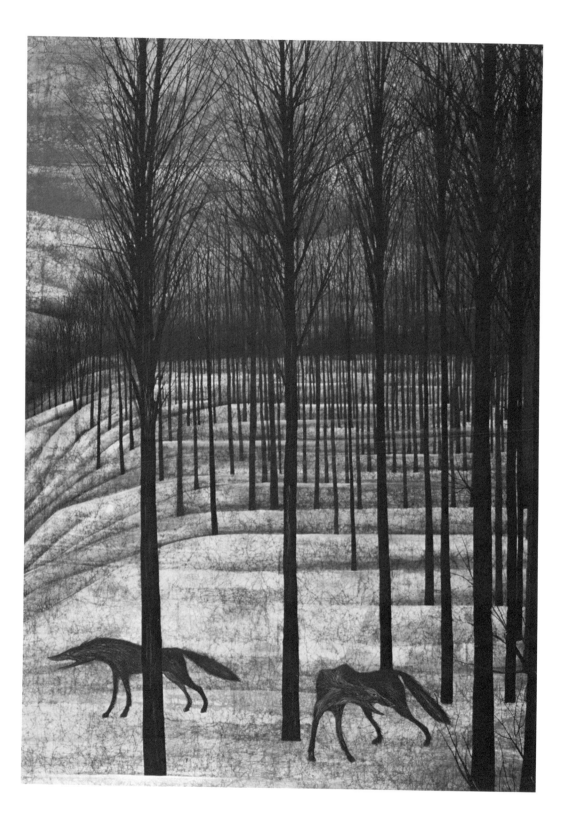

4

Japan: From the Meiji Restoration of 1868 to the Present Day

Art under the Meiji Emperor: Surrender and Counterattack

By the middle of the nineteenth century the pressure for internal reform and the challenge of the Western powers were building up to a climax. In 1854 Commodore Perry returned with his 'Black Ships' to sign the treaty of Shimonoseki, which was to throw open the doors of Japan. In 1856 Townsend Harris arrived in Shimoda as American consul general, and the Office for the Study of Barbarian Books was established. During the next four years commercial treaties and ambassadors were exchanged between Japan and the United States, and three ports were opened to foreign trade.

The shōgun's feudal administration was quite unfitted to deal with the flood of foreign ideas and goods that now began to pour into Japan or with the increasing political and economic tension that resulted. In 1867 the shōgunate was abolished and early in the following year the emperor, surrounded by young and progressive advisers, was restored to power. Long before the Meiji emperor died in 1912, Japan had achieved the astonishing feat of converting itself into a first-class industrial power on the Western pattern and had defeated in war its two great continental neighbours, China and Russia. This it accomplished by a rigorous acceptance of Western ideas and skills. Japan's leaders, at this time, saw Western art not as a possible threat to their own great tradition but simply as a useful branch of Western technology.

119

In the first fifteen years of the Meiji era, the true character of Western art was too little understood for any kind of synthesis or compromise with Japanese art to be possible: it was all or nothing. Resistance to Western art, at a time when acceptance of Western values and methods in all other fields was total, would simply have divorced art from society and the trend of the times. Besides, the forces of reaction, or conservatism, were thrown into disarray by the speed of the Western cultural invasion, and for a time they had no rallying point.

The alternative, as the modern Japanese scholar Kawakita Michiaki put it, was 'to let Japan be caught up in a tide of Western civilisation, relying on the superior adaptation and ability of her people to make rapid adjustments and to produce, eventually, a copy of the Western system'. He makes this comment on the psychology of the Japanese in a situation that was in some ways a repetition of the crisis that had faced it under the first impact of Chinese culture in the seventh century:

> The vogue for things Western in the early days of Meiji was essentially a manifesta-
> tion of this—for a Japanese, instinctive—type of reaction. The movement involved
> what seemed an almost blindly self-effacing partiality for things Western; many dif-
> ferent aspects of Western culture were taken over at a great rate, and copies were
> produced as required with astonishing speed and efficiency. It was in such a process,
> if the truth be told, that Western-style painting in modern Japan had its origin. The
> discovery of something more powerful than oneself, of something superior to one-
> self; the desire to adapt and adjust to it; the resulting blind partiality; and a final re-
> modelling of the self in the new image—such was the process involved in the funda-
> mental bias towards the West that formed one aspect of Japanese culture from Meiji
> times on, and the same circumstances presided over the birth and development of
> Western-style painting in Japan as well.

Although, as we have seen, European art had been filtering slowly into Japan through the tiny funnel of Deshima for over two hundred years, a new era began in 1857 with the arrival at Yokohama of the English draughtsman and watercolourist Charles Wirgman as staff artist for the *Illustrated London News*. Young Japanese, eager to learn about Western art from a real Westerner, gathered round him, and soon he had a little school in Yokohama. One of his first pupils was Takahashi Yuichi (1828–94), known as Ransen.

Takahashi had already had some training in Western methods under Kawa-kami Tōgai (1827–81), a former traditional artist and Restoration leader who with extraordinary perseverance had taught himself first Dutch and then the art of painting in oils, and later became director of the Official Painting Office, a post always held up till this time by a member of the official Tosa or Kanō school. In 1871 Tōgai published a guide to Western-style painting, *Seiga shinan* (Figure 79), possibly based on Robert Scott Burn's *Illustrated London Drawing*

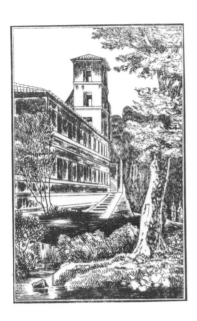

79.
Kawakami Tōgai (1827–81). A Page
from the *Seiga shinan* (Guide to Western
Painting). Tōgai compiled this practical
guide to Western drawing techniques
from a European instructional book.
While the complications of Western perspective are carefully explained, the poor
quality of Tōgai's illustrations hardly suggests the expressive potentialities of
Western art.

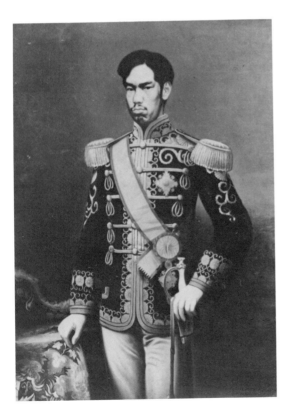

80.
Takahashi Yuichi (1828–94). *Portrait of
the Meiji Emperor.* Oil. 1870. Department
of the Imperial Household, Tōkyō. This
powerful portrait by a pupil of Kawa-
kami Tōgai and Charles Wirgman shows
how important Western-style painting
was in Japan from the beginning of the
Meiji period.

Book, published in 1852, although the illustrations are different. His devoted pupil Takahashi visited Shanghai at about this time 'to inspect conditions', it was said, but it is uncertain what contact he made there with Western art. By then Takahashi had already painted his impressive oil portrait of the young Meiji emperor (Figure 80), which firmly established the credentials of the new art.

Takahashi returned from Shanghai to found his own school at Nihonbashi in 1873. His most influential work was his *Salmon* (Figure 81), which caused a sensation when it was exhibited in Kyōto in 1877. Nothing quite like this had been seen in Japan before. Painted, like his still-lifes of this period, with a new honesty and feeling for texture—he was the first to see Western oil painting as a means of expression—this is a key work in the birth of modern art in Japan, standing out in contrast to the laboured imitations of European salon painting then in fashion.

The third of this triumvirate of pioneers was Kunisawa Shinkurō, who studied in London from 1872 to 1874. On his return to Tōkyō, he took part in Japan's first foreign-style art exhibition in 1875 and opened an atelier. A promising career came to an end with his early death in 1877 at the age of thirty.

A more influential figure, although he too died comparatively young, was Hyakutake Kenkō (or Kaneyuki; 1842–84), who spent most of the years 1872 to 1881 in London, Paris and Rome, where he managed to combine a diplomatic career with the study of painting, first with Thomas Miles Richardson, then with Léon Bonnat and finally with Cezare Maccari. His later work is solidly academic, his portraits Corotesque. He died in government service only two years after returning from Rome, at the time when the anti-Western tide in art—of which more below—was flowing strongly, so his influence was not much felt until, around 1900, the tide began to recede. He is now regarded in Japan as a neglected pioneer, although his surviving works seem rather heavy and dull.

By the mid-seventies the need for properly qualified teachers of Western art had become urgent. Accordingly, in 1876 an art school, Kōbu Bijutsu Gakkō, was added to the College of Technology in Tōkyō. Antonio Fontanesi (1812–82), a friend of the Italian ambassador in Tōkyō and professor of painting in the Royal Academy at Turin, landscape painter of the Barbizon School and admirer of Corot, was invited to head the Western painting section. He arrived before the end of the year, bringing with him Vincenzo Ragusa to teach sculpture, and G. V. Cappeletti to teach the decorative arts. Women were admitted to his classes, and, for the first time, the curriculum included drawing from the nude. At first it was difficult to find models, and a ricksha coolie who was persuaded to pose complained that he had never worked so hard in his life. The three pioneers all sent their most promising pupils to Fontanesi, one of whom was Asai Chū (1856–1907), of whom more later.

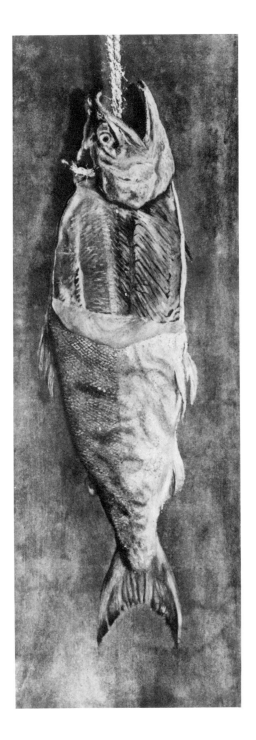

81.
Takahashi Yuichi (1828–94). *Salmon.*
Oil. About 1877. University of Arts,
Tōkyō. Although Takahashi painted
some beautiful still-lifes in oils, the large
and impressive *Salmon* is regarded as his
most important work, heralding the beginning of the westernising movement
in the 1870s.

The enthusiasm for Western art in Japan reached a climax in the late 1870s—precisely at the moment, in fact, when the fashion for japonaiserie was at its height in Paris. Regular exhibitions of oil painting and sculpture were being held in Tōkyō and Kyōto, at which Western-style artists could be sure of selling everything they showed. Tamura Sōritsu (1846–1918), a former pupil of Wirgman and director of the Western painting section of the Kyōto Art School, was being paid five to seven yen each (about £1.25 or three dollars) for his oil portraits, while at this time even the best of the traditional painters were lucky if they could earn half a yen, and two great masters, Kanō Hōgai (1822–88) and Hashimoto Gahō (1835–1908), were almost destitute. Not only were contemporary works of the traditional schools considered worthless, but the very tradition itself was in danger. Paintings by the great early Kanō masters were going begging; temples were being not merely neglected but in some cases pulled down, their treasures thrown out or sold to foreigners and their sculptures chopped up for fuel.

In 1878 Fontanesi returned, tired and ill, to Italy. His successor, a nonentity named Feretti, so antagonised the students that after one morning's classes they rebelled and quit to form a school of their own, the Jūichi-kai, which became the focus of Western-style painting for the next decade. Ragusa continued to teach sculpture, and his influence was considerable at a time when the demand for portrait busts and heroic monuments was steadily increasing, but without Fontanesi the school sank into a decline and was finally abolished in 1883.

Fontanesi had had a devoted following to whom he imparted a sound academic foundation in drawing and painting, but it is questionable whether his influence was wholly good. His own landscapes surviving in Japan are murkier than the murkiest Barbizon paintings, with none of Corot's shimmering luminosity. His pupils were inclined, after the Japanese fashion, to follow him slavishly. Asai Chū did not escape from his influence until he went to France in 1900 (Figure 82), where he exhibited at the Paris Exhibition, returning in 1902 to become the leader of the Western art movement in Kyōto, and teacher of two of the leading *Yōga* (Western painting) artists of the next generation, Umehara Ryūzaburō and Yasui Sōtarō.

The conservatives meanwhile had been watching the reckless surrender to Western art with increasing horror. It was not long before the inevitable reaction set in. For a while it lacked a focus and a leader, for in those hectic days it was a brave man who went against the tide of westernisation. But by 1878 it had both, in the person of Ernest Fenollosa (Figure 83), who had come to Tōkyō from Boston to take up the chair of political economy and philosophy at the Imperial University. Supremely self-assured and eloquent, the twenty-five-year-old professor lectured on Hegel and Herbert Spencer to students who were to become

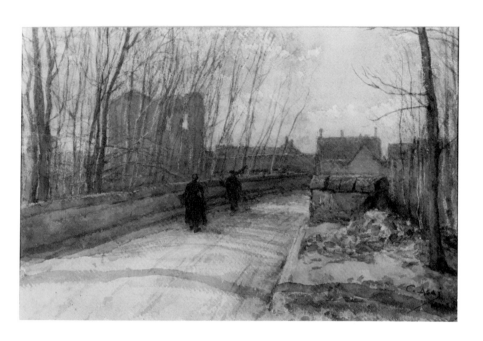

82.
Asai Chū (1856–1907). *Bridge at Gréz*.
Watercolour. 1902. Bridgestone Museum
of Art, Tōkyō. Asai Chū's two years in
Paris freed him from the influence of
Fontanesi's murky palette. The oils and
watercolours of his few remaining years
were a good influence on his two best
pupils, Yasui Sōtarō (Figure 93) and
Umehara Ryūzaburō (Figure 95).

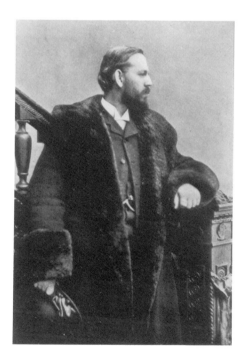

83.
Photograph of Ernest Fenollosa.

the leaders of Japan in the next generation. He had taken classes in painting in Boston, and soon added aesthetics to his courses. He began to collect Japanese works of art, though, since he was a beginner, his early acquisitions were inevitably poor stuff. A friend then introduced him to the collection of the Marquis Kuroda, and he was overwhelmed by the splendour of the Japanese heritage.

With the help of two of his students, Ariga Nagao and Okakura Kakuzō (1862–1913; Figure 84), he began to study and to compile charts of Chinese and Japanese art. He was introduced to leading members of the orthodox Kanō and Tosa schools, whose tutoring of the eager, impressionable young scholar was to yield results momentous for the future of Japanese painting. He began to steep himself in Japan's neglected artistic legacy, spending the summers of 1881 and 1882 visiting castles and temples with Okakura. In a very short time he became convinced that the indiscriminate westernisation of Japanese art was a disaster.

In this, Fenollosa was not alone. In 1879 a group of aristocrats and conservatives had founded the Dragon Lake Society, Ryūchi-kai, an exclusive society dedicated to the study of traditional art. Fenollosa was invited to join, and on 14 May 1882 delivered a stirring address to the members, denouncing the craze for everything Western. 'Japanese art', he declared,

> is really far superior to modern cheap Western art that describes any object at hand mechanically, forgetting the most important point, expression of an Idea. Despite such superiority Japanese despise their classical painting, and with adoration for Western civilization admire its artistically worthless modern paintings and imitate them for nothing. What a sad sight it is! The Japanese should return to their nature and its old racial traditions, and then take, if there are any, the good points of Western painting.

Mary Fenollosa wrote many years later that when her husband finished speaking, a great gasp came from the audience, for he had said what so many felt but none dared to say. He was heard by many influential men, among them Count Sano, founder of the Ryūchi-kai, and by the head of the Department of Education. Such was the effect of Fenollosa's words that within a few weeks official orders went out to list all art treasures in the provinces, and in the autumn, at the official painting exhibition in Ueno Park, Tōkyō, for which Fenollosa was a member of the jury, Western-style paintings were prohibited by government order.

Now it was the turn of the modernists to feel the cold. Takahashi Yuichi drafted several memorials protesting at this retreat into the past; in one he declared, 'Frivolous and illusory is the attempt to reject Western painting as a whole before gaining an impartial and full understanding of it'. But it is doubtful that he submitted them, and for the moment at least the anti-Western tide

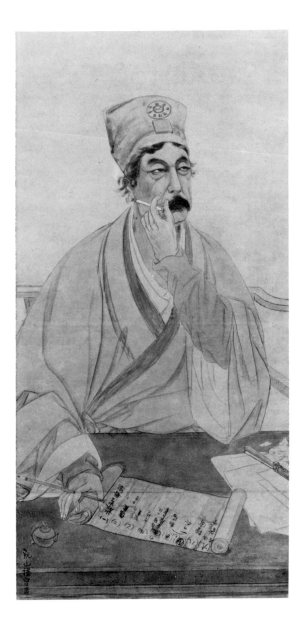

84.
Shimomura Kanzan (1873–1930). Sketch for a Portrait of Okakura Kakuzō. Ink and colour on paper. Tōkyō National University of Fine Arts and Music. Inspired perhaps by Watanabe Kazan's *Ta-* *kami Senseki* (Figure 16), Kanzan here blends Japanese brushwork and Western realism in a study for the well-known portrait of his mentor.

was flowing so strongly that they would not in any case have had any effect. In June 1883 the Western art division of the Technological Art School was closed down. That summer, the Ryūchi Society sponsored the first official exhibition of Japanese art in Paris. Again, Fenollosa was on the jury, and again Western-style art, as well as Chinese-style painting in the Literary School, *Nanga,* upon which Fenollosa heaped his scorn, was excluded.

The indefatigable young American supported his activities with expertise. He travelled busily about, generally with his mentor, Okakura, discussing and listing masterpieces, their most daring and spectacular achievement being the unwrapping of the Yumedono Kannon at Hōryūji, a wooden statue of a bodhisattva that had been concealed from view for over a thousand years. They also issued certificates of authenticity. 'The priests', Fenollosa wrote home, 'were everywhere greedy for my certificates, and I have issued more than one hundred for things which were absolutely unidentified before'.

By now Fenollosa had become an establishment figure, a rallying point for the conservatives and nationalists, the great hope and champion of the painters of the Tosa and Kanō schools, whose fortunes were at their lowest ebb. They responded by taking him to their hearts. Early in 1884 he was adopted officially into the Kanō lineage and given the name Kanō Eitan Masanobu. 'This', he wrote proudly, 'I write in Chinese characters and have special seals. I give certificates by myself for old paintings'. The eagerness with which Fenollosa at this time was accepted by high and low, from the imperial household and cabinet ministers to priests and humble Kanō painters, is a mark of his boundless self-confidence; it also illustrates that instinctive desire of the Japanese, from time to time, to surrender and adapt to 'something more powerful than oneself' that Kawakita described. The process was made less painful, and Fenollosa's task the easier, because he was appealing to a dormant, yet increasingly restless, nationalism.

We need not follow all the steps by which Fenollosa and his friends and pupils swept Western art aside and replaced it with a modernised version of the traditional schools, but merely note some of the main events. In 1884 Fenollosa helped to found the Kanga-kai, a society for exhibiting both ancient paintings in private collections and the work of contemporary traditional artists such as the neglected Kanō Hōgai. In the same year, Fenollosa, appointed to a committee to study art education, recommended that pencil and oil painting be replaced in the schools by brush and *sumi* (Chinese ink). In 1886 he left the university on his appointment, with Okakura, as imperial commissioner charged to investigate art schools and museums throughout the world and make recommendations for Japan. They returned from their world tour in 1887. In the following year a tem-

porary National Treasure Office was set up under Fenollosa, Okakura and the
aged Kanō Hōgai, whose late landscapes surprisingly reflect, though in no obvious way, his admiration for the heroic romanticism of Turner.

Eighteen eighty-nine was a year of crowning achievement for Fenollosa.
The art museum that he had advocated was opened, the art magazine *The Kokka*
was launched, and the Tōkyō School of Fine Art started classes with Fenollosa
and Okakura as managers and staffed by leading members of Fenollosa's New
Painters Group Club (Shingaku Shōkai), such as Hashimoto Gahō and Kanō
Yūshio. *Nanga* and Western art were totally excluded. 'A new art is going to
grow in the school', Fenollosa declared, 'and it will dominate all Japan in the
near future and will have a good influence all over the world'.

This new art was called *Nihonga,* Japanese painting. As exemplified in the
work of Hashimoto Gahō, it was in essence a reworking of the Kanō and Tosa
schools, based on traditional brush techniques and incorporating a new Western
realism in drawing, chiaroscuro, and perspective, and sometimes the themes
were contemporary. Being decorative and realistic, technically brilliant, new yet
rooted in tradition, it seemed for a time at any rate to be an unanswerable reply
to the challenge of Western art. For the next decade the academy and its products, as Fenollosa had predicted, dominated the art world of Japan—so much so
that when in 1893 a group of leading oil painters held a large exhibition of their
work in Kyōto, not a single picture was sold. Fenollosa would have been justified in feeling that the task he had set himself ten years earlier—no less than the
restoration and rebirth of Japanese art—was accomplished.

In July 1889 Fenollosa received an invitation to head the department of Japanese art at the Museum of Fine Arts in Boston. For some months he hesitated. In
Tōkyō he had unique status, wealth and social and political eminence, and his
position in Boston would be very different. But he could not have been unaware
that in Japan the atmosphere was changing. Nationalism and anti-foreign feeling
were growing, and the time would soon come when the Japanese artists and intellectuals would find the dominance of a foreigner intolerable; indeed, the art
programme that Fenollosa himself had drawn up for Japan was so nationalistic
that it was obvious that no foreigner could any longer take a prominent part in
it. He decided that the time had come to leave. On his departure, in July 1890,
the emperor, in an unprecedented gesture, bestowed upon him the Order of the
Sacred Mirror. 'We request now', he said at the investiture, 'that you teach the
significance of Japanese art to the West as you have already taught it to the Japanese'. Fenollosa was to return several times to Japan, always as an honoured visitor, but by now the direction of the movement that he had launched was in other
hands, chiefly those of his greatest disciple, Okakura Kakuzō, called Tenshin.

Sculpture in the Meiji Era

The notion of sculpture as a fine art is a new and foreign one in the Far East. The men who carved or cast the great Buddhist icons were regarded as master crafts-men rather than artists, and very few of their names are known. In nineteenth-century Japan, the tradition of Buddhist icon-carving still lingered on, to be dealt its deathblow by the westernising movement that followed the Meiji Res-toration. Buddhism in itself was under attack, no more commissions came from the temples, and many accomplished craftsmen were reduced to carving um-brella handles, or toys and dolls for the foreigners. Some turned to netsuke carv-ing and so made that craft for the first time a respectable profession.

When in 1876 the Italian sculptor Vincenzo Ragusa arrived in Tōkyō to open a sculpture section in the Technological Art School, students were at first chary of signing up: modelling and carving seemed to smack too much of the work-shop to have anything to do with fine art, and their friends in the painting stu-dios asked them what they proposed to do with their plaster dolls—stand them in the *tokonoma* (the recess in one wall of a room in which a scroll may be hung)? But before long Ragusa had twenty pupils, some of whom became well known as sculptors and teachers. There was already a huge demand for Western-style portraits and monuments to early Meiji leaders, which they executed skilfully enough. Ragusa's best pupil, Okuma Ujihiro (1856–1934), became his assistant and later spent a year in Rome. His best-known work is the monument to the Restoration hero Omura Masujirō, begun in 1883 and unveiled ten years later, after the sculptor's stay in Europe. It is typical of many such monuments, com-pletely European in all but its subject.

The anti-Western reaction of the 'Fenollosa era', which was itself an aspect of a much deeper current of resurgent nationalism, showed in sculpture as it did in painting. When Fenollosa and Okakura began to bring out from the secret recesses of the temples and expose to public view masterpiece after masterpiece of ancient Buddhist carving and bronze casting, sculptors turned back to the Nara period for inspiration. Notable among them were Takamura Kōun (1852–1934) and Takeuchi Hisakazu (1857–1916), who had acted as guide to the American when he visited Nara. But their Kannons and Shakas, full of archaic dignity and exquisitely fashioned, are no more than evocations of a dead past. Only occa-sionally did they break new ground, the most astonishing instance being Kōun's realistic *Old Monkey* (Figure 85), which was a highlight of the Japanese exhibit at the Chicago World's Fair in 1893.

With the founding of the Meiji Art Society in 1889, the pendulum began to swing back again, but not all the way. Now there was room for both kinds of

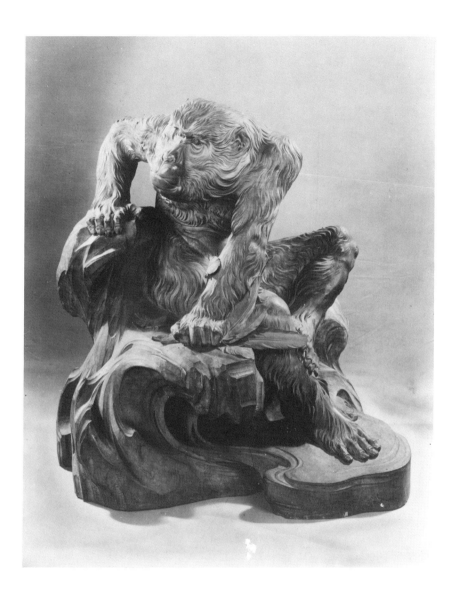

85.
Takamura Kōun (1852–1934). *Old
Monkey*. Wood. 1893. National Museum,
Tōkyō. A technical tour de force that
shows the Japanese craftsman's mastery
of the possibilities of the medium. It was
exhibited in 1893 at the Chicago World's
Fair, where it was greatly admired.

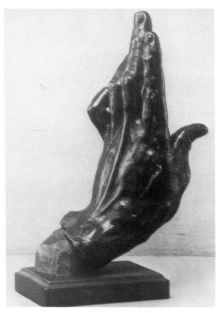

86.
Takamura Kōtarō (1883–1956). *Hand.*
Bronze. 1923. National Museum of
Modern Art, Tōkyō. A fine illustration
of the influence of Rodin, which was per-
vasive among Western-style Japanese
sculptors in the first two decades of the
twentieth century.

sculpture. Naganuma Shūkei (1857–1942), who had been in Italy from 1881 to
1887, came back to fill the gap left by Ragusa's departure in 1882 and gathered
the latter's old pupils around him. When the empress herself paid an official visit
to the Meiji Society's first exhibition in 1891, sculpture in the European style
could be seen to be fully rehabilitated. Most of it, of course, was a mere imitation of the salon style of the day, but, in 1902, Tōkyō felt the decisive impact of
Rodin.

Two years earlier an Impressionist painter named Kume Keichirō (1866–
1934) had been in Paris at the time of Rodin's great retrospective exhibition, con-
ducting a survey of art education for the Japanese government. He met Rodin
many times. He was enormously impressed, and in his report of 1902 wrote the
first detailed account of Rodin's work to appear in Japan. Six years later the
young painter Ogiwara Morie (1879–1910) saw *The Thinker* and was immediately converted to sculpture. He too wrote extensively on Rodin in Japanese
journals, stressing the inner life beneath Rodin's often rough exterior surfaces.
Ogiwara himself was a gifted Rodinesque sculptor, but died young in 1919, before he had established himself.

The banner of Rodinism was taken up by Takamura Kōun's son Kōtarō
(1883–1956; Figure 86), whose study of the master, *Rodin's Words,* had a considerable impact. Rodin himself was delighted by his success in the East and sent
three small pieces of his work to Tōkyō, where they were exhibited in 1912.
After the Second World War, Rodin came to be represented in Tōkyō by a far
greater collection of his major works, including a casting of *The Gates of Hell.*

The Twentieth Century: Japanese-style Painting

Okakura Tenshin rode to power on the crest of the wave that Fenollosa had set in motion. But Okakura's outlook was broader than his master's, and he was more willing to accept Western elements into the new Japanese paintings, *Nihonga*. He had seen European oil painting in its proper context in his travels abroad and realised that its revival and advance in Japan was inevitable; he even hoped at one time that Japanese artists would make their own contribution to oil technique. But his main effort was towards the creation of a style that would be thoroughly Japanese in its materials, techniques and subject matter and that satisfied the Japanese love of fine craftsmanship, yet had absorbed enough of Western realism to make it contemporary. Though he was not a painter himself, Okakura achieved this through his teaching and the work of his pupils at the Tōkyō Art School. But there were dark spots in his domestic life, and he had enemies among the conservatives. In 1898 they engineered his resignation from this key post. To their consternation, most of Okakura's staff and students resigned in protest, and together they set up the private Japan Art Academy (Nihon Bijutsu-in), which carried the message of the new Japanese painting forward into the twentieth century.

In his report on the progress of the academy in 1900, Okakura, thinking perhaps of the 'Six Principles' of the early Chinese theorist Hsieh Ho, set down his artistic ideals in six points: that whatever painters took from tradition or from the West must be assimilated into their unconscious and become a part of them, and not just a borrowed style—not so easy for painters traditionally trained to stress style and technique above personal expression; that they must master ancient techniques; that their passion should breathe spirit into their work; that, while without perfect technique painters cannot express themselves, originality counts for even more; that their art must be full of dignity and nobility; and lastly that further advances must be made in historical painting and in *Ukiyo-e,* that is, genre painting in the traditional style. Okakura also insisted that painters should always remain Japanese, whatever style they worked in. Caught as they were between East and West, many Japanese artists found this very difficult indeed, and it is not surprising that the great majority of them took refuge in a purely technical solution to a problem that was in essence one of personal identity.

Just as important for the growth of the *Nihonga* as the ideals behind it was the new concept of the role of art and of the artist in society that westernisation had brought with it. In the old days, painters had often worked for a single powerful patron who absorbed all their output of huge decorative screens or of small scrolls painted in monochrome ink for the *tokonoma,* and most of these

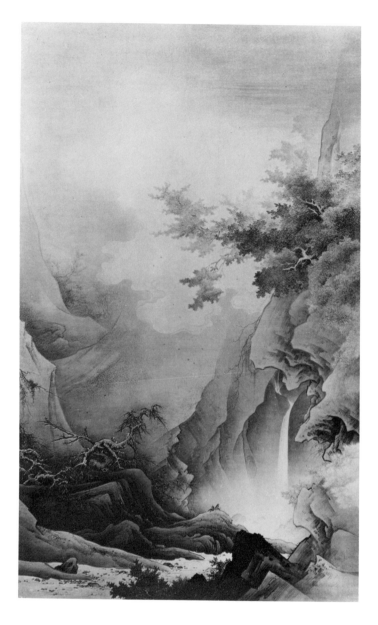

87.
Hashimoto Gahō (1835–1908). *White Clouds and Red Trees*. Ink and colour on silk. 1890. Tōkyō National University of Fine Arts and Music. Hashimoto's brilliant synthesis of Kanō style and technique with Western realism created a model for painters at an early stage in the *Nihonga* movement that was never surpassed.

painters had belonged to hereditary guilds or families such as the Tosa and the Kanō, to which their loyalty was absolute. Now, it was every man for himself. There were large and influential art associations, but they were in a continual state of flux, riddled with politics and stifled as much as they were encouraged by official support. Patronage was uncertain, but public exhibitions, unheard of before the Restoration, became a permanent feature of Japanese life, stimulating individuality and introducing a new element of competition. The exhibitions, moreover, demanded a new kind of picture, one that existed in and for itself: smaller and more personal in style than the decorative screens or sliding doors, larger and more visually arresting than the quiet, sober scrolls that hung in the *tokonoma*. As there was no place for such pictures in the traditional Japanese house, collectors had to build special galleries to house them, and cities, new Western-style museums to display them.

As early as 1890 Hashimoto Gahō (1835–1908) had achieved in his famous *White Clouds and Red Trees* a brilliant synthesis of decorative Kanō ink techniques and Western realism (Figure 87). After the turn of the century, Shimomura Kanzan (1873–1930), Takeuchi Seihō (1864–1942) and other followers of Okakura further refined this new synthetic style, extending its range of subject matter and taking their themes from Japanese history, literature and domestic life. Some of them also made a serious study of Western art. Shimomura, for instance, was in Europe from 1903 to 1905; Takeuchi Seihō in 1900 went to Paris, where he became an admirer of Turner and Corot. But their rare excursions into Western themes, such as Takeuchi's pair of screens depicting classical Rome and a Dutch windmill with cows in *sumi* ink on a gold ground (Figure 88), although miracles of technical skill, are hard to judge objectively because the subjects seem so incongruous.

If the *Nihonga* developed at all, it was in the realm of purely technical experiment, in absorbing elements from the ancient courtly Tosa style, the decorative brilliance of the Sōtatsu-Kōrin School, the realism of Ōkyo, even ancient Buddhist banner and wall painting. A notable exponent of this movement was Kobayashi Kōkei (1883–1957). In his youth a protégé of Okakura, he acquired a thorough grounding in Chinese, Japanese and Western painting (he made a special journey to London to copy the Ku K'ai-chih scroll in the British Museum). This background enabled him to produce, in addition to some semi-Western works, a series of technically brilliant scrolls on traditional themes, such as the story of the Princess Kiyo's attempted seduction of the young monk Anchin (a well-known subject in the Nō and Kabuki drama), which he painted in 1930 (Figure 89).

With each conquest of another segment of the past, however, the *Nihonga* became more deeply bogged down in tradition. Even Nakamura Osaburō's screen of a young lady in a kimono seated at a grand piano beneath an electric

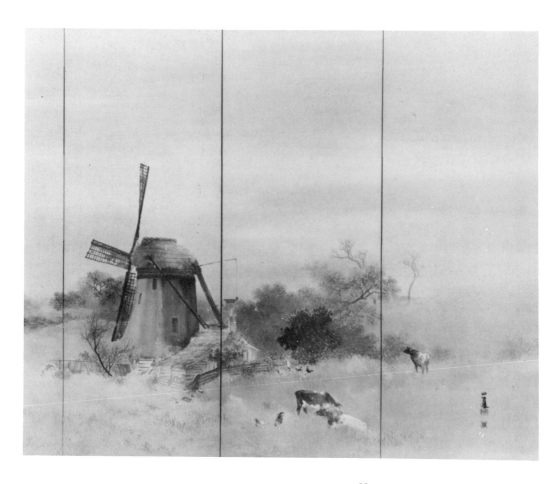

88.
Takeuchi Seihō (1864–1942). Dutch Windmill in a Landscape. Part of a screen. Ink on gold paper. 1902. Municipal Museum, Kyōto. If this experiment does not quite succeed, it is not because the subject is incongruous, but because the artist, going beyond his tradition, was unable to resolve the conflict between decoration and Western realistic drawing.

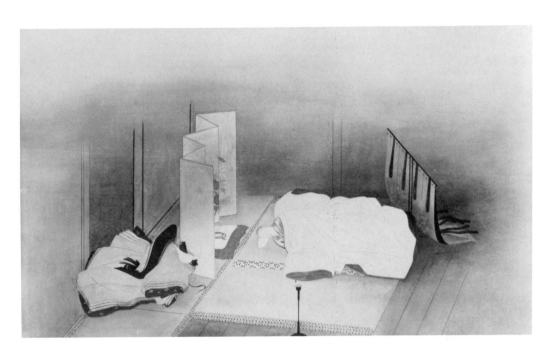

89.
Kobayashi Kōkei (1883–1957). *The Tale of Kiyohime: Scene III, In the Bedroom.* One of eight framed panels. Ink and colour on paper. 1930. Yamatora Museum of Art, Tōkyō. A skillful synthesis of Japanese and Western techniques, illustrating an incident in the legend of Kiyohime and the virtuous monk Anchin, who resisted her advances.

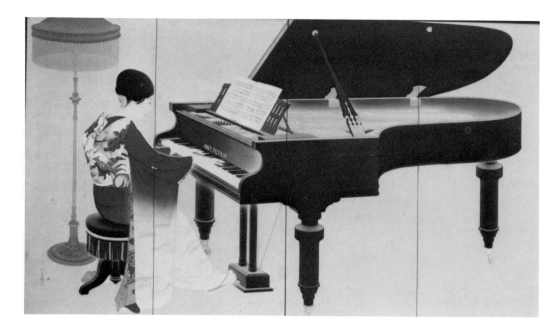

90.

Nakamura Osaburō (1898–1947). *At the Piano*. Four-fold screen. Ink and colour on silk. 1926. Municipal Museum, Kyōto. The artist employs accurate drawing and shading but avoids any suggestion of a ground, background or cast shadows, perhaps because these would have made the screen look very Western.

lamp (Figure 90), painted in 1926, which looks so 'modern', is as conservative in technique and flavour as any of the hundreds of pictures of Lord Genji or samurai warriors that graced the Inten, the official annual exhibition in Tōkyō. Yet Nakamura's screen is a successful illustration of the marriage of East and West in modern Japanese life, contemporary in theme and intensely Japanese in style and feeling—if so calculated and needle-sharp a technique can be said to express any feeling at all.

I will spare the reader an account of the ramifications of the *Nihonga* between the two world wars. Having taken what it needed from tradition and Western realism, it froze into a cold academicism, incapable of change, because all too often Okakura's ideals were forgotten and style and technique became ends in themselves. The *Nihonga* was too rigidly disciplined, too anonymous in touch, to convey the turbulent emotions of creative artists in the years leading up to Pearl Harbour, and it was too narrowly academic to come to terms with the Western movements, notably Cubism and Surrealism, then fashionable in cosmopolitan circles. If it had not been for the Second World War, the *Nihonga* artists might have gone on producing these perfect, yet lifeless, pictures indefinitely.

But it was not always that way, and even in the 1920s and 1930s there were exceptions—artists who refused to be confined by the perfect formal language created by Takeuchi Seihō and his contemporaries: men of the Kyōto School such as Murakami Kagaku (1889–1939), who expressed himself freely in ink line; Hata Teruo (1887–1943), a bohemian whose dark nude in a forest, *Pool of Blood,* seems utterly remote from *Nihonga* ideals; and Tokuoka Shinsen (1896–1972), whose steady development into a 'modernist' helped to bridge the chasm of the Second World War. But on the whole the pioneers of the 'Okakura era', as it has been called, had been too successful. It was difficult for all but a handful of their followers to be anything but superb craftsmen. As we shall see, it took Japan's defeat in 1945 and its chaotic aftermath to break the mould and bring the *Nihonga* to life once more.

The Twentieth Century: Western-style Painting

Once the anti-Western reaction of the 1880s had passed its peak, European-style painting began to advance again, and this time there was no need of a Fenollosa to hold it in check, for conservative taste and nationalistic sentiment were amply catered to by the flourishing *Nihonga* movement.

In 1887 Yamamoto Hōsui (1850–1906) returned from nine years in Paris, where he had been a pupil of Gérôme, and in the same year Harada Naojirō (1863–1906), a pupil of Gabriel Max, came back from Munich. Both were conservative salon painters who brought no fresh life to the Western movement. But in 1893 Kuroda Seiki (1866–1924), a more considerable figure, returned from Paris with a light *pleinairiste* style that he had learned from Raphael Collin. To a culturally obedient public, schooled against all their better instincts to regard the murky browns and heavy impasto of Fontanesi and his pupils as the latest and best in Western art, Kuroda's cheerful lyrical palette must have come as a very welcome change (Figure 91). 'What a pleasure it was in those days!' one of Kuroda's students later exclaimed. 'An artist travelling along a pitch-dark road suddenly saw before him a bright column of light'.

Acceptance was not by any means universal, however. A frank, solid nude painted by Kuroda in Paris in 1893 was banned by the police from an exhibition in Tōkyō ten years later, and prominent writers supporting him protested in vain. The nude had appeared in Western-style art since the 1880s, though sometimes

91.
Kuroda Seiki (1866–1924). *At the Lakeside*.
Oil on canvas. 1897. Bijutsu Kenkyūjo
(National Property), Tōkyō. Kuroda acquired his light *pleinairiste* manner from
his teacher, Raphael Collin, in Paris. This
picture is regarded by some Japanese critics as the first oil painting that is truly
Japanese in feeling. Kuroda was the first
Japanese Western-style painter to be appointed a court artist.

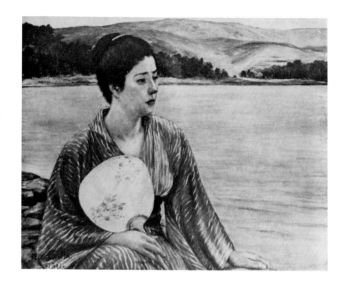

92.
Aoki Shigeru (1882–1911). *Ladies of the
Nara Court, Tempyō Era*. Oil on canvas.
1904. Bridgestone Museum of Art,
Tōkyō. Aoki is greatly admired in Japan
today for an air of mystery and romance
in his work suggestive of G. F. Watts and
Burne-Jones, with hints of Monet and
Gustave Moreau. He died young, was
forgotten, then rediscovered after World
War II.

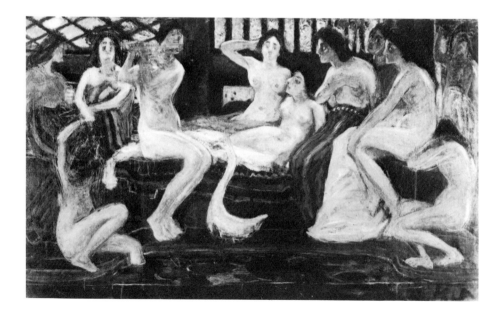

in odd places—surely the oddest being Aoki Shigeru's *Ladies of the Nara Court, Tempyō Era* (Figure 92), painted in 1904, in which a group of very European naked ladies, painted in a muddy Impressionist technique, are posed languidly in the manner of Albert Moore. Okakura must have had this sort of thing in mind when he exhorted painters to remain Japanese. Although Aoki's most famous work, *Harvest of the Sea,* is strong in form and draughtsmanship, more often this ultraromantic indulged in woolly textures that remind us of G. F. Watts. Long neglected in Japan, Aoki has recently come to be admired for undertones of mystery and romance and for hints of Burne-Jones and the Symbolists that glimmer through the rather congested surfaces of his oil paintings.

In 1896 Kuroda had been appointed the first professor of Western painting at the Tōkyō School of Fine Art, and in the same year he and a number of his pupils formed the White Horse Association (Hakuba-kai), for the promotion of Western painting, lyrical in mood, varyingly Impressionist in technique. So successful was it that the old Meiji Art Society was eclipsed. But with the return from Europe of a group of painters who had studied at the Académie Julian under J. P. Laurens, there came to Tōkyō a more solid modernism than the lyrical manner of Kuroda and the followers of Raphael Collin. Among the leaders of the new Pacific Western Painting Society (Taiheiyō Gakkai), founded in 1902, were Fujishima Takeji (1867–1943), who had also studied portraiture under Carolus-Duran in Rome, Mitsutani Kunishirō (1874–1936) and Nakamura Fusetsu (1866–1943).

The splitting off of the Pacific Western Painting Society was a sign of the beginning of the intense sectarianism that has plagued Japanese art movements in the twentieth century. It was partly to stop this rivalry that in 1907 the Ministry of Education established an annual art exhibition modelled on the Paris Salon, with three sections: Japanese painting (*Nihonga*), Western painting (*Yōga*) and sculpture. First called the Bunten, later Teiten, then finally Nitten, the annual exhibition in Ueno Park is still the focus of officially accepted art of modern Japan. The Bunten gave many young artists their first public success, notably Wada Sanzō (1883–1967), whose scintillating *South Wind* is a masterly, if in Western terms rather conventional, work of a then almost unknown pupil of Kuroda. Japanese practitioners of Impressionism seldom tried to come to terms with traditional painting, which was on the whole just as well, for the two arts were almost irreconcilable: the one thick, plastic, sensuous; the other smooth, clear, transparent and without surface texture. The few painters who succeeded in giving their work something of a Japanese flavour—such as Suzuki Shintarō (b. 1895) and Yasui Sōtarō (1888–1955), who had studied in Paris from 1907 to 1914—did so chiefly by infusing into their brushwork some of the calligraphic freedom that they had acquired from the study of Chinese literary ink painting—

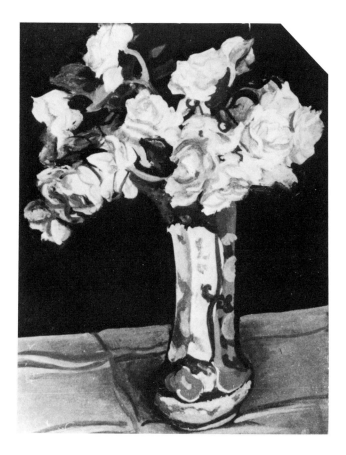

93.
Yasui Sōtarō (1888–1955). *Roses.* Oil on canvas. 1932. Bridgestone Museum of Art, Tōkyō. Yasui, who studied in Paris from 1907 to 1914, gives to this otherwise thoroughly Western painting some of the linear movement that derives from his earlier training in calligraphy.

an unlikely alliance indeed. Yasui's *Roses* of 1932 (Figure 93) would stand comparison with any European flower painting of the same kind. Kishida Ryūsei's (1891–1929) series of solidly painted portraits of his little daughter, Reiko (Figure 94), is completely Western in style, a slight emphasis on the decorative texture of materials being the only concession to Japanese taste.

One of the most successful syntheses was achieved by Umehara Ryūzaburō. Born in 1888 into a prosperous merchant family in Kyōto dealing in kimonos, Umehara grew up among textile designers and printers and said later that he knew all about the great seventeenth-century decorative painters Sōtatsu and Kōrin before he went to primary school. Umehara showed early talent as an artist and studied under Asai Chū, a pupil of Fontanesi, who was then teaching at the Technological School in Kyōto. Asai died in 1907, and in the following year

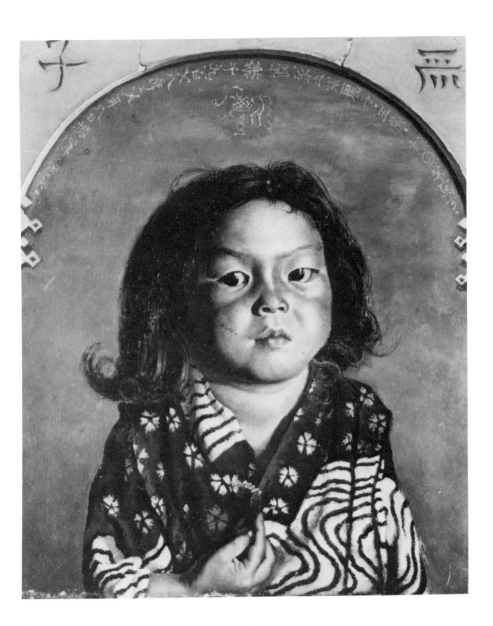

94.
Kishida Ryūsei (1891–1929). *Reiko at
Five Years Old.* Oil on canvas. 1918. National Museum of Modern Art, Tōkyō.
Between 1918 and 1924 Kishida painted
many portraits of his little daughter, of
which this is one of the strongest.

Umehara set off for Paris. The day after he arrived, he saw a Renoir for the first time. 'These paintings', he wrote, 'are exactly what I'm seeking and seeing in my dreams'.

In February 1909 the young Umehara took his courage in both hands and set off to Cagnes to pay his respects to Renoir. Later he wrote movingly of his first visit, and of the thoughts that ran through his head on the way south:

> If I visit him, what should I do? Will he let me in? I've heard that when people knocked at Degas' door, he would open his narrow eyes and if it was a stranger or someone he disliked he would slam the door again. How awful it would be if the same were to happen to me! If I'm allowed in, what shall I say? There isn't much hope of engaging the master's interest if I can't even manage as well as the halting speech of my three-year-old child. Sometimes my timidity whispers to me, 'you'd better stop bothering the man you admire'. But my desire to see him is even stronger. Courage! I'm worthy of being seen by him. I like his art so much. He must know that.

They met, and Renoir was so affected by the spirit of the young painter that he agreed to give him lessons. Umehara stayed for months at Cagnes and became Renoir's favourite pupil in his later years.

In 1913 Umehara returned to Japan, self-confident, master of a palette as hot as Renoir's, which he applied with an easy, firm touch. The pictures that he painted in the next decade may appear at first sight thoroughly European, but his upbringing was not to be denied. It may seem almost impossible that he could admit the *Yamato-e,* Sōtatsu or Kōrin styles to his own manner, but he succeeded—by the simple device of adding gold to his palette. Whether he was painting a nude (Colour Plate 7), a still-life or a landscape (Figure 95), he would set down his highlights in firm strokes of semitransparent gold paint that allowed the colour to glow through it, giving the canvas extraordinary vibrancy and luminosity. In his late works, such as the landscapes he painted when, nearly eighty, he was back on the Riviera for the third and last time, blobs of gold paint take their place in a rough, vigorous pointillism. By now he had moved a long way from his early Post-Impressionism. But in spite of the seductions of his medium, he never descended to mere decoration, the bane of some Japanese painting, for he drew with colour like van Gogh, and his brushwork is always expressive. Umehara's synthesis of East and West is uniquely successful partly because it is the expression of a powerful artistic personality who had lived in both worlds.

Beside Umehara, most of the other *Yōga* artists seem mere imitators. Kanayama Heizō (1883–1964) and Nakagawa Kazumasa (b. 1893), for example, carried Impressionism into the 1920s; Yamamoto Kanae (1882–1946) and Morita Tsunetomo (1881–1933) were faithful followers of Cézanne; Nakagawa Kigen

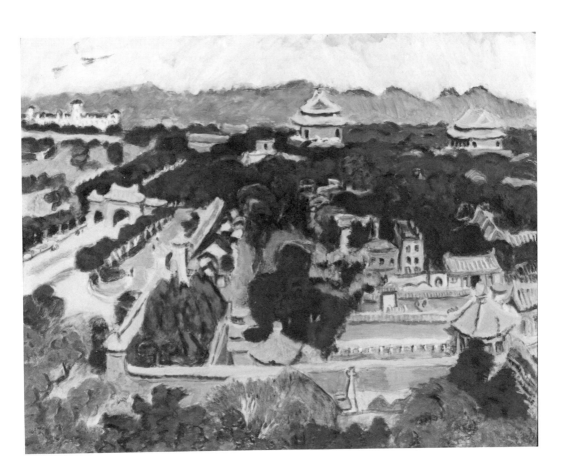

95.
Umehara Ryūzaburō (1888–1986).
Chang-an Street, Peking. Oil on canvas.
1940. National Museum of Modern Art,
Tōkyō. The artist had visited China sev-
eral times before and during the Pacific
War. As in his figure subjects (Colour
Plate 7), his bold handling of colour was
stimulated by his close association with
Renoir.

(1892–1972) was influenced by Matisse and Dérain; Yorozu Tetsugorō (1885–1927) was for a while notable among many Japanese Cubists.

Even though they worked in the manner of the School of Paris, sheer talent and confident handling of the chosen idiom raised several of the Western-style artists of this period to a high level. Notable among them were Nakamura Tsune (1887–1924) and Koide Narashige (1895–1933), in whose work we can see the influence of André Lhote, Klee, Dérain, Matisse and even Rouault. Although the influence of Picasso appeared in the work of the Kimura Shōhachi (1893–1958) as early as 1915, Picasso was too unpredictable a master to have a consistent following in Japan, where he had few champions. The flowing line and decorative colour of Matisse must have seemed far more accessible. His work was vigorously promoted by the Shirakaba-ha Group's enthusiasm for Post-Impressionism. The influence of the Fauves between the wars was much greater, perhaps because, as Kawakita put it, 'in the fauvist medium the Japanese artist could simply let himself go'.

In the meantime, the Japanese had discovered Surrealism. In 1930 Takiguchi Shūzō had translated André Breton's *La Surréalisme et la peinture,* which made a deep impression on the art world of Tōkyō. An even deeper impression was made by the comprehensive exhibition of the work of Ernst, Masson, Miró, Tanguy and Arp shown by the Union of Rising Art in 1932. Though not many Japanese painters fully understood the psychological basis of the movement, Surrealism became the dominating avant-garde art of the 1930s, culminating in Takiguchi's international 'Surrealism Overseas' exhibition in 1937. He himself believed, as he said later, that 'Surrealism should not be considered just another Western modernism, but a vital force that could revive the creative and artistic force of Japan'. Whether this would have happened is doubtful, for by then the Surrealist movement was already past its peak in Europe, and Japanese painters were quick to follow trends in Europe. In any case the advent of the Second World War dealt a heavy blow to all avant-garde movements in Japanese art.

It would, however, be wrong to dismiss the Japanese Surrealists, any more than the Fauves and Cubists, as mere imitators. Japanese Surrealism—in such works, for example, as Kitawaki Noboru's *Spikenards* (Figure 96)—had a special flavour, blended with romanticism, decoration and the irrationality of Zen; moreover, it expressed a deep desire to break out of the narrow confines of Japanese tradition and to be modern and cosmopolitan. It was also an escape from the agonies of the present into a world where the spirit was free, for the liberal climate that had developed in the 1920s was giving way to a bleak authoritarianism. In 1931 Japanese armies had occupied Manchuria; in the following year Japan was at war with China, and by 1936 it had become a military dictatorship. The first casualty was the left-wing art of the early 1930s—revolutionary paintings of little aesthetic merit by artists such as Yabe Toroe (b. 1892), who had

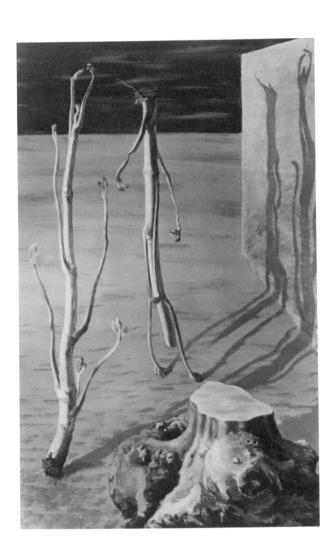

96.
Kitawaki Noboru (1901–51). *Spikenards*.
Oil on canvas. 1937. National Museum
of Modern Art, Tōkyō. Surrealism in
Japan was less a revelation of the subconscious than an expression of the artist's
yearning for spiritual freedom at a time
of growing militarism.

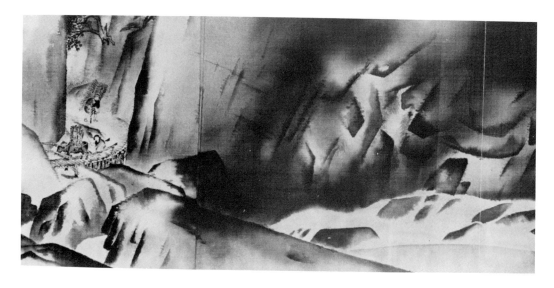

97.

Yokoyama Taikan (1868–1958). Wheel of Life. Detail of a handscroll. Ink and a little gold on silk. 1922. Eisei Bunko (Hosokawa Collection), Tōkyō. In his most famous work, Taikan combines a hint of Western realism and chiaroscuro with a re-creation of the styles of early masters of ink painting such as Sesshū and Sesson.

spent a year in Soviet Russia. Now the flame of freedom and internationalism in the arts was smothered, and henceforward, until the end of the Second World War, only a conservative, patriotic art was given any encouragement, although the Surrealists, Abstractionists and Expressionists continued to exhibit unofficially until about 1941.

The war naturally created a vogue for realistic paintings in oils depicting Japan's early triumphs against China, America and Britain—works indistinguishable in style from those being produced in Germany at the same time. But as Japan's fortunes sank, there was less and less place for this kind of art, while the Western-style avant-garde, cut off from Europe, dried up too, as people hankered for something more Japanese in spirit. Perhaps the art of these dark years is best symbolised by the indomitable old master Yokoyama Taikan (1868–1958). In the early decades of the twentieth century Taikan had achieved a brilliant re-working of the *Yamato-e* and of the ink style of Sesshū in his long scroll *The Wheel of Life,* painted in 1922 (Figure 97). He had made bold experiments in the use of colour, and on his visit to Italy in 1930 had studied Leonardo's sfumato. Now he had returned to purely Japanese themes, from which the Western elements had all but vanished. Again and again he painted his beloved Mount Fuji, symbol of the unconquerable Japanese spirit. In these works he seems, perhaps unintentionally, to put the clock back fifty years. By the end of the war the fires of creativity for him, and indeed for most Japanese painters, had all but died out.

Japan after the Second World War

Exhausted by the war, occupied by a victorious army, its people half starving, its cities in ruins, Japan in the immediate postwar years hardly seemed a likely setting for an artistic rebirth. But several factors contributed to a surge of creative activity that began when the dust of Hiroshima had barely settled. The Japanese, with that remarkable adaptability that they had shown eighty years earlier, almost overnight became enthusiastically pro-Western, while the American administration was on the whole liberal and humane, anxious to win the Japanese people over to its side. Americans were among the first patrons of the artists who had survived the war and opened a direct channel of communication to the outside world. The waves of Abstraction and Action Painting that radiated out from New York, the new capital of the avant-garde, were very quickly picked up by Japanese painters impatient to establish their credentials in the world of international modern art.

When we consider how much suffering the Japanese people had inflicted and had themselves endured during the previous decade, it is extraordinary how little of this is reflected in postwar painting. A handful of artists, such as Fukuzawa Ichirō and Abe Nobuya, depicted defeat, hunger, the plight of the refugees, but on the whole the reaction in these early years was a deeply personal one. Is there a hint of the national calamity in Kudō Kōjin's surrealist landscapes of the 1960s? Hardly; his *Withered Leaves* (1963) and *Hands and Eyes of Earth* (1964; Figure 98) are too close to the nature of things and too elegantly composed to suggest any inward suffering. Oyamada Jirō's weird expressionist oil paintings, such as *Sketch of an Ossuary* (1964; Figure 99), and grimly primordial images, such as *Fortunes of the Sea,* a watercolour of 1956, seem to be the expression not of the agony of the war but of a very private kind of hell.

It seems that several years had to elapse before most of the major artists could bring themselves to recollect their wartime experiences. One of the most powerful of them was Kazuki Yasuo (1911–74). From 1945 to 1947 he had been a prisoner of the Russians in Siberia, where he saw his companions die one after

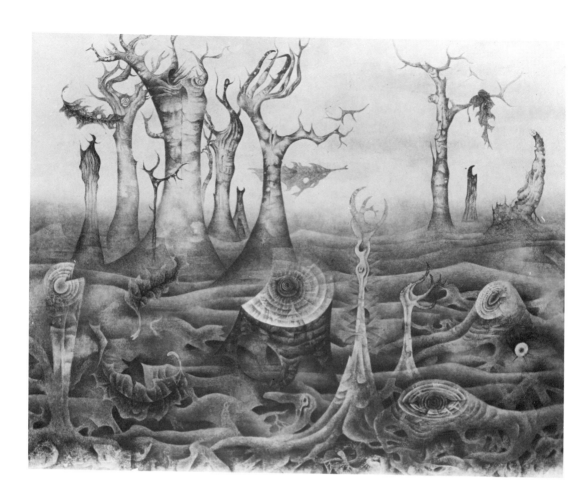

98.
Kudō Kōjin (b. 1915). *Hands and Eyes of Earth*. Colour on paper. 1964. Although 'surrealist', this Daliesque fantasy is too elegantly composed, too decorative, to be psychologically disturbing.

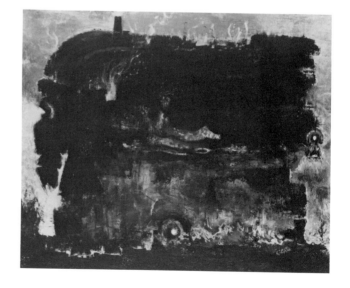

99.
Oyamada Jirō (b. 1914). *Sketch of an Ossuary*. Oil on canvas. 1964. Iida Gallery, Tōkyō. One of the most powerful expressions of the horrors of the Nazi concentration camps to come out of postwar Japan.

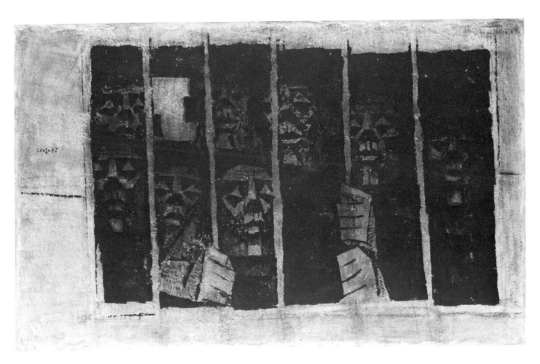

100.
Kazuki Yasuo (1911–74). *To the North,*
to the West. Oil. 1959. Photo by Shi-
nohosha, Tokyo. Kazuki had been a prisoner of the Russians in Siberia, but his
great series of paintings of prisoners tran-
scends time and place.

another from maltreatment, starvation and cold. Yet it was not until 1959 that he
was able to begin work on his great 'Siberia Series' (Figure 100)—mainly the
images of haunted faces and imploring hands, which seem to express the fate of
millions in Asia and Europe during those terrible years. By then, the effects of
the atomic bomb at Hiroshima had been unforgettably recorded in the panels
painted between 1950 and 1953 by Maruki Iri (b. 1901) and his wife, Toshiko.

Within a year of the end of the war the Japanese Ministry of Education had
reorganized the official annual exhibition, renaming it Nitten. In 1947 two large
exhibitions of Western art from Japanese collections were held in Tōkyō, while
the Japan Avant-Garde Club organized its first show. Surrealism and Abstraction were in vogue again. By 1951 the lines were open to Paris, and a collection
from the Salon de Mai was followed by exhibitions of the work of Picasso and
Matisse. In the same year the Museum of Modern Art opened at Kamakura,
while Japan was represented by no less than forty-six painters, sculptors and
printmakers at the São Paolo Bienal.

In 1952 the peace treaty became effective, and there were signs that Japan's economic recovery was gaining momentum. The Bridgestone Museum, with its notable collection of European painting, formed by Ishibashi Shōjirō, opened in Tōkyō in 1952. The new National Museum of Modern Art, designed by le Corbusier to house the Matsukata Collection, opened in 1959. No remotely comparable collections of Western art existed then, or exist today, in any other Asian country. In 1959 Tōkyō held its first Biennial. A large Braque exhibition was brought to Tōkyō by the Yumiuri newspaper in 1952, followed by a collection of Western art put on by the Mainichi Press. Within eight years of Japan's catastrophic defeat, Tōkyō was already becoming one of the art capitals of the world.

During the 1950s young painters naturally tended to copy everything that was being done in Paris and New York. Tōkyō galleries were full of the work of almost indistinguishable young followers of Soulages and Mathieu, Pollock and Kline. It was the 'old masters', men like Umehara and Yasui, who gave some stability to the postwar scene, while several survivors of the war, notably Okada Kenzō (b. 1902) and Tsutaka Waichi (b. 1911), helped to transform the imported Abstract Expressionism, through a return to the calligraphic roots of their own tradition, into a movement in which they could as Japanese feel thoroughly at home.

For a time it looked as if the *Nihonga* was faced with extinction. Neither the artists nor the public wanted to see the continuation of a style that had achieved a static perfection decades earlier and had since become identified with all that Japan was repudiating. The first Tōkyō Biennial of 1952 showed that the new generation, as in the 1870s, was surrendering too hastily and uncritically to the latest from abroad. If the *Nihonga* could somehow be made relevant to the artistic climate of the day, some critics felt, the balance might be redressed.

Deliberately, it seems, *Nihonga* painters such as Yamamoto Kyūjin and Yoshioka Kenji set out to modernise traditional painting, not by the obvious device used before the war of making it more realistic and depicting contemporary subject matter, but, on the contrary, by making it more abstract, using new colour harmonies and applying pigment all over the surface in the manner of Western oil painting. Many of these artists were concerned more with means than with ends—a common failing—but there are honourable exceptions. Hashimoto Meiji, under the influence of Fernand Léger, strengthened and thickened the delicate *Nihonga* line till it became a dominant element in the design, flattening his colour in the manner of Matisse (Figure 101). In the 1950s Kayama Matazō painted a series of winter landscapes showing bare trees and birds, which successfully combine an intensity of expression and completeness of realisation that suggest Flemish painting. His *Winter* of 1957 is not simply a

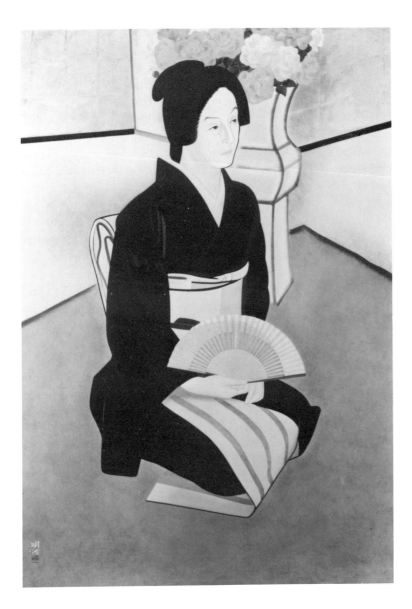

101.
Hashimoto Meiji (b. 1904). *Portrait of Marichiyū*. Ink and colour on paper. 1954. Shimbashi Embujō Theatre, Tōkyō. This portrait of a well-known geisha in Tōkyō combined Japanese feeling with a firmness of linear design that suggests Léger. It is surprising that Hashimoto should have spent ten years as chief of the copyists of the eighth-century Buddhist wall paintings in Hōryūji.

parody of Brueghel; it converts Brueghel into Japanese terms (Colour Plate 8). Here and in his *Bare Trees in Winter* of the same year, superbly disciplined craftsmanship does not stand in the way of deep feeling for nature.

A much older master, who in his postwar painting brought a new solidity to the *Nihonga,* is Tokuoka Shinsen. Born in 1896 and trained in Kyōto, Shinsen took the *Nihonga* a stage further towards Abstraction in *Harvested Ricefield in Rain* (1960) and *Rain* (1964; Colour Plate 9), a poetic, elusive, yet solidly painted study of a garden pool with a rock in the rain, a sight so familiar in Japan. In Japanese terms it seems impressionistic, but beside Monet's *Nymphéas* series, which must surely have at least partly inspired it, there is about it a serene Oriental timelessness that is the very antithesis of Impressionism. In abandoning the thin, sharp line and slick graded tones of the earlier *Nihonga,* Shinsen has brought the style much nearer to Western painting, but the somewhat melancholy beauty of the garden in the rain, so redolent of that quality the Japanese call *shibui,* has a very Oriental flavour.

During the early 1930s Yoshiwara Jirō had been a lonely, largely self-taught pioneer of modernism, and one of the first Japanese painters who understood and admired Kandinsky. Twenty years later he was associated with a group of fifteen young artists who founded the Gutai (Concrete Form) Group, dedicated to the most advanced forms of Action Painting and 'creative happenings'. Michel Tapié, visiting Japan in 1957, found them practising his Art Autre, and described Yoshiwara as the animating spirit of the group. Tapié wrote:

> He prepares unusual exhibitions (in parks, in the dockyards of Kōbe, even in honourable municipal buildings), an extremely avant-garde yet completely popular spectacle where artists create the skits, make everything, including sets, costumes, and complicated machines, and themselves act in crowded theatres, thrilling a public which is almost one hundred percent working class. Yoshiwara produced the unique miracle of a group created *as a group,* which includes more than half the authentic *names* belonging to the avant-garde.

If some of the workmen who saw the group tearing up huge sheets of paper or watched Shiraga Kazuō painting with his feet were ever bewildered, they must, being Japanese, have been reassured that this was art and therefore to be admired, while to anyone familiar with Zen its irrationality and spontaneity had an obvious appeal. Yoshiwara's own Minimal Art sums up the Gutai spirit at its most Japanese: 'I have been working on variations of circles [Figure 102]. It is difficult to say what this style represents. Some say it is Zen painting. Indeed, a Zen monk once asked me what prompted me to paint in such a manner. When I replied, "Since I did not have time, this was the best I could do at the moment", he remarked, "What you have just said contains an essence of Zen"'. To attempt

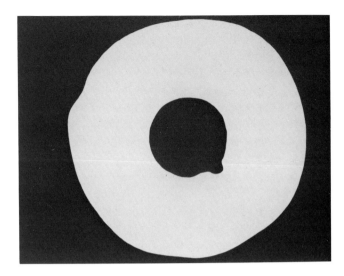

102.
Yoshiwara Jirō (1905–72). *Circle*. Oil on canvas. 1968. This work reflects both Western Minimalism and the Zen reduction of form to essentials of universal significance. It is reminiscent of the monk-painter Sengai's circles, squares and triangles.

to interpret this anecdote, or even to assert that it has any meaning at all, would be to fall into the trap that followers of Zen set for the unwary.

In 1957 the American Action Painter Sam Francis was invited by the Gutai Group to exhibit in Tōkyō. While he responded to Japanese traditional painting and calligraphy, the Japanese were equally excited by his freedom and daring in the use of oil paint, by 'his regard', as a critic put it, 'for the happy accident and his discovery of forms through the paint itself'. One of his most important works to date is the huge mural that he painted for the Sōgetsu Institute, where Teshigahara Sōfū was teaching the art of abstract flower arrangement that he had invented.

In postwar Japan the marriage of Zen, calligraphy and Action Painting was both inevitable and irresistible, winning converts even among well-established traditional painters. 'Abstract calligraphy', an art in which the forms hover between the ideograph and pure abstraction, has had a considerable vogue. But it is more than a vogue. Although Abstract Expressionism has been superceded by other trends, the link formed through calligraphy seems to be a lasting one, because the relation between form and meaning expressed in the ideograph has become central to modern aesthetics. As early as 1951, the Japanese-American sculptor Isamu Noguchi (of whom more below) had shown to the calligrapher Morita Shiryū (b. 1912) some photographs of the work of Franz Kline, which Morita promptly published in his new journal on calligraphy, *Bokubi* (The Beauty of Ink). Suddenly—although Kline himself always denied that he was influenced by the Orient—a bond had been established at a deep level between Eastern and Western art.

Another leading exponent of abstract calligraphy is Inoue Yuichi (b. 1916), a close associate of Morita's, whose bold rendering of the Chinese character *shu* (to belong) carries the swift 'draft script' (*ts'ao shu*) almost to the point of total illegibility (Figure 103). Perhaps the most remarkable metamorphosis took place in the work of Dōmoto Inshō. Born in Kyōto in 1891, Inshō by 1927 was a member of the judging panel of the Imperial Fine Art Exhibition (Teiten) and in 1944 was chosen to become one of the official artists to the imperial household. He executed a series of monumental screens and sliding doors for Buddhist temples in the traditional style, beginning at Tōfukuji in Kyōto in 1933. His conversion to Abstraction culminated in the huge screens inspired by the Pacific Ocean and the Inland Sea painted in 1963 for Chikurinji Temple in Kōji City, which a Japanese critic has called 'the first great work of abstract art in Japan'.

After this leap into the present it is surprising to find that at about the same time as Inshō was carrying out the Chikurinji commission, he was also painting the figurative Gloria of Santa Maria with Japanese martyrs for the cathedral in Ōsaka, and only a year earlier had painted a still-life in a synthetic Kōrin-Matisse manner. In his bold abstractions of the 1960s, such as *Establishment* and *Four Seasons of a Garden* (Colour Plate 10), Inshō overlays strong ink brushwork with colour in a manner remotely derived from that of the seventeenth-century Kanō masters. But he often surrenders to the temptation to produce somewhat self-conscious, even pretty effects by the addition of patches and dots of gold and long trailing gold lines that wander across the composition and destroy much of its power—a device beloved of Japanese poster designers.

When we consider Inshō's oeuvre as a whole—and he is by no means untypical—we cannot help being astonished at the ease and speed with which a Japanese painter acquires a repertoire of different, and sometimes conflicting, styles and manages to combine them in one picture. This of course is nothing new. In the eleventh-century *Tale of Genji* there is a description of a landscape painting of which the top half was in the old Chinese manner, the bottom half in the new native style (*Yamato-e*) just then coming into fashion, and we have already seen how adept the eighteenth-century 'modernists', such as Shiba Kōkan, were at this kind of synthesis.

The number of postwar Japanese painters who have succeeded in reconciling East and West in their work runs into hundreds, and we can only mention a few. Among those who were already active before the war are Saitō Yoshishige (b. 1904), Kumagai Morikazu (1880–1977) and Yamaguchi Takeo (b. 1902). Yamaguchi had been associated with Zadkine in Paris in the 1920s and later became an abstract painter. Of his compositions in powerful flat shapes (Figure 104), he says, 'I am little concerned with the problem of communication. In fact, I try to avoid it, because communication is needed only when something is lacking in content'—a remark that seems to put the philosophy of abstract art in

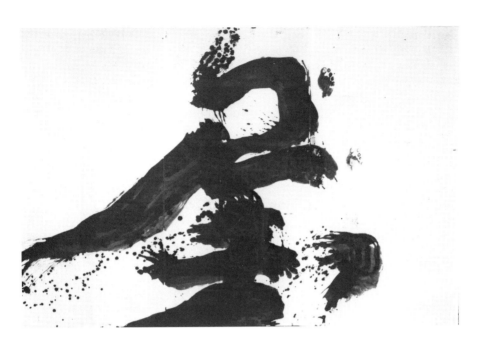

103.
Inoue Yuichi (b. 1916). *Shu* (Chinese
character for 'to belong': in Japanese,
shoku). Ink on paper. 1967. Artist's collection. Calligraphy is a form of abstract
art. In his 'abstract calligraphy', Inoue
carries the character almost, but not
quite, to the point of total illegibility.

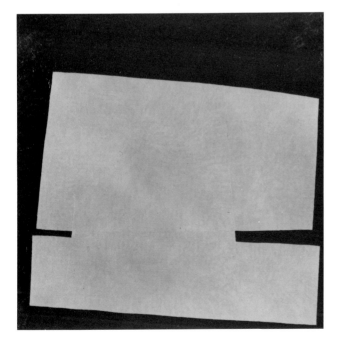

104.
Yamaguchi Takeo (b. 1902). *Turn*. Oil.
1961. National Museum of Modern Art,
Tōkyō. Yamaguchi studied from 1927 to
1931 in France, where he was associated
with Zadkine. Here he is influenced by
postwar American Minimalism.

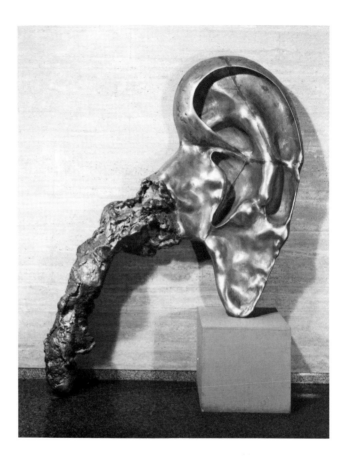

105.
Miki Tomio (b. 1917). *Ear.* Cast aluminum. 1964. Hakone Open Air Museum, Kanagawa. Miki was for a time fascinated by the form of the human ear, its detachment from the head, seeing it as a symbol of the futility of aesthetic communication—something that before the impact of the West no Asian artist would have thought of.

a nutshell. Asō Saburō, influenced by Mark Tobey, paints subtle abstractions in oils, less calligraphic and more decorative than those of the contemporary Chinese painter in Paris Zao Wou-ki.

The reaction against Abstract Expressionism did not leave the Japanese unprepared; indeed, the anonymity and technical discipline of Op Art, Kinetic Art and Hard-edge Abstraction appealed to a love of precise craftsmanship that is perhaps more deeply rooted in the Japanese than calligraphy, which was originally a Chinese art form. More recent developments still—such as the 'body art' of Shinohara, the reliefs of endlessly repeated ears of Miki Tomio (Figure 105) and the work of the Superrealists, Photorealists and their successors—is not a minute behind New York and may, in the helter-skelter search for something new, even be ahead. Miki spoke of his obsession with the ear as 'the least integrated part of the human body', a symbol of 'the absurdity of a world in which communication is impossible'—and a symbol too, perhaps, of that sense of isolation, of alienation, that a modern city such as Tōkyō can produce.

Nor is South Korea lagging. Her artists seem to have leaped into the turbulent world of the avant-garde—no less than fifteen were represented at the
1982 São Paolo Bienal—without having passed through, still less digested, the
intermediate stages in the response to Western art. If the works in the latest
idioms produced by Japanese and Korean, American and European artists sometimes seem almost indistinguishable from each other, that is because a shared
technology makes the advanced cultures of East and West more and more alike.
Only a rise in political tensions, and a return to cultural chauvinism, is likely to
reverse this trend. In the meantime, the avant-garde artists have become a supra-
national fraternity, often communicating more readily with each other than
with their own people.

The Modern Japanese Print

In the complex pattern of acceptance, synthesis and surrender in Japanese art, the
modern woodcut stands apart with a quality entirely its own, for it is a Japanese
art form that has been virtually abandoned, then revived and revolutionised,
while retaining its essential Japanese character. By the late nineteenth century
the *Ukiyo-e* was in a sad state of decline. There was no place for it in an art world
oscillating between European salon painting on the one hand and the revived
Kanō and Tosa schools on the other, while its function as illustration was being
taken over by modern photographic reproduction processes. There were one or
two attempts to modernise the woodcut during the Meiji period. Kobayashi
Kiyochika's portrait of the journalist Fukuchi Genichi, his very successful landscape and industrial prints of the 1880s—most strikingly, *Ryōgoku after the Fire of
1881* (Figure 106)—and the work of his pupils Ogura Ryūson and Inoue Yasuji
show what might have been achieved if they had had any following. But their
efforts were premature, and by the end of the nineteenth century the woodcut as
an art form in Japan seemed to be dead.

The revival was largely the work of one man: Yamamoto Kanae (1882–1946),
who had spent the years from 1912 to 1916 in Europe and returned to take up a
career as a Western-style painter and printmaker. Hasegawa Kiyoshi (1891–1980)
was another pioneer, but as he settled in Paris in 1918, his work is much better
known in the West than in his native country. In 1919 Yamamoto produced his
famous colour print, *Breton Woman* (Figure 107), which made an immediate and
profound impression. Though the blocks were cut in Japan, the subject was
foreign enough. But the cool, flat colours, the emphasis upon the line, the
simplification towards essential forms (carried a good deal further than in the
Kobayashi portrait) and the frank acceptance of the two-dimensional surface all

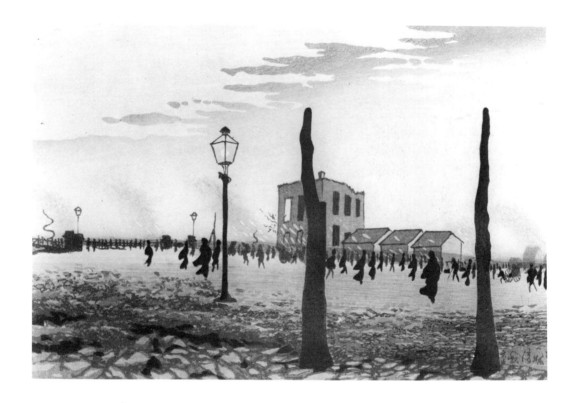

106.
Kobayashi Kiyochika (1847–1915).
Ryōgoku after the Fire of 1881. Colour
woodblock print. Santa Barbara Museum
of Art. Photo by O. E. Nelson.
Kiyochika, trained in photography, Japanese painting and Western techniques (by
Wirgman), turned out a large number of
conventional prints, but occasionally, as
in this striking composition, he is far
ahead of his time.

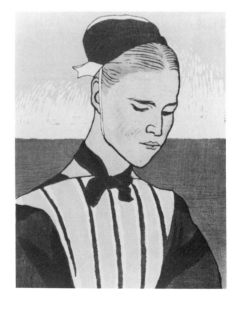

107.
Yamamoto Kanae (1882–1946). *Breton
Woman*. Colour woodblock print. 1920.
Courtesy of the Shōbi-Sō Gallery, Ueno.
Founder of the creative print movement,
Yamamoto made this revolutionary print
after nearly four years in Europe. Al-
though by no means his first 'modern'
print, it was to have an enormous influence
on the art of the younger generation.

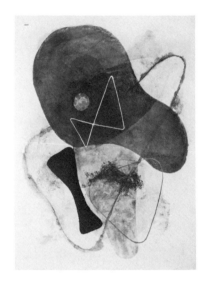

108.
Onchi Kōshirō (1891–1955). *Poem Number Nineteen: The Sea*. Colour woodblock print. 1952. James Michener Collection, Honolulu Academy of Arts, Hawaii. An important print from the period of the dramatic revival of modern Japanese art after World War II. Onchi here successfully integrates a Japanese sense of design with influences from several contemporary Western abstract artists.

showed that Yamamoto had recovered the essentials of the *Ukiyo-e*. With this mild but revolutionary work, the modern Japanese print was born.

In 1916 Yamamoto founded the Japanese Creative Print Society (Nihon Sōsaku Hanga Kyōkai). The emphasis was upon the word 'creative'. For what distinguishes the modern Japanese print from the *Ukiyo-e* is that it is no longer a popular art form, a picture translated into a print by anonymous craftsmen, but a work of art in its own right carried out entirely by the artist, who makes very few impressions, or a monotype only. Modern printmakers frankly engage in a dialogue with their medium, exploiting its limitations and possibilities to the full.

It has often been remarked that Japanese artists are at their best when they have to overcome the resistance of the medium—they are carvers in wood and ivory rather than modellers in clay—and modern Japanese printmakers share with carpenters and woodworkers a love and understanding of their material that is unique in the world. As Kawakita put it, 'The Japanese have always shown a special ability in those arts that involve a compromise with recalcitrant material. . . . There are certain aids and handicaps affecting the artist as he fashions his work, that function independently of his own will'. But, he goes on, 'if one looks for a fault in the contemporary print one will find it in those cases where the artist, becoming overpreoccupied with his skill at coping with physical resistance outside himself, has become bogged down in mere cleverness'.

After the initial stimulus, direct Western influence on the modern Japanese print became relatively unimportant, although it was Americans in Japan who first patronised the printmakers after the war and the appreciation of foreigners that gave the movement such status as it initially acquired at home. The abstract prints of the first truly modern master, Onchi Kōshirō (1891–1955; Figure 108),

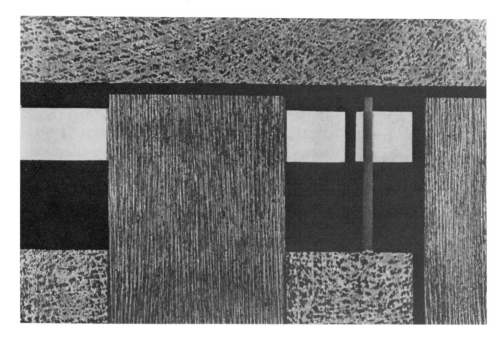

109.
Saitō Kiyoshi (b. 1907). *Wall*. Colour
woodblock print. Saitō was already
making 'modern' colour woodcuts in the
1930s. He was a leader in the postwar
woodcut movement, when the Western
influence on his work was no longer
Gauguin, but Mondrian.

were influenced by Picasso, Kandinsky, Munch and Miró, and the bold, expres-
sionistic, figurative style of Munakata Shikō (1903–75) by Japanese folk art and
Matisse, while at a very early age Munakata resolved to become 'the van Gogh
of Japan'. Saitō Kiyoshi (b. 1907) had originally been led to the creative print by
Gauguin, who in turn had been inspired by Hokusai (Figure 109). But the very
nature and demands of the medium precluded that swift and indiscriminate surrender to successive fashions in Western art to which the Japanese oil painters
had been so vulnerable. Although the woodcut has its expressive limitations, it
is the most purely Japanese and therefore the strongest Japanese contribution to
the international movement in modern art. So it is not surprising that it was the

prints by such masters as Sugai Kumi, Munakata and Saitō shown at the Venice and São Paolo Bienales in the early 1950s that first persuaded Western critics that modern Japanese art must be taken seriously.

By the 1980s the print had come to reflect the two mainstreams in modern Japanese art: on the one hand, the *Shin Hanga* devoted to landscapes, beauties and Kabuki actors in updated versions of the styles of Hiroshige, Utamaro and Sharaku; on the other, total freedom in the handling of every technique practised by the modern printmaker anywhere, such as Noda Tetsuya's disturbing cityscapes and haunting pictures of his little daughter, achieved in a combination of mimeograph, woodblock and silkscreen. As the modern print becomes somewhat polarised between these two extremes, we cannot help looking back, a little wistfully, to the early postwar work of Saitō, Munakata, Onchi and their contemporaries, in which any self-consciousness about style and technique seems to have been overwhelmed by the urge, after years of suppression, to express feeling and create anew.

Japanese Artists Living Abroad

It is rare to find a Japanese painter who comes to the West asserting his 'Japaneseness'. Generally, the acceptance of Western art is wholehearted, for that is after all what they come for. Hasegawa Kiyoshi and Ogisu Takanori were successful Post-Impressionists in Paris between the world wars; Fujita Tsuguharu, who settled in Paris, became in essence a French painter, and died a French citizen. Oda Hiroki also settled in Paris, where he came under the influence of Chagall. Kuniyoshi, who went to America in 1906 at the age of eighteen, crowned a successful career as an American painter by being elected the first president of the Artists' Equity Association in 1947. He died in 1953 without ever having returned to his native land and never thought of himself as a Japanese artist.

Since the Second World War a second generation of Japanese painters living abroad have made their contribution to the international modern movement, notably Inokuma Genichirō, who settled in New York in 1961, attracted thither by the complete freedom from the group pressure and group loyalties that plague the Japanese art world and by the businesslike relationship between artist and gallery that he found there. He returned to Japan in 1969. Kito Akira achieved a reputation in Paris, as did Sugai Kumi, whose bold abstract forms and 'abstract calligraphy' secured him a first prize at the São Paolo Bienal in 1965 (Fig-

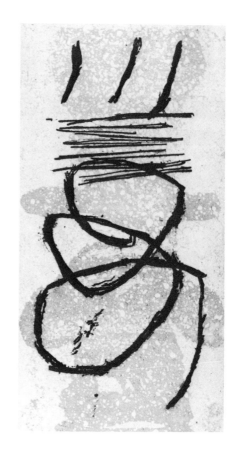

110.
Sugai Kumi (b. 1919). *Snow*. Copperplate etching. 1965. Sugai, who has lived
in Paris since 1952, is a representative of
the internationalism of some movements
in modern art, yet the flavour of his work
is still Japanese.

ure 110); Azumi Kenjirō was long associated with Marini and became his assistant in Milan. And one could name many more. For all of them, to a greater
or lesser degree, involvement with Western art and adjustment to Western society has brought a crisis of identity, a crisis that was most clearly and movingly
articulated by Isamu Noguchi.

Born in America in 1904 of a Japanese father and an American mother (he
was known as Isamu Gilmour till he grew up), educated in Japan and then again
in America, apprenticed disastrously to Gutzon Borglum (who said he would
never become a sculptor), trained in New York and in Paris under Brancusi,
Noguchi visited Japan again in 1931 almost as a stranger. Sculpture as he then
found it in Tōkyō had no message for him. Takamura Kōun was carving Buddhas in the style of the Nara period; his son Kōtarō was working in the manner
of Rodin. But in the Kyōto Museum Noguchi discovered the ancient clay figures, called *haniwa*, that had stood around the great tombs of the prehistoric period. 'They were in a sense modern', he said later, 'they spoke to me and were
closer to my feeling for earth'. He moved into a cottage and began to make ter-

racottas and to discover the beauty of gardens and the Japanese countryside. Of this period he said, 'I have since thought of my lonely self-incarceration then, and my close embrace of the earth, as a seeking after identity with some primal matter beyond personalities and possessions. In my work I wanted something irreducible'.

Noguchi was back in New York, building a solid position for himself with sculpture and stage designing, when there came the shock of Pearl Harbour. Suddenly he realised that he was not American but Nisei, or second-generation Japanese. Yet he was not truly Japanese either. When he visited Tōkyō again after the war, he expected to be treated as a foreigner, and up to a point he was. But gradually he became reconciled to his dual origin and drew strength from it. 'Why do I continuously go back to Japan', he wrote, 'except to renew my contact with the earth? There still remains the familiarity with earthly materials and the skill of Japanese hands. How exquisitely functional are their traditional tools. Soon these, too, will be displaced by the machine. In the meantime I go there like a beggar or a thief, seeking the last warmth of the earth'. Of his situation—one can no longer call it his predicament—he said, 'My own contradictions, enhanced perhaps by my mixed parentage, are probably shared by most artists to some degree. We all look to the past and the future to find ourselves. Here we find a hint that awakens us, there a path that someone like us once trod'.

Noguchi's *Black Sun* (Figure 111) of 1969 is a work of great nobility, simplicity and strength. But not all the work of this amazingly prolific and resourceful artist has been an equally successful blending of East and West. Where he has consciously attempted a synthesis, as in the UNESCO garden in Paris, of which one level is modern and formalistic, the other more purely Japanese, the symbolic meeting of the two cultures seems too contrived, too intellectually conceived to be wholly satisfying. Perhaps his greatest achievement, because it is most basic, is his landscaped 'garden' for the National Museum outside Jerusalem (Figure 112). Here, with terraces and retaining wall, he sculpted a hilltop into something spacious, inevitable, 'irreducible'. Nothing is imposed; the materials, and the shapes that they are given, are natural to the site itself, as in the finest of Japanese gardens. Noguchi's own words express movingly his awareness of the garden as a common ground between people, nature and art that is one of Japan's chief contributions to civilisation:

> I like to think of gardens as sculpturing of space: a beginning, and a groping to another level of sculptural experience and use: a total sculpture space experience beyond individual sculptures. A man may enter such a space: it is in scale with him; it is real. An empty space has no visual dimensions or significance. Scale and meaning enter when some thoughtful object or line is introduced. This is why sculptures, or rather sculptural objects, create space. . . . What may be incomplete as sculptural entities are of significance to the whole.

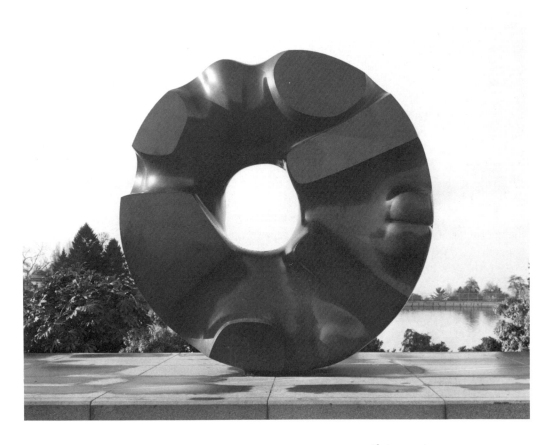

111.
Isamu Noguchi (b. 1904). *Black Sun*.
Tamba granite. 1969. Seattle Art Museum, Washington. Noguchi sees the sun
as a 'coiled magnet, the circle of ever-
accelerating force'. Is there also some
deeper reference to Amaterasu, the Sun
Goddess, the legendary founder of Japan?

112 (facing page).
Isamu Noguchi (b. 1904). *Water Source
Sculpture*. Red granite. 1965. Bezale
National Museum, Jerusalem. Of this
project, Noguchi wrote, 'Here you have
a sculpture . . . weighing a million tons.
No, it is a piece of the earth itself, extending all the way to China. This is
what I have sculptured, and one may
walk upon it and feel its solidity under
foot and know that it belongs to all of us
without limit and equally'.

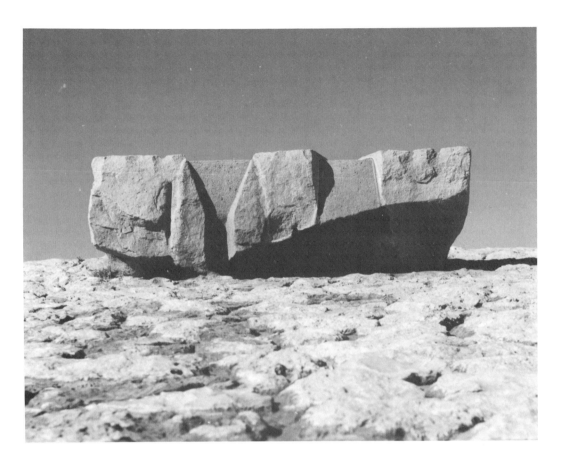

That Noguchi's most profoundly 'Japanese' garden does not look Japanese at all suggests that in the transmission of art from one culture to another it is not the forms and materials themselves that are important, but the ideas and attitudes that lie behind them, for these, in a new setting, can give expression through a new set of forms and different materials and yet retain much of their original character.

The 1960s had been a period when Japanese artists threw themselves with a quite uncritical abandon into the international modern movement. 'Japan itself', wrote the critic Kawakita at this time, 'is completely caught in the sick condition of this sick generation. On reflection it would seem that there is nothing left to attempt in the world of art'. Indeed, it seems that every possible style and medium, and combination of them, was attempted. But in the 1970s the atmosphere began to change. As Japan grew economically stronger and more self-confident, the number of exhibitions of Western avant-garde art began to decline.

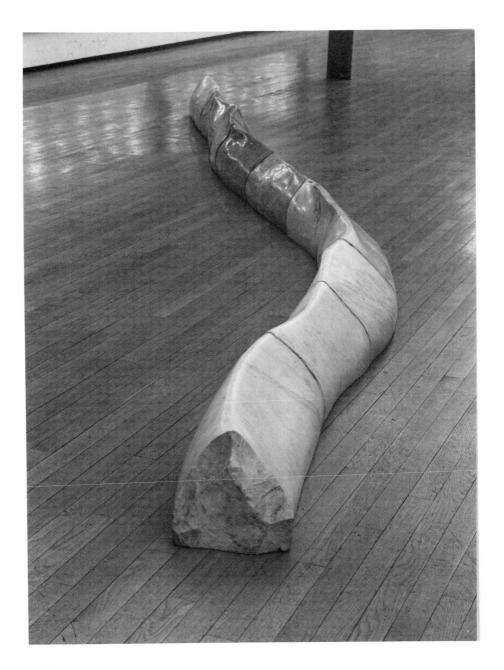

113.
Nagasawa Hidetoshi (b. 1900). *Colonna.*
Eleven different kinds of marble on polished wood floor. 1972. Nagasawa represents a recent rejection by some Japanese
artists of foreign styles and a return to a
native reverence for craftsmanship and
the material.

Art became, to some degree, nationalistic—not in the political sense, for the militarism of the 1930s and 1940s and its consequences could not be forgotten—but in a search for identity, for the roots of Japanese culture, such as Noguchi had embarked upon in his earlier pilgrimage to his homeland. Besides, among the young, who had so eagerly surrendered to the West, there was—particularly after Vietnam—some disillusionment with Western ideas and values.

Japan was becoming a leader in the high technological culture of the world, and there could be no retreat into cultural isolationism. But, around 1969, a group of artists who called themselves the Mono-ha, the School of the Thing or Object (*mono*), began to rediscover the virtue of natural, unprocessed and unfinished materials. Abandoning Surrealism, Dada, Body Art, and other Western movements, they worked with stone, paper, cotton, wood, iron. The leader of the Mono-ha, the naturalised Korean U-Fan Lee (or Ou-fan Lee), demanded that his followers totally reject Western modernism and return to what Minemura called 'a candid vision of an undisguised world'. Lee undoubtedly oversimplified the situation: few artists today can reject everything but the instinctive dialogue with the material, and in fact Lee's art, and that of others in the group such as Suga Kishio and Nagasawa Hidetoshi, is not immediately identifiable as Japanese. Lee for instance laid a rough-hewn cube of stone on a sheet of plate glass; Nagasawa laid a winding snakelike form seven metres long, carved in marble, on a polished wood floor (Figure 113); Enokura Kōji draped huge sheets of oil-impregnated cotton cloth along the wall of a gallery. None of these ideas were either very original or very Japanese, but the feeling for the form, texture and behaviour of the materials the artists were working with is acute and sensitive in a particularly Japanese way. Perhaps, in the increasingly international character of contemporary art, this is the most one should expect.

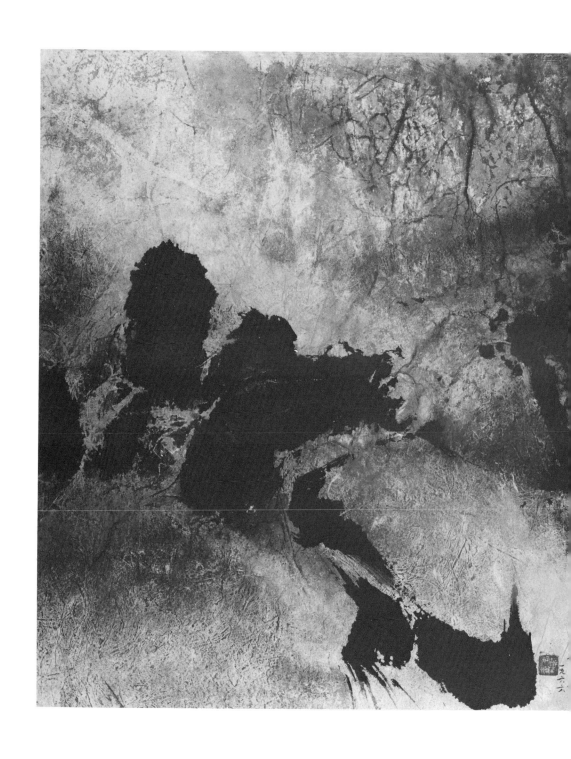

Plates

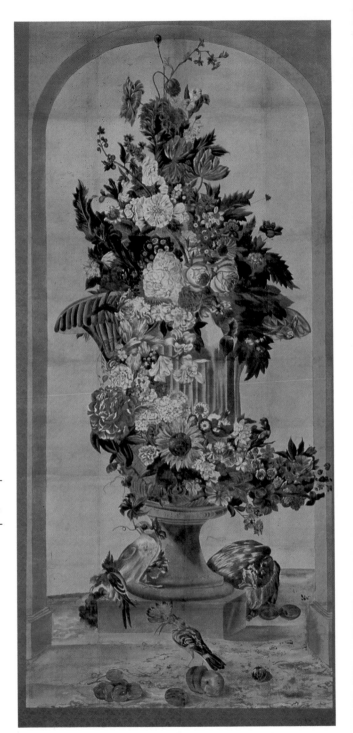

Plate 1.
Tani Bunchō (1763–1840). *Flowers in a
Vase, with Birds.* Ink and colour on silk.
Municipal Art Museum, Kōbe. This
enormous painting, 91 inches high, is a
copy of a floral still-life by the Dutch artist Willem van Royen that had been presented by the Dutch factor in 1729 to the
shōgun Yoshimune. There is another version by the Ishikawa brothers, Tairō and
Mōkō.

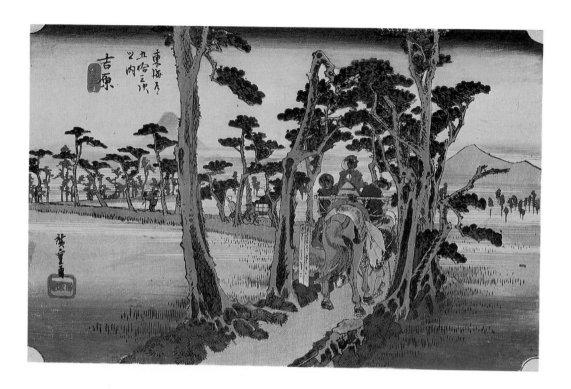

Plate 2.
Andō Hiroshige (1797–1858). *Mount Fuji
from Yoshiwara*. From the *Fifty-three
Stages of the Tōkaidō*, 1833–34. Colour
woodblock print. Victoria and Albert
Museum. A striking example of the Japanese printmaker's skill in combining
Western three-dimensional space with
traditional design.

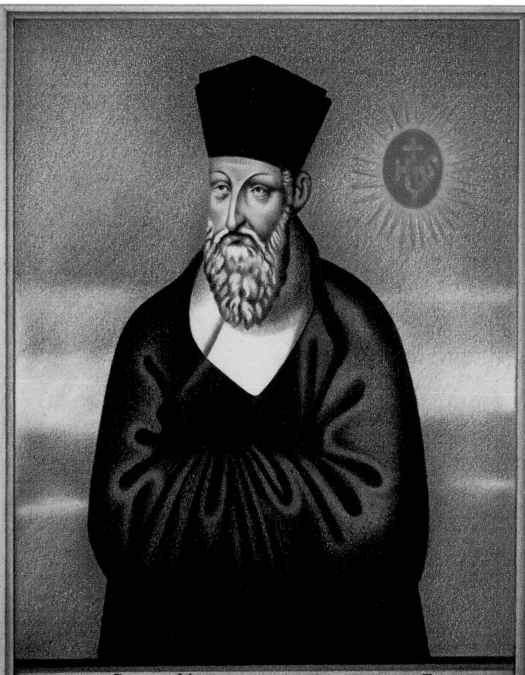
EMATTHEVS RICCIVS MACERATENSIS QVI PRIMVS E SOCIETAE
ESV EVANGELIVM IN SINAS INVEXIT OBIIT ANNO SALVTIS
1610 ÆTATIS 60.

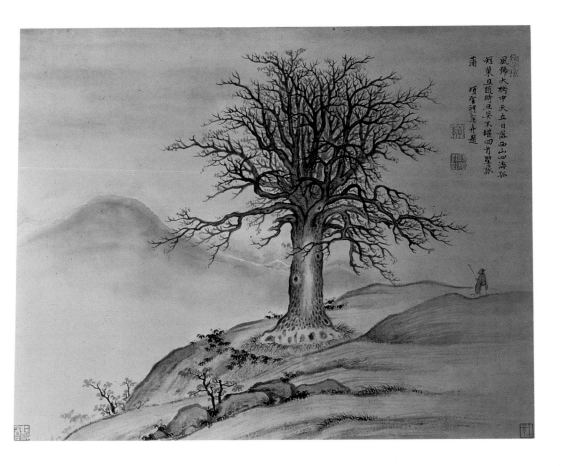

風獅大樹中天立日落西山四海弧
短棠且題時旦吳不堪四育聖孫
蒲
項聖謨寫幷題

Plate 3.
Yü Wen-hui (Mañoel Pereira). *Portrait of Matteo Ricci*. Oil. c. 1610. Istituto Storico della Compagnia di Jesu, Rome. Yü Wen-hui, trained in Japan, returned to China where this portrait of the great Jesuit missionary could well have been painted from life. Probably the oldest surviving oil painting by a Chinese artist, it looks as if it had been heavily and rather clumsily restored.

Plate 4.
Hsiang Sheng-mou (1597–1656). Bare Solitary Tree. Leaf dated 1649 from an album. Ink and colour on paper. J. T. Tai Collection, New York. The tree stripped bare at the centre of the world stands for China after the Manchu conquest. The heavy symbolism of this strange picture is helped by a touch of Western realism. There is another version of this painting in the Nü-wa-chai Collection, New York.

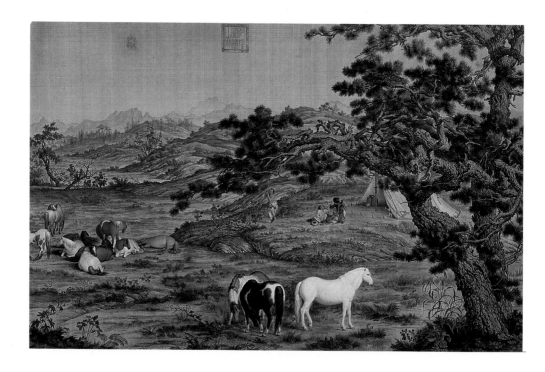

Plate 5.
Lang Shih-ning (Giuseppe Castiglione; 1688–1766). *A Hundred Horses in a Landscape*. Detail of a handscroll. Ink and colour on silk. 1728. National Palace Museum, Taipei. The Italian artist uses shading to make the horses and tree trunks more solid but reduces to a mere hint the cast shadows that Chinese viewers found unacceptable.

Plate 6.
Anonymous. A Court Lady and Her Attendants. Panel on silk. Eighteenth century. Courtesy of Mr and Mrs Peter Quennell, London. The delicate charm of the Rococo interior and the figures suggests the hand of Attiret, although the little dog looks very like one of Ch'ien-lung's pets, of which Lang Shih-ning painted a portrait.

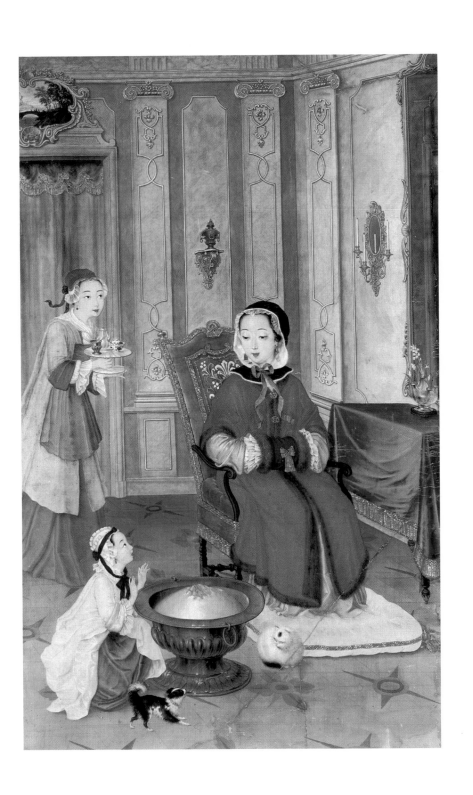

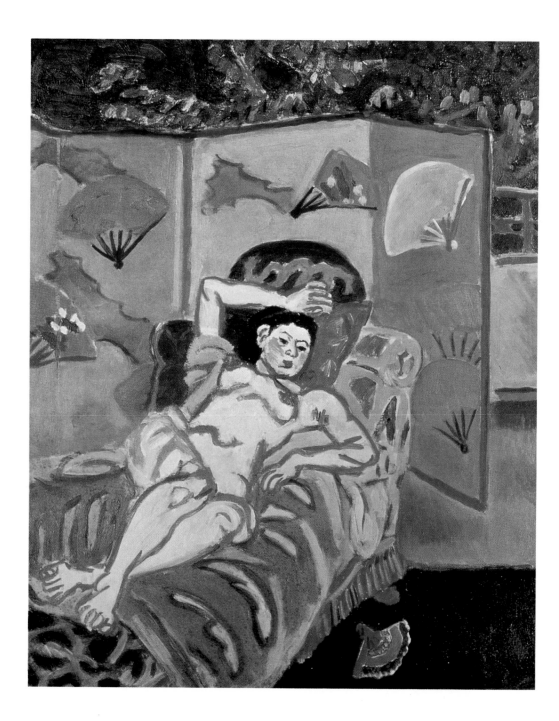

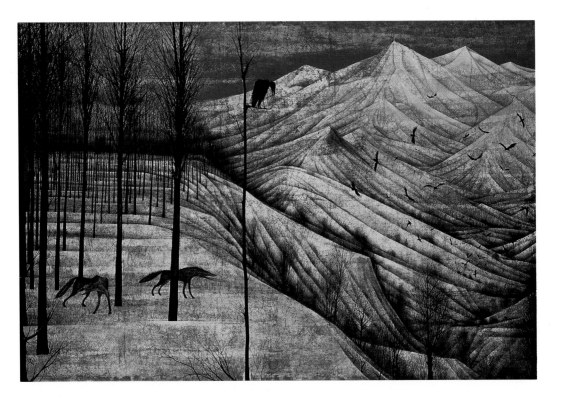

Plate 7.
Umehara Ryūzaburō (1888–1986). *Nude with Fans.* Oil on canvas. 1938. Ōhara Museum of Art, Kurashiki. Pupil of Asai Chū and of Renoir, admirer of van Gogh and of Rouault, Umehara in this vibrant picture seems to be recalling also the japonaiseries of Whistler and Monet.

Plate 8.
Kayama Matazō (b. 1927). *Winter.* Ink and colour on paper. 1957. National Museum of Modern Art, Tōkyō. A brilliant transformation of the theme and composition of Brueghel's *Hunters in the Snow* into Japanese terms.

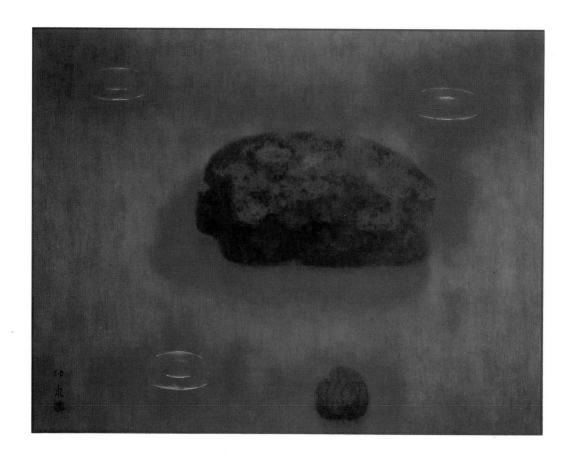

Plate 9.
Tokuoka Shinsen (1896–1972). *Rain*.
Colour on paper. 1964. Collection of
Zauhō-Kanko-Kai Publishing Company,
Tōkyō. It was the influence of modern
Western art after World War II that
helped Shinsen, a pupil of Takeuchi
Seihō, to regenerate the *Nihonga* School,
which had stagnated between the wars.

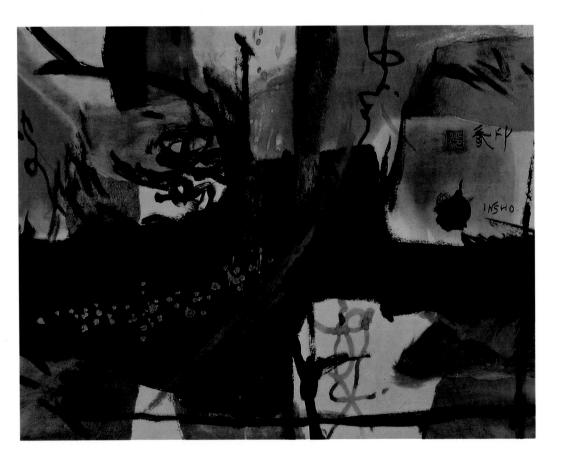

Plate 10.
Dōmoto Inshō (1891–1975). *Four Seasons
of a Garden*. Ink and colour on paper.
1964. Private collection, Kyōto. The conversion of this very conservative Kyōto
painter to the imperial household into
an Abstract Expressionist is a striking instance of the influence of the New York
School on Japanese art in the 1950s.

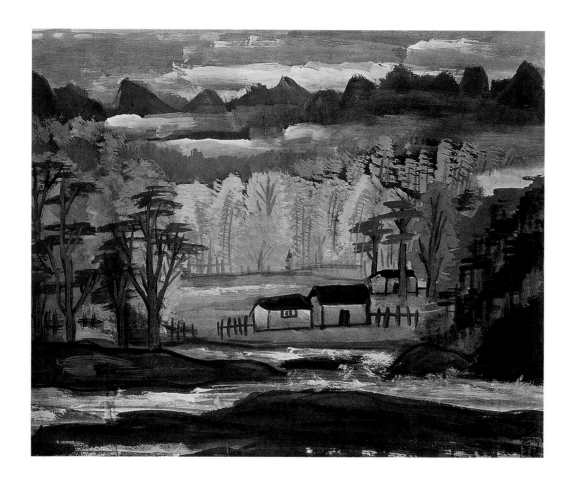

Plate 11.
Lin Feng-mien (Lin Fengmian; b. 1900).
Before the Village. Chinese ink and gouache
on paper. This work by the artist who
has done more than any other to create
a modern school of Chinese landscape
painting combines Chinese liveliness in
the brushwork with a bold Western use
of expressive colour.

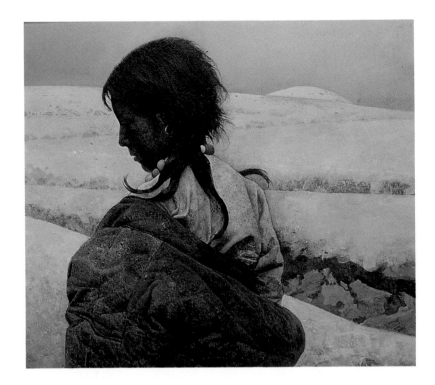

Plate 12.
Ai Hsüan (b. 1947). *A Not Too Distant
Memory*. Oil on canvas. 1983. Private collection. Many of the post-1976 school of
Szechwan realists recall in their works the
bitter times of the Cultural Revolution in
a style that reflects the influence—which
they freely acknowledge—of the modern
American artist Andrew Wyeth.

Plate 13.
Huang Yung-yü (b. 1924). *Southern Landscape*. Gouache and Chinese ink on paper. 1977. Private collection, Oxford, England. This vibrant painting reflects the new freedom to be found in the work of many Chinese artists liberated after persecution during the Cultural Revolution of 1966–76. Here style is not deliberately chosen but created in the act of painting.

Plate 14.
Liu Kuo-sung (b. 1932). *Abstraction*. Ink
and colour on paper. 1966. Private collection, Oxford, England. Liu Kuo-sung,
a founder of the Fifth Moon Group in
Taipei, here carries the expressive calligraphic gesture and free blending of
colour and ink almost to the point of
pure abstraction, but his work can still be
'read' as a landscape in the Chinese way.

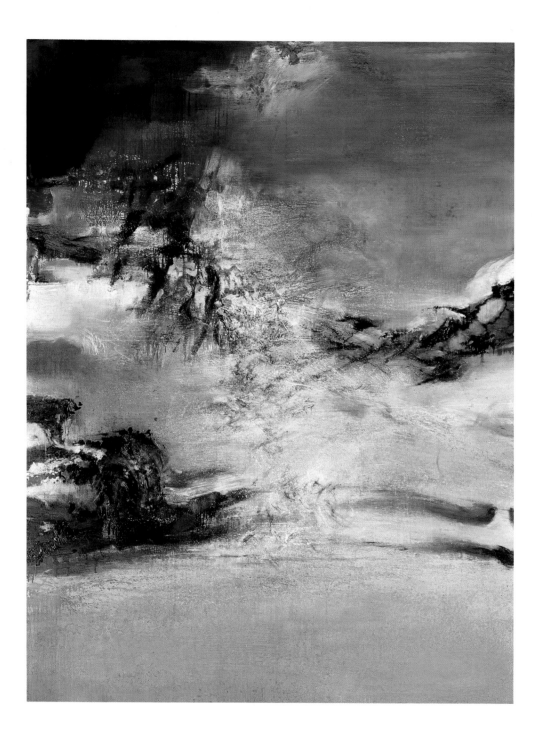

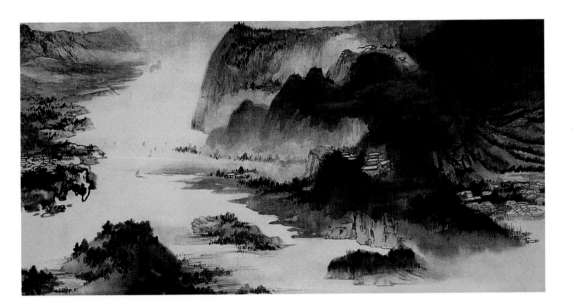

Plate 15 (facing page).
Zao Wou-ki (Chao Wu-chi; b. 1920). *Abstraction, 21.4.1980*. Oil on canvas. Property of the artist. By the 1960s, Zao Wou-ki, having absorbed what he needed from Klee and Abstract Expressionism, was creating the notable series of semi-abstract landscapes in which space, atmosphere and the calligraphic gesture with the brush all play their part.

Plate 16.
Chang Ta-ch'ien (Chang Dai Chien; 1899–1983). Ten Thousand Miles of the Yangtse River. Detail of a handscroll. Ink and colour on paper. 1968. Chang Ch'un Collection, Taipei. The traditional painter par excellence, Chang Ta-ch'ien in his later years responded to the challenge of Abstract Expressionism and of the 'creative accident' in his free blending of ink and mineral colours.

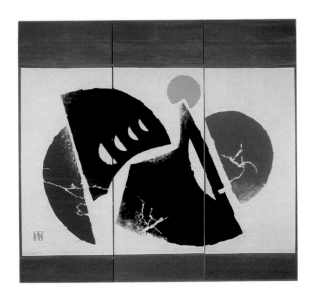

Plate 17.
Ch'en T'ing-shih (b. 1919). *Abstraction*. Print from blocks cut from sugar-cane fibreboard. 1967. Private collection. Poet and painter, Ch'en has created his own kind of abstraction. His prints have a monumental simplicity and strength that reminds us of rubbings from ancient stone reliefs.

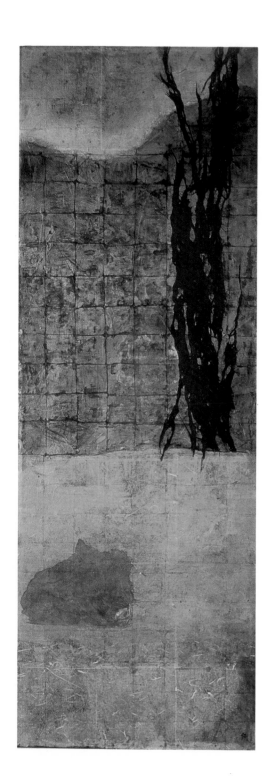

Plate 18.
Tseng Yu-ho (b. 1923). *At Second Sight*.
Ink and collage on gold paper. 1962. Mr
and Mrs Jacquelin Hume collection, San
Francisco. In this very contemporary
synthesis of East and West, Tseng Yu-ho
replaces calligraphic brushwork with a
collage of seaweed that gestures towards
the rock against a background of gold
leaf borrowed from Japanese screen
decoration.

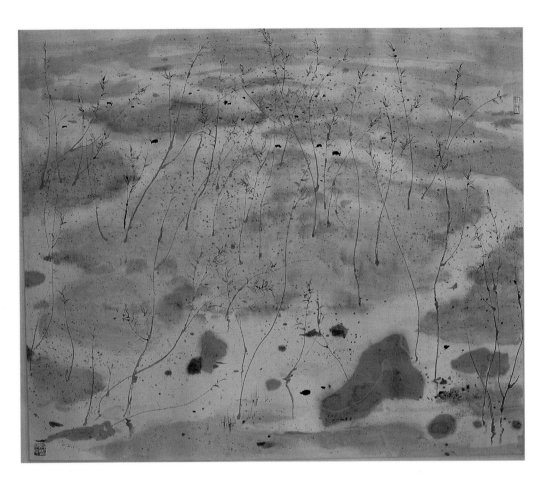

Plate 19.
Wu Kuan-chung (Wu Guanzhong;
b. 1919). *Autumn*. 1983. Chinese ink and
colour. Property of the artist. A completely successful, because natural and
spontaneous, synthesis of Chinese brush
technique and Western feeling for continuous recession, achieved by an artist
trained in Hangchow and Paris, who is
equally at home in the Chinese and Western media.

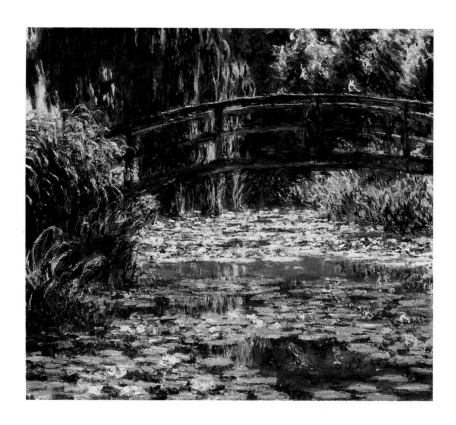

Plate 20.
Claude Monet (1840–1926). *Japanese Bridge at Giverny*. 1900. From the *Nymphéas* series. Musée de l'Orangerie, Paris. Although Monet's technique is anything but Oriental, the idea of the garden as a source of inspiration to the artist, the sense of continuous space and the colours reminiscent of Kōrin show that Monet had absorbed the message of Japanese screen painting.

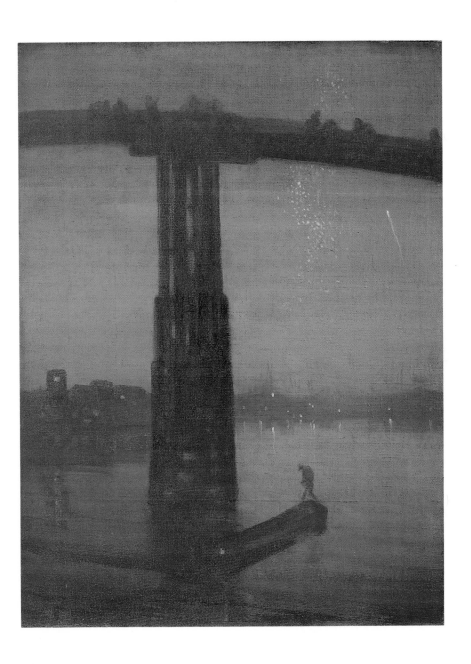

Plate 21.
James Abbott McNeill Whistler (1834–1903). *Old Battersea Bridge: Nocturne in Blue and Gold*. Oil on canvas. 1872–73. Tate Gallery, London. Whistler, like Pissarro, was inspired by Hokusai and Hiroshige.

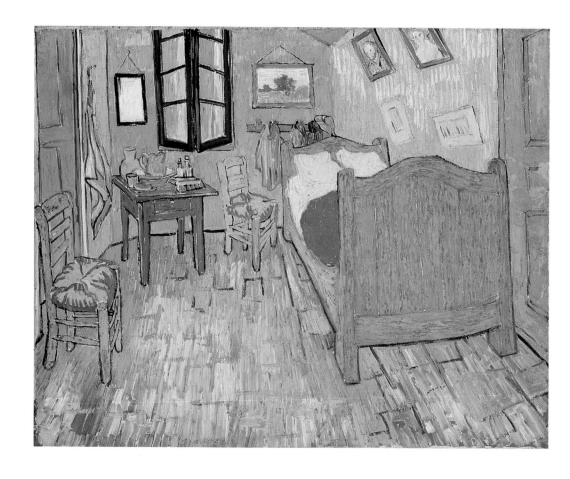

Plate 22.
Vincent van Gogh (1853–90). *The Artist's Bedroom at Arles*. Oil on canvas. 1888.
Art Institute of Chicago. Van Gogh
wrote of this picture to his brother Theo,
'Here colour is to do everything. . . . It
is painted in free, flat tints like Japanese
prints'.

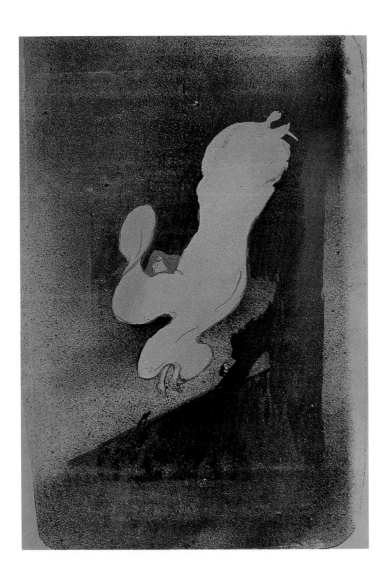

Plate 23.
Henri de Toulouse-Lautrec (1864–1901).
*Miss Loei Fuller Performing Her Fire
Dance*. Lithograph. 1893. Edition published by Marty. To create the effect of
the electric footlights, here used in the
theatre for the first time, Lautrec borrows the Japanese device of applying gold
with a cotton pad to each impression
after printing.

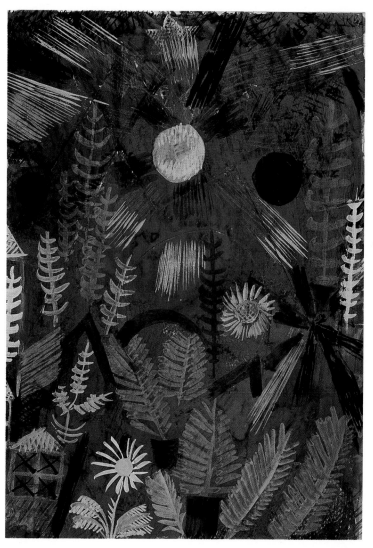

1918 60 .   Sonne im Garten

Plate 24.
Paul Klee (1878–1940). *Sonne im Garten*.
Watercolour. Private collection, Basel.
Painted at a time when Klee was deeply
immersed in Chinese poetry, this picture
is not obviously Oriental. Yet there is a
Chinese feeling in the sense of space, in
the forms of the plants and trees, and in
the suggestion that these images stand for
a reality that lies behind the surface of the
picture.

The Revolution in Chinese Art

Art in China from 1800 to 1949

We have seen how before modern times Western art was no more than a light wind blowing over the stream of Chinese painting; it rippled the surface for a while, then it was gone, and the Chinese tradition, as represented for example by late nineteenth-century masters such as Jen Po-nien, Wu Ch'ang-shih and Chao Chih-ch'ien, seemed to continue its slow progress through time as though it had never felt the breeze at all. Even today there are many painters whose art is totally unaffected by the impact of the West: amateurs who paint delightful landscapes in the manner of Wang Hui, rendering bamboo or birds and flowers in a variety of traditional styles. There is no more incongruity in this than in a Western gentleman playing Bach or Chopin in his free time. For many Chinese painters, even today, the traditional style, embodying as it does the arts of painting, calligraphy and frequently poetry as well, is so completely satisfying a mode of expression that it cannot be enriched by the infusion of Western techniques; it can only be changed in a way that robs it of its essential character, for Western realism, because it demands an analytical approach to the subject, gets in the way of both free calligraphic expression and the intuitive generalisation from experience that gives to Chinese painting its timeless, universal quality.

The eighteenth-century gentleman-painters had regarded Western art as something of a curiosity, and they were not in the least interested in European civilisation itself. But in the nineteenth century, as China suffered one humiliation after another at the hands of the European powers, she was forced to adopt more and more from the West in self-defence. China's leaders insisted that Western science and technology should only be the 'shell', while Confucius and Mencius remained the 'kernel' of Chinese culture, and there was no wholesale surrender to Western values such as the one that caused such violent oscillations of feeling in Meiji period Japan. In China westernisation was a slow and at first almost haphazard process, and until the Revolution of 1911, and the establishment of the Republic, it was scarcely reflected in art at all. Well into the twentieth century Western-style art was confined largely to the treaty ports, and above all to the French Concession in Shanghai. What went on in these enclaves was not thought of as having much to do with China, and high Chinese officials and others in positions of power (generally warlords), unlike their Meiji counterparts, tended to be conservative and anti-Western in cultural matters. Western railways and machine guns were one thing, Western painting—unless realistic and utilitarian—was quite another. The alternating rhythm of hunger for foreign culture and rejection of it that we find in Japanese civilisation is far less evident in China. From time to time China has, strictly on her own terms, accepted foreign ideas and forms—Buddhism and Buddhist art being the obvious example—but slowly and inexorably she has digested them, made them part of herself and continued on her own majestic way. Mao Tse-tung's dictum, quoted everywhere in China during his lifetime, 'Make foreign things serve China'—with all that is implied in the word *serve*—sums up a way of dealing with the culture of the Outer Barbarians that China has practised successfully for more than two thousand years.

In view of China's Olympian attitude to other civilisations, it is all the more interesting to see how she has responded to the latest and most critical of all the cultural challenges that have faced her throughout her history. I have quoted the views of Ch'ing dynasty savants about Western art, which may be summed up by saying that while they admired its realism, they could not take it seriously as painting because it showed so little skill and feeling in the use of the brush. Traditional painters hold this view today. In the work of leading masters such as Ch'i Pai-shih (1863–1957) and Huang Pin-hung (1864–1955), there is not even a hint of Western influence. The Western challenge indeed seems, as it did in Japan, to have provoked something of a revival in traditional painting. While the educated class long continued to think of Western art as mere craft, it was a useful, indeed an essential, tool in China's slow path to modernisation. As in Japan at a much earlier stage, it was through books and manuals on technology and through magazines and newspapers such as those published by F. Major at the Tien-shih-chai Press in Shanghai from 1884 onwards (Figure 114) that the literate public became accustomed to Western pictorial techniques.

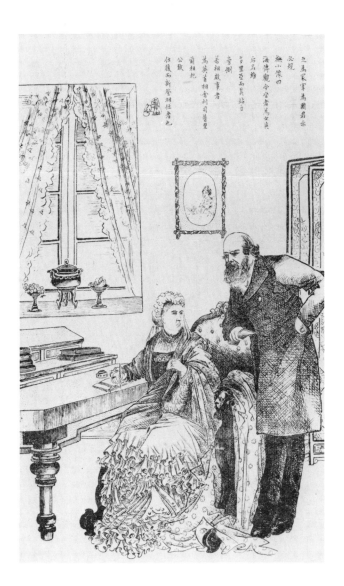

ㄴ為家筆為圖君示
次規
撫傳寵四
海傳寵令堂者為女庶
后名雖
辛墨墨而其詰言
亭僻
若相敵事者
為英自相官利司慧里
前相批
公戲
仕後而新登相任者也

114.
Wu Yu-ju (late nineteenth century).
*Queen Victoria Being Advised by Her Prime
Minister, Lord Salisbury.* A page from the
Tien-shih-chai hua-p'u, September 1885.
Western pictorial techniques took permanent hold in China only when they were
found useful for communicating information about foreign countries, events
and technology that traditional Chinese
painting methods could not handle. Note
the Chinese ornamental bronze on the
window-sill.

But it was not until 1906 that the first department of Western art was opened, in the Kiangsu-Kiangsi Normal School in Nanking, followed by another in Peking in 1911. In the next three years several Chinese painters who had studied in Tōkyō returned to set up their studios in Shanghai. Chou Hsiang, who had been trained by the now reestablished Jesuits at Ziccawei (l'Université Aurore), outside the city, opened a little private school in Shanghai. His star pupil, Liu Hai-su, later founded the Shanghai Art Academy, which became the focus of more conventional Western-style oil painting during the 1920s and 1930s. Until 1919 most of the teachers of Western art in Chinese art schools were Japanese, and the more enterprising Chinese students, such as Liu Hai-su, went to Tōkyō for further study. At this time, even in Shanghai, there were almost no Western paintings to be seen, and aspiring young art students, as Wang Ya-ch'en later remembered, were reduced to looking for colour reproductions in magazines in the secondhand bookstores on the Peking Road.

In 1919 Japan tried to seize the former German Concessions in China. This aroused a violent wave of anti-Japanese feeling, and young painters, for the first time, turned their eyes away from Japan and towards Europe. Many of them were fired by the liberal ideas of Dr Ts'ai Yüan-p'ei, president of Peking University, who opened the minds of a whole generation of Chinese students to a world beyond China's frontiers, invited Bertrand Russell, Rabindranath Tagore (Figure 115) and the American pragmatist John Dewey to lecture in Peking, and himself believed in a spiritual regeneration of China according to five principles of education, of which aesthetic education was one. His passionately held belief that art is the one universal language came to be shared by many young men and women and helped to free them from the cultural chauvinism of their elders. His influence in helping to create the climate for the acceptance of foreign art and music in modern China was to be far-reaching.

The vernacular literature movement, launched by Hu Shih in 1917, had been another powerful stimulus, for by liberating writers from the scholarly complexities of the old literary style, it enabled them to explore a range of feelings and emotions not previously thought of as expressible in literature at all. Much of what they produced was ephemeral and self-indulgently romantic, but this discovery of the self in literature was passionately sincere and soon found its way into art. The significance of the vernacular movement and all that it gave birth to is that although some of the forms and techniques employed in the arts, such as oil painting and the sonnet, were borrowed from abroad, it was a Chinese movement, expressing purely Chinese feelings.

To Paris the painters flocked in such numbers that one of them, Chou Ling, later founded the Association des Artistes Chinois en France. Some of its members remained in France and became Post-Impressionists in all but name; some sank into poverty and obscurity; others returned to China to establish a little

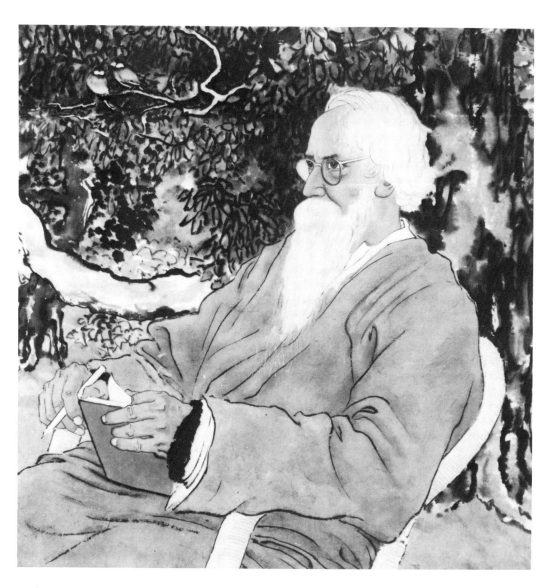

115.
Hsü Pei-hung (1895–1953). *Rabindranath
Tagore*. Ink and colour on paper. 1940.
Chinese collection. While Tagore's guest
at Shantiniketan, Hsü Pei-hung painted
this portrait of the Indian poet, who had
lectured in China twenty years earlier. It
is a good example of Hsü's skill in blending Chinese and Western techniques.

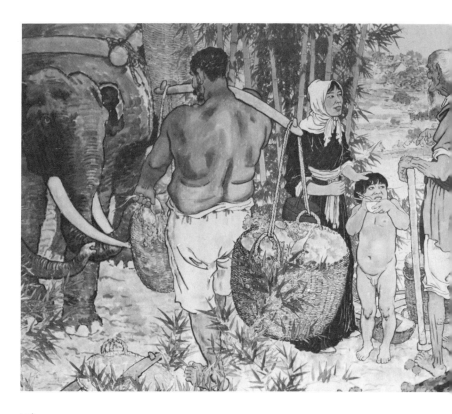

116.

Hsü Pei-hung (1895–1953). *The Foolish Old Man Removes the Mountain*. Handscroll. Chinese ink on paper. c. 1940. Chinese collection. Here Hsü attempts to show how a knowledge of the nude acquired in Europe can be combined with the Chinese medium and scroll format to produce a picture with the message 'achieve the impossible'. This curious work was much admired by Mao Tse-tung.

Quartier Latin in the French Concession of Shanghai and to set up art schools on the Beaux-Arts model: Yen Wen-liang in Soochow, Hsü Pei-hung in Nanking and later Peking and Lin Feng-mien in Hangchow. Lin Feng-mien's school later became, with that in Peking, one of the two national art academies and the centre of the most progressive art movements in China.

Students returning from Europe formed little cosmopolitan bridgeheads, such as T'ien Han's Académie du Midi (Nan-kuo I-shu Hsüeh-yüan) in Nanking, dedicated chiefly to the spread of drama, art and literature. In 1927 T'ien invited Hsü Pei-hung to open a department of fine art, which later became the art school of National Central University. Hsü Pei-hung was at that time a thor-

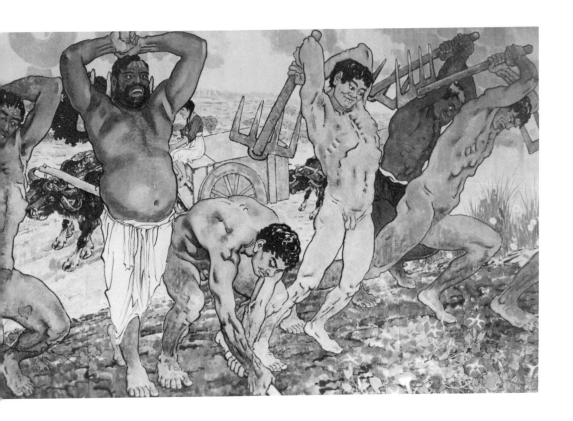

oughly academic oil painter, having studied in Paris (where he gallicised his name as Ju Péon) and in Berlin under Kamph; among his first works on returning to China were oils on Chinese historical subjects in the manner of Meissonier and Gérôme, who had also influenced an earlier generation of Japanese painters. But the pressure of his own culture was strong, and soon Hsü Pei-hung began to develop a brush technique that was both calligraphic and realistic; it is typified by the endless series of horses that he painted in the 1930s and 1940s. A curious example of this synthetic style is his scroll *The Foolish Old Man Removes the Mountain* (Figure 116), painted in about 1940. After 1950 this successful formula, combining realism and Chinese brushwork, seemed to be just what the

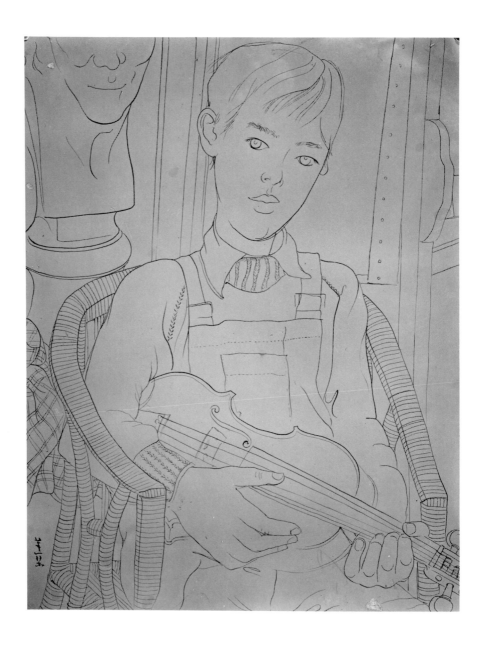

117.
P'ang Hsün-ch'in (1903–85). *Portrait of the Artist's Son*. Chinese ink on paper. 1944. Painted when the artist was a refugee in West China, this sensitive study suggests the influence of Picasso, whose work P'ang had come to admire as a student in Paris.

People's Republic required of its painters, and Hsü Pei-hung crowned a successful career by his appointment as director of the National Academy of Art in Peking, a key post that he held till his death in 1953.

For the more imaginative painters, however, reconciliation of East and West was not a matter of technique, but of vision and feeling. To them, their sense of alienation from their own society was often a spur. When P'ang Hsün-ch'in returned in 1930 from Paris, where he had been a friend of Fujita and Matisse, and saw how incomprehensible his paintings were, even to the comparatively sophisticated Shanghai public, he burned them all and retired to the country for a year to consider where he stood. When he took up painting again, it was not to revert to the traditional style nor to attempt to express himself as a Chinese in the modern idiom. Henceforward, his work—except for his delightful but somewhat archaistic T'ang dancers—always remained sincere and a little tentative, as though he was not wholly sure of his identity, which indeed was the case. In the 1930s and 1940s, he and Lin Feng-mien were probably the most successful artists in showing how Chinese painting could be 'modern' in form and style and yet essentially Chinese in feeling—this indefinable quality being preserved through a somewhat generalised rendering of form, a suppression of shadows and a fresh, sensitive handling of the brush (Figure 117). But it was in the work of Lin Feng-mien that the New National Painting Movement (*Hsin kuo hua*) found its clearest and most lyrical expression.

In Canton, Japanese influence was stronger and had a longer history. As early as 1903 Kao Chien-fu (1879–1951) had studied Western drawing and painting under a French teacher at Canton Christian College in Macao—which makes him the true pioneer of modern art in China. In 1906 he went to Japan, where during a two-year stay he is said to have joined Kuroda's White Horse Society, although no purely Western paintings by him exist today. A far more potent influence on him was Okakura's *Nihonga* movement, particularly the work of Takeuchi Seihō and Hashimoto Gahō. Back in Canton, he and his brother Kao Ch'i-feng later founded the Ch'un-shui (best translated as Spring Awakening) Art Academy to do for China what the *Nihonga* had done for Japan: revitalise traditional art by injecting into it realism and modern subject matter (Figure 118)—in the heroic pursuit of which Kao Chien-fu, in 1920, even made some sketches from an aeroplane.

Though a revolutionary in his ideals, Kao Chien-fu was not a revolutionary painter. Although *Two Monsters of the Real World,* his picture of an aeroplane hovering like a dragonfly over a tank in a traditional landscape, for the first time makes warfare a theme for traditional-style painting, it is, as a work of art, singularly feeble. In surrendering to Japanese eclecticism, he denied himself the calligraphic expressiveness of the Chinese brush—which was no doubt why

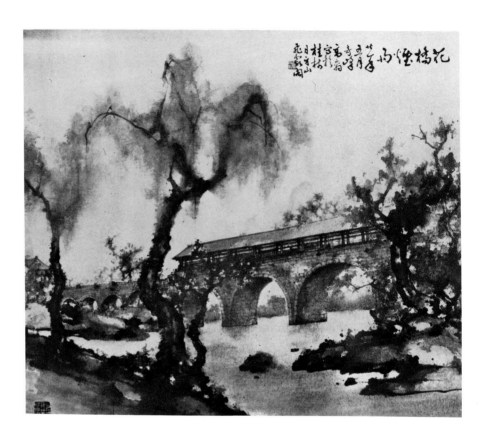

118.
Kao Ch'i-feng (1889–1933). *The Bridge in Drizzling Rain.* Chinese ink and colour on paper. 1932. Artist's collection. The Kao brothers in Canton were pioneers in combining Oriental techniques with Western devices such as perspective, shading and reflections in the water, which they had learned in Japan. But the result is too deliberate a synthesis to convey much feeling.

conservative critics contemptuously labelled the work of Kao Chien-fu and his Lingnan (Cantonese) School 'cheap imported Japanese goods'. Whatever its achievements and failures, the Lingnan School illustrates in both its paintings and its polemics and ideals the dilemma of artists of this formative period who strove consciously to be both modern and Chinese.

The second generation of Chinese painters who returned from Europe were more at home in Western art than their predecessors; they had greater skill in using it and were able to adapt it more freely to their own expressive needs. But the response to European art at this time was still somewhat confused. While Japan by now had had fifty years to come to terms with it, the whole Western tradition, including a bewildering succession of modern movements, was dumped into China's lap at once. Can it be any surprise that many painters had a hazy notion of the movements since Cézanne, calling them all 'Futurism'? On the whole they played safe. A cautious Impressionism, Romanticism and a vague sort of Symbolism flourished; Dada and Cubism were avoided, while Surrealism, introduced in 1935 into Shanghai and Canton from Japan, was savaged by the critics and died a quick death. Picasso's violent distortions were uncongenial. Chinese modernists, like their Japanese counterparts, on the whole responded more easily to the linear rhythms and cheerful colour of Matisse and to Vlaminck's expressive brushwork.

In the early 1930s it seemed that a new Chinese painting, native in spirit, contemporary in theme, borrowing techniques freely from East and West, was about to take root—promoted by Lin Feng-mien and his pupils in the Hangchow Academy of Art (Colour Plate 11), while a new cosmopolitanism was beginning to colour the art journals. In 1931 the sculptor, poet and critic Li Chin-fa had founded *Mei-yü tsa-chih* (Mi-yo Magazine), which reflected the Western leanings of his circle. It was scarcely an organ of the avant-garde. Croce and Lamartine appear in its pages, side by side with reproductions of Bouguereau and Bourdelle. More ephemeral, though more progressive, were such journals as *I-shu hsün-k'an* and *I-shu* (Art), in which we find discussions of Surrealism and a study of Herbert Read's *The Meaning of Art* by the scholar and critic T'eng Ku.

Meantime the debate about Western versus Chinese art went on, as it still does today. In 1924 Tai Yo, who had translated Stephen Bushell's *Chinese Art*, wrote that artists should turn to Western art because the native tradition had three major defects: it only used generalised type-forms, its imagery bore no relation to today's world and its techniques were 'irrational and unscientific'. Two years later, P'an T'ien-shou, who later became a distinguished traditional painter, gave four reasons for the interest in Western art: European taste had moved towards painting in colour and line, 'tending', as he put it, 'towards the spiritual taste of the Orient'; the influence of the political reform movements had

taught that anything not new or foreign was not worth studying; Chinese painting had passed its high point and it was not easy to open new paths without
influence from abroad; and the materials and modes of Western painting offered
new possibilities of experiment.

Much of the opposition came from chauvinists and conservatives, who
brought no fresh ideas to the question. But in 1934 the well-known critic Tsung
Pai-hua raised the level of debate in his defence of Chinese painting by stressing
its philosophical and metaphysical basis, citing the yang-yin dialectic, the *I-
ching*, Lao Tzu and Chuang Tzu, pointing out that the Chinese painter seeks
'inner rhythms', despising the literal representation of nature, and that China's
'lack of perspective', far from limiting the artist's expression, gave him un-
restrained and free communication with nature. Tsung Pai-hua was therefore
one of the first Chinese critics to define a concept of 'reality' for the artist that
would finally bring East and West together. It is perhaps not altogether surprising that at this time it was not the Western-style painters dedicated to visual realism but a handful of traditional painters and critics like Tsung Pai-hua, who
understood the message of Kandinsky, and particularly his stress on the 'inner
necessity' and spontaneity of expression—although it is hard to distinguish the
direct influence of Western Expressionism in the work of the traditional masters
before the 1960s. What really stimulated the revival of traditional painting was a
resurgent nationalism.

In 1928 P'ang Hsün-ch'in and a group of his friends had founded the Société
des Deux Mondes to keep open the lifeline to Paris. In the stormy wilderness of
Shanghai they felt very isolated, for the rich merchants (almost their only patrons) wanted only flattering portraits and the odd piece of ornamental sculpture. Unlike their Japanese counterparts, the Chinese middle class in the coastal
cities felt no obligation to welcome Western art. Although some with their cars
and radios were westernised in material ways, they never saw any good Western
painting—there was none in the Chinese museums—and they naturally thought
their own painting vastly superior.

Meanwhile China was in crisis. Caught between their Kuomintang rulers
on the right and the Communists on the left and oppressed by the growing
menace of Japan, the internationally minded artists and intellectuals felt that the
attitude represented by the Société des Deux Mondes and other cosmopolitan
groups in Shanghai was becoming more and more untenable. Already in 1926
the archaeologist Kuo Mo-jo had quit his ivory tower and launched an attack on
all the foreign 'isms' in modern Chinese literature. In 1932 some of the modern
painters, notably P'ang Hsün-ch'in and Ni I-te, formed the Storm Society, dedicated to bringing art closer to the people. But what art? And to which people?
'The people' were the urban proletariat and the illiterate peasantry, whose cause

was best served not by the followers of van Gogh and Matisse but by the wood-engravers, led by the writer Lu Hsün, who were creating out of an ancient Chinese medium a truly popular art that rapidly developed into a powerful weapon of left-wing propaganda. During the first years after the forming of the woodcut movement in 1929, the engravers had been inspired by Russian Socialist Realism, Georg Grosz, Franz Mazereel and Käthe Kollwitz (Figure 119), whose

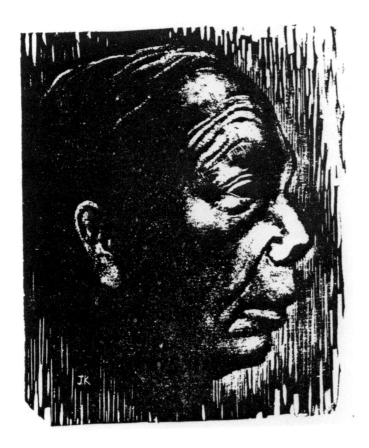

119.
Jung K'o (b. 1923). *Käthe Kollwitz.*
Woodcut. c. 1940. This adaptation from
Kollwitz's self-portrait (a lithograph) is
symbolic of one of the main sources of
inspiration of the left-wing woodcut
movement founded by the writer Lu
Hsün.

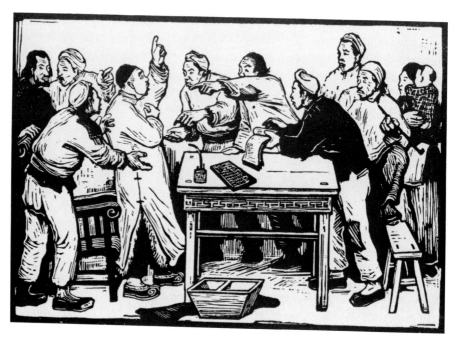

120.

Ku Yüan (b. c. 1910). *Demanding a Rent Reduction*. Woodcut. c. 1950. A typical product of the woodcut movement, which drew on a variety of Western ex- amples—European, Russian and Ameri- can—to create a powerful weapon in revolutionary propaganda.

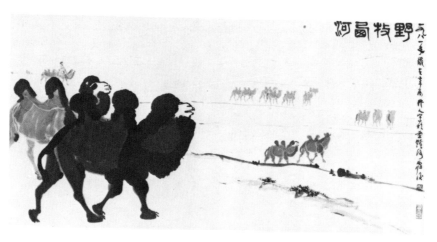

121.

Wu Tso-jen (b. 1908). *Camels*. Ink on paper. 1977. Chinese Culture Center, San Francisco. Wu Tso-jen, who paints with equal facility in oils and Chinese ink, here exemplifies China's discovery— which began in World War II—of its Far West.

graphic work Lu Hsün published in 1936, but soon their woodcuts began to take on a national character (Figure 120). One of their slogans was 'Out of the salons and into the streets!'. By the mid-1930s the modern art movement had become polarised.

The dilemma of liberal artists and writers in the New Art Movement was abruptly resolved by the Japanese attack on Peking in July 1937. Eight years of war followed, during which all the centres of modern art were occupied by the enemy, ties with Europe were severed and painters, deprived of canvas and oil paints, became refugees and moved far into the interior, where they rearranged their lives in a new and strange pattern. For the Japanese people the war was the culmination of a decade of increasingly oppressive militarism, and as they moved inexorably towards defeat, creative art in any form became almost impossible. For the Chinese, in spite of the suffering and hardships, government censorship and isolation from foreign contacts, the early war years were a period of unity, expansion, even—for some—exhilaration, as painters discovered a new world in the remote western provinces, Central Asia and Tibet (Figure 121). They responded with sincerity to their wartime experience and in so doing created new styles in which Western realism was at last successfully absorbed.

The styles practised in China after the People's Republic took power in 1949 were very largely those created by such artists as Chang An-chih, the cartoonist and illustrator Hsiao Ting (Figure 122) and Hsü Pei-hung's pupil Wu Tso-jen in West China between 1937 and 1945.

Meantime, the painters dreamed of returning to the coastal cities and of a new life after the war when contacts with the outside world would be renewed. For a brief time in 1945 and 1946 it seemed as if the modern movement might get under way again, and even that China might, like Japan, feel the impact of the New York School and give birth to an Abstract Impressionist movement. But the Kuomintang regime was fast disintegrating, inflation was out of control, Shanghai was a sink of corruption and painters were filled with a despair so deep as to make the renewal of artistic ties with Europe and America an impossible dream for most of them. One of the fortunate exceptions was Chao Wu-chi, a gifted young pupil of Lin Feng-mien and P'ang Hsün-chin in Hangchow, who left China in 1947 for Paris, where he is known as Zao Wou-ki. I shall have more to say about him presently. When in the summer of 1949 the Communist armies arrived in Shanghai, they were welcomed by the majority of intellectuals and artists with open arms.

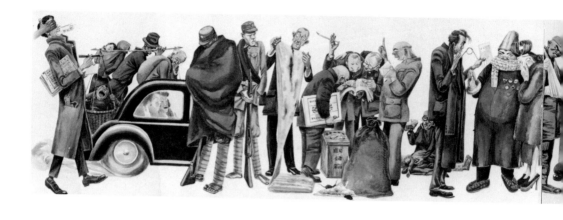

Art in China since 1949

We might expect that a Marxist China would have rejected out of hand poetic, conventionalised traditional art and embraced an uncompromising socialist realism. There was indeed a great deal of socialist-realist art that was entirely Western in style: innumerable portraits of Chairman Mao, for instance, and huge paintings and posters celebrating China's achievements on the land, in industry and in self-defence. But these are not the whole story. Certain crucial elements of traditional art have proved indestructible, though their traditional nature may seem to be obscured by their radical content.

For a short time after 1949 the old Beaux-Arts training continued in the art schools. By 1953, however, the art schools had been 'reformed', their 'bourgeois' directors replaced by hard-line wood-engravers trained in the revolutionary Yenan Academy of Art. The critic Hu Ch'iao-mu described the new regimen in the National Academy in Hangchow—how Lin Feng-mien and other 'followers of Matisse' were sent with their students to farms and factories to paint

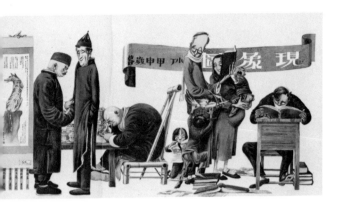

122.
Ting Ch'ung (Hsiao Ting; b. 1916). *Life
Today*. Handscroll. Chinese ink and
colour. 1944. Gift of William P. Fenn,
Spencer Museum of Art, Lawrence, Kansas. When Hsiao Ting painted this scroll
satirizing the corruption of the Kuomintang régime and its dependence on
American support, he was strongly influenced by the Mexican revolutionary artists, notably Diego Rivera.

what they saw instead of basing their work only on Greek sculpture and the
nude. 'The first-year and second-year students', Hu Chiao-mu reported, 'have
to draw portraits of the "living men" besides studies of Greek sculptures. Likewise the third-year and fourth-year students have to draw "models in clothes" in
addition to studies of nudes'. This does not sound very revolutionary; indeed, in
matters of style and technique the Chinese academies remained a good deal
more conservative than many Western art schools. Nor was the difficulty in per-
suading students to draw what was before their eyes in itself anything new. In
the early 1930s students in Peking, set to draw a street scene, had asked their
teacher for photographs of figures that they could copy into their pictures. They
were helpless without a ready-made formula. But now it was not a question of
how they drew but of what they drew, and, as we shall see, the problem of dependence on a ready-made schema was not solved by substituting heroic peasants for Greek casts.

China's leaders recognized that aesthetic problems cannot simply be ignored and that it would be impossible to impose a crude socialist realism along the lines of the Russian model. For one thing, such a course would not be Chinese; for another, the Chinese are far too intelligent to wish to avoid theoretical and philosophical issues, and their pride in their nation's heritage is strong and deep. Mao Tse-tung made it clear that traditional forms need not be abandoned; what had to be changed was the attitude of social and intellectual exclusiveness that was characteristic, for example, of the ink painting of the Ming and Ch'ing literati and survived in their twentieth-century successors. 'We do not refuse', he said, in one of the famous *Yenan Talks on Literature and Art* in 1942, 'to use the literary and artistic forms of the past, but in our hands these old forms, re-modelled and infused with new content, also become something revolutionary in the service of the people'. His attitude to Western art was equally unambiguous. 'Making foreign things serve China' meant that, in theory, any Western art form might be adopted, or adapted, to meet China's needs, while the use of the word *serve* showed that the foreign element, however important, would always be considered as the offering of an inferior, just as the gifts brought by foreign ambassadors were always regarded as 'tribute'.

After 1950 there was a reaction against the landscape painting of the literati in favour of the far older tradition of figure painting, which has its roots in the didactic wall paintings in the palaces of the Han emperors. Here too, what was wanted was not objective 'realism', but something of a much loftier kind: heroic figures depicted, as Mao Tse-tung put it, 'on a higher plane, more intense, more concentrated, more typical, nearer the ideal, and therefore more universal than actual everyday life'. Sir Joshua Reynolds, writing on the sublime in art, could not have expressed himself more succinctly. 'Revolutionary romanticism' was the name given to this kind of art in China. But not all of it carried so obvious a message. Ch'eng Shih-fa, formerly an individualistic painter of traditional scenes of bamboos and rocks, after 1950 painted a series of lyrical pictures, chiefly of the peoples of China's Tibetan borderlands, which use the Chinese medium and brush line in an entirely new way, expressing the idea of peaceful abundance with great charm and originality.

While the new society must be idealised, the old could be depicted with gruesome realism, and here Western techniques were invaluable. A famous example of this trend is the *Rent Collection Courtyard* (Figure 123), a life-size sculptural group running round the courtyard of the mansion of a former rapacious landlord at Ta-i in Szechwan, created in 1965 as a reminder of the days when, to pay their rent, the tenant farmers had sold their daughters and mortgaged their crops up to sixty years in advance. This dramatic work is a good illustration of Mao's dicta I quoted above, for in style it is thoroughly Western, yet it also draws on an ancient Chinese tradition of realistic sculpture that could be seen,

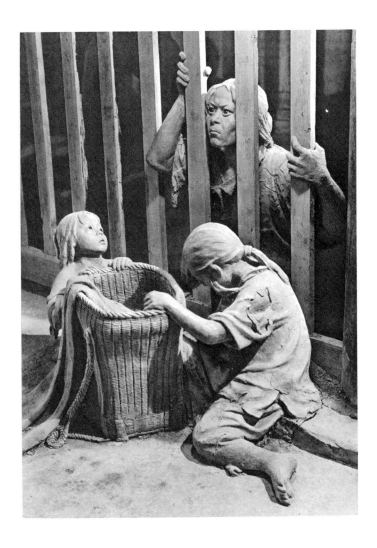

123.
Group of anonymous Szechwan artists.
The Mother Imprisoned. Section of a life-
size tableau, *The Rent-Collection Courtyard,* modelled in clay at Ta-i, Szechwan.
1965. If the vividness of this group owes
something to Western realism, it also
owes something to the ancient Chinese
tradition of clay modelling, found in
tomb figurines and in the dramatic portrayals of the punishments of Hell in
Buddhist temples.

for instance, in the vivid portrayals in coloured plaster of the horrors of the Eighteen Hells in Buddhist temples.

Eight years before the *Rent Collection Courtyard* was completed, Chinese artists had caught a brief glimpse of freedom, instantly blotted out. In 1957 Mao Tse-tung, confident of the support of the artists and intellectuals, launched the Hundred Flowers Movement in the belief that he could control and exploit the flood of individualism and protest that followed—or did he intend, as many now believe, to provoke it, simply in order to identify and suppress it? The Hundred Flowers Movement came to an abrupt end; many painters who had demanded more freedom were branded as 'rightists' and were to remain in political disgrace for the next nineteen years.

In 1964 Mao Tse-tung declared, 'If we stick to our old ways and do not study foreign literature; . . . if we do not know how to listen to foreign music, that is not good'. But within a year he was insisting that only Western technology was acceptable; Western arts and literature must be utterly rejected. When the Cultural Revolution exploded in the summer of 1966, one feature of the campaign was an attack on everything Western on the part of thousands of young people who felt they were 'out in the cold' with no hope of a future in the elite of the Party, the universities or the professions. In the ensuing terrible years many artists who had studied abroad or had a taste for foreign things were sent down to the country for 'reeducation' through hard labour; some were killed, some committed suicide.

The Cultural Revolution severed all China's remaining artistic contacts with the West. The art academies and museums were closed, the art magazine *Mei-shu* shut down. The Cultural Revolution ended officially in 1969, but now the warring factions united to persecute artists and writers even more thoroughly under the fanatical Chiang Ch'ing (Mme Mao). As far back as 1961 Chou En-lai had tried to stem the excesses of the anti-rightist campaigns, and, while never compromising on his basic Marxist beliefs, he continued almost up to his death in January 1976 to protect artists from the tyranny of the Gang of Four. But he could do little to help them. Their sufferings, which did not end till well after the death of Mao in September 1976, left a scar on Chinese cultural life that it will take a generation to heal.

In 1977 the doors to the outside world began cautiously to open. *Mei-shu* had resumed publication in 1976, but not until March 1978 was any foreign art reproduced or discussed, the safe choices being the realists Courbet and Millet. The political rapprochement with the United States is reflected in an article on Henry Eakins, another realist. Two issues of 1979 deal with Rodin. Since then, the range of acceptable Western artists has spread to Bonnard, Klimt, Matisse, Thomas Hart Benton and Andrew Wyeth. Wyeth's strong influence—particularly on a school of realistic oil painters in Szechwan of whom Ho To-ling

(He Duoling) and Ai Hsüan (Ai Xuan; Colour Plate 12) are two of the most talented—is due not to any ideological appeal but, on the contrary, to the fact that Wyeth's realism appears to be totally free of ideology, being visual and psychological. Early in 1988 a Peking art journal carried an article on Balthus, while some young modernists were deserting Wyeth for Francis Bacon.

At the same time exhibitions of foreign art have been a powerful stimulus. A collection sent from the Boston Museum of Fine Arts in 1981 included, over strong official objections, works by Olitski and Jackson Pollock, while in 1983 the National Art Gallery in Peking staged the first exhibition in China of original works by Picasso. Lest the Chinese public and readers of *Mei-shu* should think that all Western art is acceptable, however, there came a vigorous attack on Marinetti the and Futurists, quoting Lu Hsün's strictures on anarchism and on 'upholding the strange', while the works of Christo were roundly condemned.

For several years after 1976 the cultural authorities were able to hold the line through their control of publications and exhibitions. But by the end of the decade artists were going abroad once more: no longer to the Soviet Union and the Eastern bloc countries, but to America and Europe. Lin Feng-mien returned to Paris in 1984 after an absence of forty-five years; Huang Yung-yü (Colour Plate 13) toured America; Wu Tso-jen visited San Francisco. By the mid-1980s it was reckoned that about two hundred Chinese artists of the younger generation were studying in the West—most of them in the United States—and an even greater number of talented students were competing fiercely for the chance to study abroad.

Chinese painters working outside the People's Republic have been another powerful stimulus to the acceptance of contemporary art in China. For nearly thirty years after 1949 their work was ignored at home. Today, partly on account of their international reputation, these painters are beginning to be accepted and to become an important influence on the growth of a modern movement in China. Zao Wou-ki, an Abstract Expressionist and former pupil of Lin Feng-mien who has lived in Paris since 1948, was invited to exhibit in Peking and to paint decorative panels for the hotel in the Western Hills designed by the Chinese architect I. M. Pei, who lives and works in the United States. The semi-abstract landscapes of Liu Kuo-sung (Colour Plate 14), one of the founders of the modern Fifth Moon Group in Taiwan, now living in Hong Kong, have received critical approval at an exhibition in Peking. When the Taiwanese Photo-realist Yen Ch'ing-cheng, who has worked in New York since 1970, held an exhibition in Peking, the critics asked why this technique should not be used by local artists to depict their capital city. By the time this book appears, it will be surprising if the work of the Taiwanese sculptor Chu Ming has not been recognised in the People's Republic. Chu Ming started life as a poor carver of wooden images for Buddhist temples. With intense dedication, and the encouragement of the sculptor Yang Ying-feng, he has developed in early middle age into a carver of extremely powerful figures, the most notable being his series of men performing the traditional t'ai-chi movements (Figure 124); these show a remarkable understanding of the medium, while they are both Chinese in theme and contemporary in spirit.

In some respects the atmosphere for art in the post-Mao era has been reminiscent of that of sixty years earlier, when eager young men and women flocked to Paris, some to get caught up in movements they barely understood. The same issues are being debated once more: the nature of beauty, the duty of the artist to society, how foreign styles can meet China's needs, and questions of individualism and abstraction.

While politics reigned supreme, aesthetics inevitably were a blend of Marx and Mao, unbelievably naive and crude. But some more sophisticated Marxist writers such as Chu Kuang-ch'ien found sanction for their repudiation of abstraction and art-for-art's-sake in the age-old Chinese belief that art is not an isolated activity but part of a larger whole, that artists whatever their gifts share the values of society and like everyone else are responsible for upholding them. Huang Yung-yü (Colour Plate 13), when I asked him what he thought of the abstract painting he saw at the Whitney Museum in New York answered, 'It has no meaning'; in other words, it is merely form. But surely, one might argue, the highest Chinese art, calligraphy, is 'merely form'? Not so, says Chu Kuang-ch'ien, echoing a view that goes far back into the early history of Chinese aesthetics; the beauty of the writing is inextricably bound up with the content of the passage written—no unedifying text could inspire beautiful calligraphy—and with the moral worth of the calligrapher, which is revealed in his or her handwriting. Who would assert, asked Chu in an article, that the beauty of a young girl's blush is not connected with her modesty? Even the 'dissidents' of the Star Group, who held their audacious protest exhibitions in Peking in 1979 and 1980, firmly believed that they did not stand outside society but were its voice, its conscience.

By the mid-1980s, after the brief but disturbing 'anti-pollution campaign' of late 1983, the ideological clouds had lifted—whether permanently or temporarily, no one dared predict—and Chinese artists were approaching foreign art with the same mixture of curiosity and enthusiasm that they had shown in the 1920s and 1930s, but now they were accepting it from a position of far greater strength and confidence. Less often today are Chinese oil painters attacked for betraying their national heritage or faced with a crisis in personal identity. Moreover, as China follows Japan in its technological development, the outward, visible face of Chinese life becomes more like that of the West. The differences lie beneath the surface.

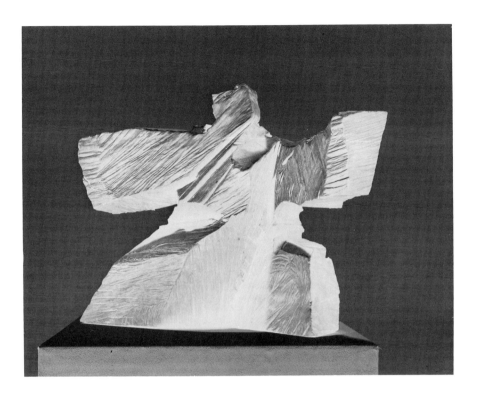

124.

Chu Ming (b. 1938). *Single Whip*. T'ai-chi figure. Bronze casting from wood carving. 1985. Max Hutchinson Gallery, New York. Though liberated from tradition by the impact of contemporary Western art, Chu Ming's figures have their roots in popular Chinese culture. His direct attack on the medium he learned in Taiwan as an apprentice carver of temple images.

One problem, however, has not been solved, and perhaps never will be. Between the Chinese approach to picture making and that of the West since the Renaissance there is a fundamental and, it seems, irreconcilable difference, for Chinese artists left to themselves would always tend to create, or adopt, a pictorial convention distilled from experience, theirs and their forebears' going back for centuries, rather than to depict accurately the particular model before them. Many painters trained in the traditional way were unable to paint subjects, or objects, for which there were no conventions in their repertoire. The painter Ch'ien Sung-yen, for example, described how he went to the Taihang Mountains not, as one would expect, to draw them as he saw them, with fresh eyes, but to 'check his texture-strokes' as he put it, to see that they matched the

rocks of Taihang. Once having done this, having revised and updated his pictorial vocabulary and—much more difficult—having created new conventions
for things never before painted, the artist need never, in theory, leave his studio
again. To this method of painting, Western art presents a constant challenge,
opening the way to the exploration of the real world and the direct expression of
experience. It is no wonder that many young painters, such as Ai Hsüan (Colour
Plate 12), have abandoned the traditional style altogether, considering it 'too abstract'. They do not believe they are surrendering their identity as Chinese, as
some Chinese and foreign critics have claimed; on the contrary, they feel that
painting in the Western manner is the only way in which they can fully express
themselves *as* Chinese.

Yet the place of Western styles and techniques will always be a matter of
debate in China, for it is reasonable to ask whether movements that emerged in a
particular historical context in Western art have any place outside Western culture. But it must also be asked how conservative Party officials in China, while
promoting the 'four modernisations', can reject modernism in art and literature
out of a fear of 'spiritual pollution'. Many Chinese cultural bureaucrats feel very
uncomfortable about this, and control of the arts is beginning to slip out of their
hands. In the meantime, although conditions for artists and writers are generally
improving, they can hardly feel completely at ease in the climate of alternating
restraint and release that authority still creates around them.

Chinese Painters on the International Scene since the Second World War

Artists such as Zao Wou-ki in Paris and Cheong Soo-pieng in Singapore, whatever manner they painted in, have never ceased to think of themselves as Chinese.
This awareness of their origin may reveal itself, if at all, only in a particular kind
of sensibility in the use of the line, a tendency to give colour a subordinate role
or a subtly poetic feeling for space and depth, recognisable only to someone familiar with Oriental art. But, however imperceptible, the consciousness is there
in these artists, and in a variety of ways, direct and indirect, they cannot help but
express themselves as Chinese, and in so doing make a Chinese contribution to
the East-West dialogue.

As long as the differences between Chinese and Western art were clear-cut,
the Western public tended to be not merely critical but often positively hostile
towards Chinese artists who painted in the Western idiom and judged their
works harshly. Westerners dismissed Chinese painters who continued to work
in the traditional style as conservative and uninteresting, yet if they detected the
influence of Picasso or Klee they accused the painters of 'copying', although

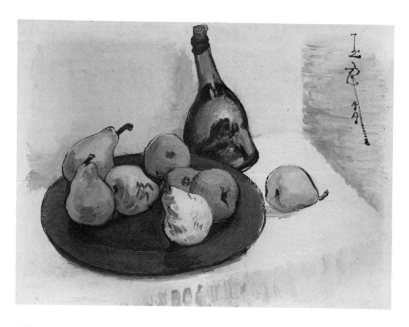

125.
P'an Yü-liang (1905–83). *Still-life*. Oils. 1944. Private collection, Paris. Only the composition, in which the artist's signature plays an essential part, proclaims this as the work of a Chinese painter.

they would applaud Oriental influences on Western painters. For Zao Wou-ki to be stimulated by Jackson Pollock showed how derivative he was; for Mark Tobey to be influenced by Chinese calligraphy showed how receptive he was.

Faced with this sort of prejudice, some Chinese painters abroad became 'professional Chinese', for there is always a living to be made by teaching ink painting or designing calendars and greeting cards. Others—P'an Yü-liang and Liao Hsin-hsüeh, by contrast—became solid Post-Impressionists in Paris, though both preserved something of their heritage: even at her most Cézann-esque, P'an Yü-liang revealed a Chinese expressiveness in her brush line, and her signature is placed unerringly in the Chinese fashion (Figure 125).

Abstract Expressionism and Action Painting put the Oriental painter in a totally new relationship with Western art. Now suddenly Calligraphic Abstrac-tion became respectable, and no serious critic would accuse Dōmoto Inshō or Zao Wou-ki of merely 'copying' Pollock or Kline, although these painters would in most cases admit that it was the impact of the New York School after the war that drove them to discover, or rather to rediscover, the Abstract Ex-pressionist element in their own tradition. Art since 1945 has in any case become international, and today the stimulus is as likely to go from East to West as in the other direction. The complaint that the work of some Oriental painters is no longer really Oriental has ceased to have any meaning.

The successive stages in the evolution of Zao Wou-ki's painting offer a good illustration of the flowering of the new Abstract movement in Far Eastern art. His early work in Hangchow, chiefly portraits in oils and very sensitive and original small landscapes in the Chinese manner (Figure 126), shows an imaginative young painter making a series of tentative explorations in a new direction while remaining essentially Chinese. On his arrival in Paris in 1948 he felt the full impact of modern Western art for the first time. Although his first loves had been Cézanne and Matisse, for a while his work was strongly influenced by Paul Klee, whose 'landscapes of the mind' have appealed to many modern Oriental artists.

Meantime, Zao Wou-ki was moving towards Abstraction. He began to work in oils on a much larger scale, sometimes incorporating archaic ideographs, or suggestions of ideographs, taken from Shang bronzes and oracle-bone inscriptions. In so doing, he was paying homage to the ancient Chinese belief that the arts of painting and writing came into existence together and are of divine origin. This idea has a strong appeal to all educated Chinese painters, and others have followed Zao Wou-ki, finding that incorporating the ideograph gives their painting a richness of symbolic content and association that Western abstract painting so conspicuously lacks. Such is the beauty and power of the characters themselves that many a lesser painter than Zao Wou-ki has been tempted into using them in a purely decorative way. Others, particularly in Japan, have taken the ideograph as a springboard for 'Abstract Calligraphy', in which the form may suggest an idea or call up an association without itself being legible as a character.

Zao Wou-ki's contribution to nonobjective art went still further, however. His large abstract oil paintings combine calligraphic liveliness with an atmospheric depth that owes nothing to Pollock or Kline, but is the expression of his instinctive Chinese feeling for three-dimensional space (Colour Plate 15). In the same way, some of the paintings of Chu Teh-Chun (Chü Te-ch'ün), who went to Paris from China and Taiwan in 1955, are not pure abstractions, but suggest rather some cosmic event, evocative of the Chaos at the beginning of the world.

The Chinese artist is never concerned with the surface of things. He is always aware of what lies behind it, and the misty distances that fill so many traditional paintings hint at a reality that exists beyond what the eye can see. Zao Wou-ki is delighted if we can 'read' his abstractions as landscapes, for that is what they are. It only needs a touch here and there—a few trees, a cottage, a fisherman—and we have come full circle to the landscapes of the late T'ang 'action painters' and the Zen ink-flingers of the thirteenth century.

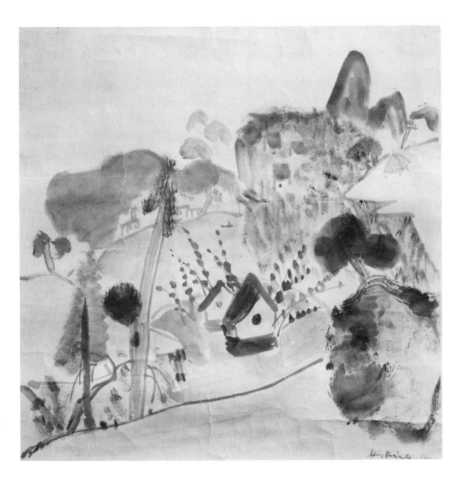

126.
Zao Wou-ki (Chao Wu-chi; b. 1920).
Landscape. Watercolour. Exhibited in
Paris, 1948. Artist's collection. Painted
just before his departure for Paris, this
rather tentative work shows the influence
of Paul Klee blended with a subtle sense
of space and atmosphere that is very
Chinese.

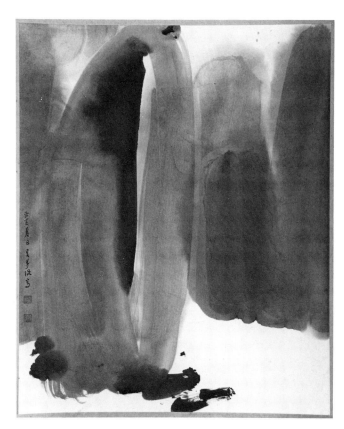

127.
Lui Show Kwan (Lü Shou-k'un; 1919–
76). *Cliffs and Rocks*. Ink on paper. 1962.
Collection of the late Major Barker. Lui,
founder of the modern movement in
Hong Kong in the 1950s, developed from
a very conventional Chinese artist into a
painter of semiabstract landscapes that
depend for their life on the sweep of the
brush and the transparent luminosity of
the ink.

This step was in fact taken by a number of Chinese painters in the 1960s, for
example by Lui Show Kwan (Lü Shou-k'un) in Hong Kong, whose swirls with
the brush—the fact that they are more luminous and transparent than those of
Soulages is only partly due to the medium employed—are transformed into
suggestions of landscapes by the addition of a few rocks, or trees, or a fishing
boat (Figure 127). The most surprising convert to this way of painting was
Chang Ta-ch'ien (Chang Dai Chien; 1899–1984). Although in appearance, dress
and manner the very embodiment of tradition, this bearded, long-robed master,
who once spent two years copying Buddhist frescoes at Tunhuang, responded
with tremendous verve to the march of events. In 1953, at a famous meeting in
Antibes, he exchanged paintings with Picasso, a personality with whom he had
much in common. In 1968 he painted a long handscroll of the Yangtse River in
which ink washes and strong mineral colours are allowed to mix, to confront or
repel each other in a daring and apparently accidental fashion, after which, by

the addition of telling accents and precisely drawn details, the composition is turned into a stupendous panorama that sends us on an imaginary journey down the river from its source in Tibet to where it loses itself in the China Sea (Colour Plate 16).

The modern movements, notably the Fifth Moon Group founded in Taipei in 1965, have sprung from the happy marriage of Abstract Expressionism and Action Painting on the one hand and the Chinese calligraphic tradition on the other. They have also been united in their aim of breaking free both from Western art and from dependence on the traditional formal vocabulary. Liu Kuo-sung and Chuang Che, for example, rejected the *tien* (dots) and *ts'un* (texture-strokes) altogether. Later, some followers of Lui Show Kwan in the In Tao (*Yüan Tao,* or 'Original Way') and Circle groups in Hong Kong, notably Wu-cius Wong (Figure 128) and Lawrence Tam, went a step further, reacting against calligraphic gesture painting, and began to create a new formal vocabulary. The possibilities of these new explorations seem inexhaustible, producing a wide range of work, from the free, sweeping forms of Lui Show Kwan and the earlier Kline-like gestures of Chuang Che to the elegant, carefully controlled semi-abstract landscapes and cloudscapes of Hung Hsien (Figure 129).

In the late 1960s Op Art, Pop Art and Kinetic Art appeared as the inevitable reaction against the expressive limitations of pure Abstraction. Their exponents were not content simply to copy the styles and methods of Vasarely or Lichtenstein, but were deeply concerned with the relevance these movements might have to the Chinese tradition, for only when this had been established could the style have any meaning for them. This conscientious heart-searching has prevented the uncritical surrender that took place in postwar Japan. In Hong Kong I have heard the dynamic confrontation of areas of pure colour in Hard-edge painting interpreted as an expression of the interaction of opposites enshrined in the yang-yin concept, and Kinetic Art as an expression of the state of eternal flux that both Buddhists and Taoists see in the natural world. For painters like Chuang Che in Taiwan, who came to feel that the lyrical abstractions of Liu Kuo-sung and others in the Fifth Moon Group were too elitist, too remote from the feelings of a society in ferment, there was, for a short time, Pop Art. Most Chinese artists shrank from it as vulgar and as a denial of the calligraphic basis of their tradition, but in a rigidly censored society such as that of Taiwan, Pop Art was about as close as a painter could approach to an art of social protest.

These artists and other independent painters, such as Cheong Soo-pieng in Singapore, have made an important and unquestionably Chinese contribution to the international modern movement. Poised between East and West, they are searching not only for a style but for their own identity, which they are finding in their painting. This is not to say that their work, in terms of the international

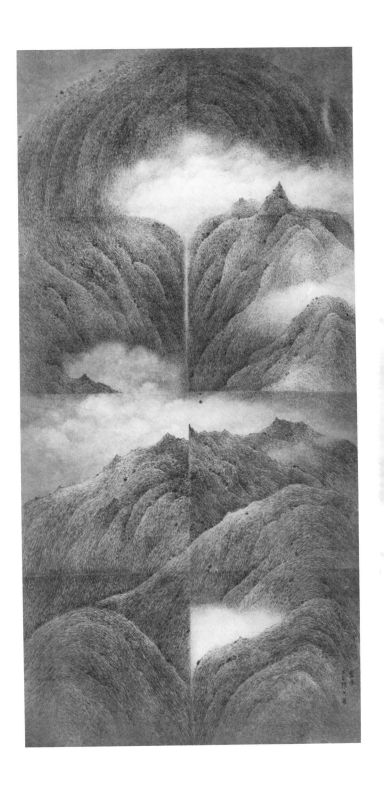

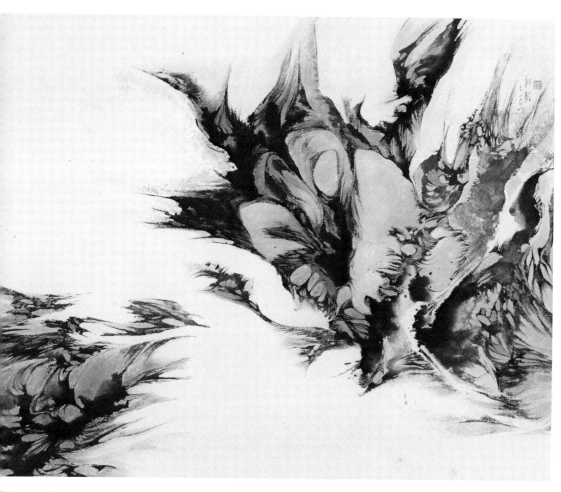

facing page).
Wu-hsiu (Wucius Wong; b. 1936).
Harmony. Hanging scroll. Ink and
on paper. 1978. Hong Kong Mu-
of Art, Hong Kong. Wang belongs
Hong Kong group that reacted
st Calligraphic Expressionism, seek-
achieve an intense poetic realism,
d in his case both by the seven-
-century master Kung Hsien and
experience of flying over the
tains of south China.

129.
Hung Hsien (b. 1933). *Cliff with Clouds.*
Ink and colour on paper. 1970. Art Institute of Chicago. While in Taiwan, Hung
Hsien was a pupil of the orthodox traditional master P'u Hsin-yü, cousin of the
last Manchu emperor. An elegant and
disciplined brushwork survives in the
style she developed after she went to live
in America in 1958, when she came
under the influence of Tobey, Miró,
Gorky and Tchelichew.

202

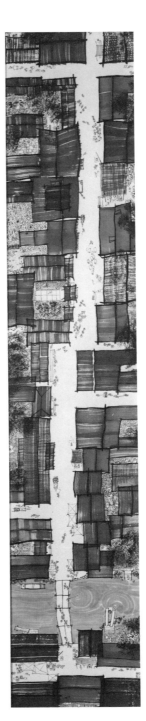

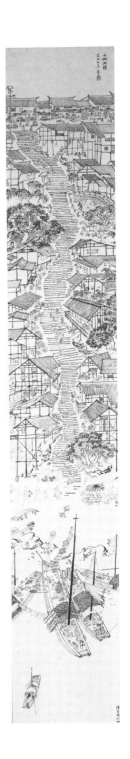

130 and 131.
Ch'en Ch'i-k'uan (b. 1921). *Street* (1952)
and *Chungking Steps* (c. 1954). Ink and
colour on paper. Private collections.
Both these paintings display not only
Ch'en Ch'i-k'uan's original viewpoint on
the world, but also his Western training
as an architect and a Chinese sense of
continuous movement in space.

modern movement, is always entirely original. There may be precedents for Liu Kuo-sung's *Which Is Earth* series of the late 1960s, for example, in Adolph Gottlieb's *Blast* (1957); for some of Lui Show Kwan's abstractions in Mark Tobey's series of calligraphic abstractions of 1956–57; for Hung Hsien's techniques in those of Pavel Tchelichew; for Ch'en T'ing-shih's prints (Colour Plate 17) in the compositions of Saitō Yoshishige; and for Ch'en Ch'i-k'uan's *Street* and *Chungking Steps* (Figures 130 and 131) in the set of aerial views of Kyōto painted by the *Nihonga* artist Maeda Seison with uncharacteristic freedom as long ago as 1916. In no case, of course, can we prove that one was derived from or suggested by the other. But with the extraordinary speed of the movement of art today and the infinity of choices open to the artist, such derivations are much less meaningful than they used to be. The effort to be original has in any case become the pursuit of an illusion, as Jackson Pollock showed when he hurled a book of Picasso reproductions across the room and shouted, 'God damn it, that guy thinks of everything!'.

Sometimes the homage of the modern Chinese painter to tradition reveals itself in a more direct yet still very subtle way. Tseng Yu-ho as a girl in Peking studied what we might call the 'academic literary style' under P'u Hsüeh-chai, a cousin of the last Manchu emperor. With this thoroughly traditional equipment, she was flung by her marriage to the art historian Gustav Ecke and her subsequent removal to America into the mainstream of modern Western art. The results were startling (Colour Plate 18). Between 1955 and 1965 she produced a series of paintings in which she managed to convey with astonishing freshness of vision the form and texture of the Hawaiian landscape in the language of the Chinese scholar-painters, notably that of the morose seventeenth-century eccentric Kung Hsien, whose stippling technique is well suited to depicting the strange geology of the Hawaiian Islands. The ominous atmosphere and dense textures of Max Ernst, who visited Honolulu in 1952 and gave a series of lectures on modern art at the University of Hawaii, was another, rather elusive, influence upon her. Later she painted a series of landscapes in which she paid homage to the Sung masters and to the great individualists Shih-t'ao, Pa-ta Shanjen and Hung-jen (Figure 132), suggesting their characteristic compositions and even their brush techniques, while working in a completely modern idiom—a striking instance of the power, and indeed of the obligation, of a Chinese scholar-painter to keep the tradition alive by a creative reinterpretation of it.

Although conservatives in the Chinese cultural establishment would like to see the import of modern Western art styles strictly controlled—and this can be done to some extent by their control of what is exhibited—they can no longer prevent Chinese artists from knowing what is happening elsewhere in the world and responding to it. The result has been since 1979 a vast enlarging of the range

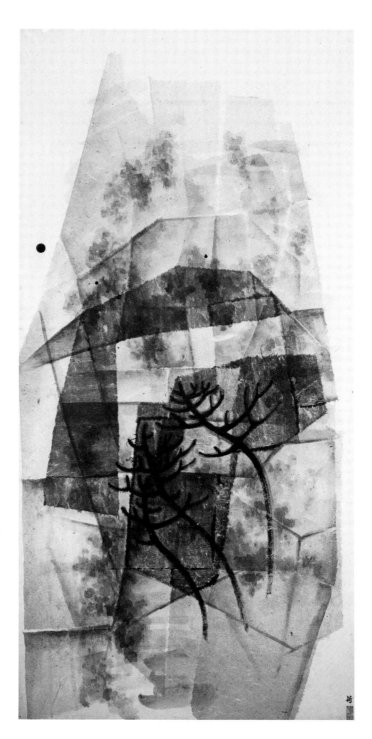

132.
Tseng Yu-ho (b. 1923). *Landscape II
in the Spirit of Hung-jen*. Ink and
colour on paper. 1958. Artist's collection. A very sophisticated reinterpretation of the landscape style of
the seventeenth-century master, influenced, as are so many modern
Far Eastern works, by Paul Klee.

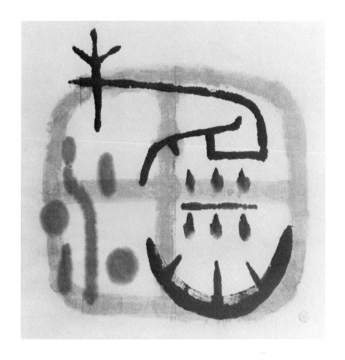

133.
Yang Yen-p'ing (Yang Yanping; b. 1934).
Paddy Field. Chinese ink and colour on
paper. About 1982. Artist's collection.
Photo by Michael Shavel. The artist not
only makes a beautiful abstract design
with the archaic graph *tao* (paddy) super-
imposed on *t'ien* (field), but by doing so
evokes the fundamental connection in
Chinese culture between writing and pictorial art.

of expression in modern Chinese art and enthusiastic experiment in all the
modes and techniques being practised in Japan and the West. We can see the
effects in the work of, for example, Wu Kuan-chung, who spent the years
1950–55 in Paris, was persecuted under Mao, and later became in his writings
the courageous champion of Abstraction, although his own landscapes stop well
short of the nonobjective (Colour Plate 19). Completely in tune with traditional
Chinese thinking about the purpose of art is his insistence that the thread con-
necting the forms in a painting with real objects, however thinly stretched, must
not be broken altogether. Liu Kang-chi (Liu Gangji), another champion of Abstraction during the thaw of 1980, also urged people not to be afraid of it, but,
he insisted, 'Abstract handling and deformation of the object must be beautiful,
and not weird or ugly', while Abstraction should be only one school in Chinese
art, because 'this school cannot completely satisfy the whole people's demand in
regard to art'—a perfectly reasonable view.

Among a host of young and middle-generation painters whose eyes and
minds are wide open to the West is Yang Yen-p'ing (Yang Yanping), a sensitive
and imaginative painter whose sources of inspiration lie deep in the ideograph
and in her native landscape, although her handling of them is certainly influenced by Western art (Figure 133). Wang K'o-p'ing (Wang Keping) is a powerful

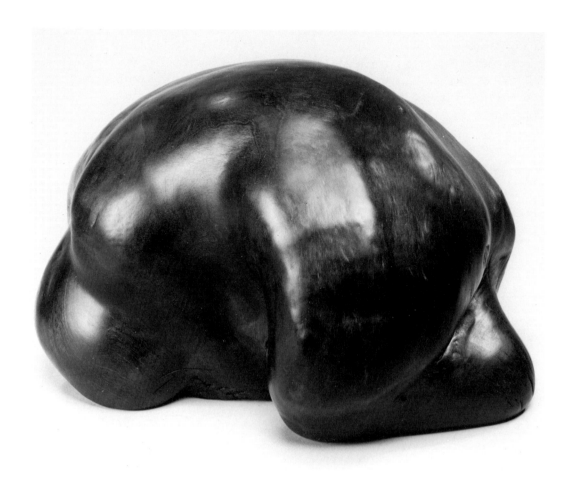

134.
Wang K'o-p'ing (Wang Keping; b. 1949).
Crouching Woman. Wood. About 1983.
Author's collection. A powerful piece by
a member of the dissident Star Group of
1981–83, whose untraditional choice of
style and subject matter was an indirect
gesture of protest against the conservatism of officially sponsored art.

sculptor in wood (Figure 134), formerly a dissident of the Hsing-hsing (Star) Group, who in 1984 went to live in Paris, where he is free from the heavy-handed patronage of the Chinese Artists' Association. Chinese art in the 1980s is in a state of fluid transition, rapid development, uncertainty and hope, as Chinese artists begin to find a place in the international world of modern art while remaining at heart Chinese.

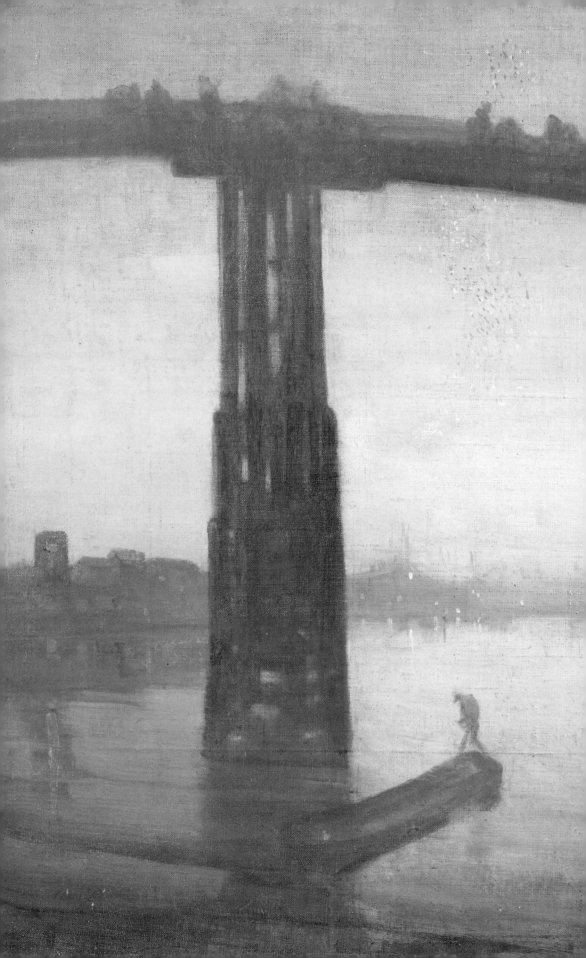

Europe and America: From 1850 to the Present Day

Japan and the Impressionists

It is often said that the tide of *japonisme*[1] that swept over and outward from Paris in the 1860s and 1870s started from very small beginnings in 1856, when the designer and etcher Félix Bracquemond discovered in the workshop of his printer, Delâtre, a little book of woodcuts after Hokusai's drawings. Bracquemond eventually acquired this volume of the famous *Manga* (Figure 135) and carried it everywhere with him, showing it enthusiastically to his artist friends, who included Manet, Degas, Fantin-Latour and Whistler. Bracquemond himself returned again and again to Hokusai for inspiration for his porcelain decorations.

It is an attractive notion that the Japanese influence on Western art was inaugurated in so exact a fashion. Certainly it was France that chiefly responded to the challenge of Western art, and the Impressionists who most learned its lessons. But the impact on the painters must also be seen as part of a fascination with Japan at mid-century that stretched far beyond the artists themselves. Indeed, at first, awareness of Japan was stronger in America and London than it was in Paris. The account of Commodore Perry's expedition, which had thrown open the doors of Japan, made a deep impression when it was published in

---

1 On Japanese influence on the Impressionists I have used three terms that sound similar but mean very different things. *Japonaiserie* has to do with the creation of a Japanese effect in a picture by adding fans, kimonos, vases, screens and other oriental paraphernalia; Monet's *La Japonaise* is a good example. *Japonisme* involves serious concern with Japanese pictorial techniques and may or may not include Japanese accessories; Manet's *Zola* is a fairly primitive example, van Gogh's *Bedroom at Arles* is a very advanced one. *Japonerie* is a word applied chiefly to rather frivolous objects made in the Japanese manner.

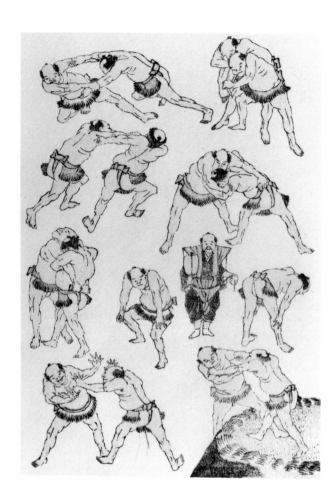

135.
Katsushika Hokusai (1760–1849). A
Page from the *Manga*. Woodblock print.
Hokusai got the idea of filling a page of
an album with studies of nature and the
human figure from European works such
as de Lairesse's *Groot Schilderboek*. In
turn, a copy of the *Manga* circulating
among the Impressionists was to play
a key role in spreading enthusiasm for
Japanese art in France.

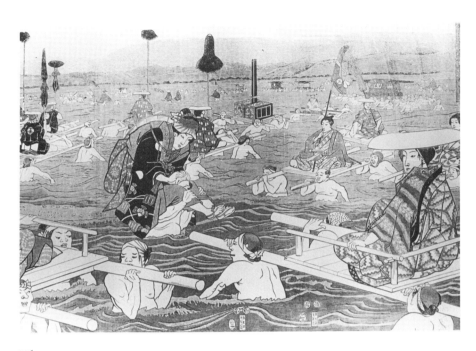

136.

Persons of Distinction Crossing the Oho-e-gawa. Copy of a print by Kunisada. *Illustrated London News,* 13 December 1856. The text notes that the Japanese 'can picture the ludicrous, and good-naturedly laugh at clever caricature' and that they have a knowledge of perspective. These full-page illustrations in the *Illustrated London News,* which reached a wide public, must have helped to awaken English taste for things Japanese at a very early stage.

Washington and London in 1856. The *Illustrated London News* for December 13 of that year carried an article on Japanese painting and, three weeks later, a translation of a Japanese tale, *The Folding Screen,* illustrated with large copies of Japanese prints (Figure 136). The first official display of Japanese prints in the West, from the collection of Sir Rutherford Alcock, was held in 1862 not in Paris but in the Japanese Court of the International Exhibition in London. Around 1860, therefore, the climate was being created for a sympathetic response to the art of Japan. Yet it is true that only in Paris did painters really begin to study it. In America the first enthusiasm, felt by the painter John La Farge, who bought prints on his visits to Paris in 1856, and reflected in the Japanese-style pictures he painted between 1859 and 1864, quietly subsided, while in Britain the influence on painters, apart from Whistler, was negligible.

The main events in this rising tide of *japonisme* are well known. In 1862 Mme Desoye (or de Soye) and her husband, recently returned from the Orient, opened their shop on the Rue de Rivoli, where they dealt in Far Eastern arts and crafts of all kinds. Another shop, long established, was La Porte Chinoise at 36 Rue Vivienne, which had opened as early as 1826 as the Salon des Thès. These establishments became meccas for artists, collectors and the fashionable world in general. Manet, Fantin-Latour, Tissot, Whistler, Baudelaire, the Goncourt brothers and many of their friends might be seen there rummaging for fans, textiles, colour prints, blue-and-white porcelain. Soon every studio and up-to-date salon had its pile of kimonos, its fans and woodcuts pinned to the wall. All the Impressionists owned Japanese fans or prints, or both, some many hundreds, and they often appear as accessories in their portraits and interiors. Whistler, studying in Paris between 1855 and 1859, was one of the first painters to fall under the spell of Oriental art. Not only did he collect prints, but he had a passion for Chinese and Japanese blue-and-white porcelain, which he later carried with him to London.

The French hunger for things Japanese was whetted by the Japanese exhibits at the Exposition Universelle in 1867, among which were a hundred prints that were later offered for sale. It was more literally assuaged by the founding in the same year of the Société Japonaise du Jing-lar, whose members, chiefly painters, collectors and critics, held monthly dinners with sake and chopsticks, and each had his own menu card designed by Bracquemond in a pseudo-Japanese manner.

Although other dealers soon began to exploit the craze for *japonerie*—notably Samuel Bing, with whom van Gogh and his brother had dealings some years later—Mme Desoye's establishment, La Jonque Chinoise, remained for many years the centre of the cult. In 1875 the Goncourts in their *Journal* described 'la grasse Mme Desoye', enthroned in her 'bijouterie de l'idole japonaise. Une figure presque historique de ce temps, car ce magasin a été l'endroit, l'école, pour ainsi dire, òu c'est élaboré ce grand mouvement japonais, qui s'étend aujourd'hui de la peinture à la mode'. Mme Desoye's shop has long since disappeared, but the reverberations of what a critic called 'cette grande explosion japonaise' could still be heard in the first decades of the twentieth century.

The Goncourts claimed in their *Journal* (1868) that they had 'discovered' Japan as early as 1860, but the fashion can be traced to no single source. Zacharie Astruc's articles on 'the Empire of the Rising Sun' in the same year probably made as wide an impression as the Goncourts' advocacy, while exhibitions helped too. There were Japanese paintings again in the Exposition Universelle of 1872, and in Vienna in 1873. Fenollosa's Ryūchi Society, founded in Tōkyō in 1879, sent a representative and paintings for exhibitions in Paris in 1883 and 1884; Samuel Bing was appointed local representative of the society and augmented its shows with paintings from his own collection.

In his defence of Manet, published as early as 1867, Emile Zola had cited the 'élégance étrange' and the 'taches magnifiques' of Japanese woodcuts. Meier-

Graefe thought that this was the first occasion on which the influence of Japan was mentioned, but this seems doubtful. The main flood of literature on Japan, however, came in the 1880s and 1890s with, for example, Théodore Duret's *L'Art Japonais* (1882) and Samuel Bing's influential periodical *Le Japon Artistique,* launched in 1890. Edmond de Goncourt's sympathetic study of Utamaro appeared in 1891 and his much less successful book on Hokusai, six years later. Many of van Gogh's ideas about Japan, true and false, were derived from Pierre Loti's *Madame Chrysanthème,* which he read in 1888. The writings of men who had lived in Japan, such as Lafcadio Hearn, Whistler's pupil Mortimer Menpes, Ernest Fenollosa and the collector Emile Guimet, all helped to reveal a new world—one that was exotic and remote, yet growing in power and importance, gratifyingly pro-Western, and an inspiration in all aesthetic matters.

By contrast, China at this time was seen as weak and corrupt, helpless under the heel of the Western powers, antiforeign and, according to the missionaries, inhumane. It is little wonder that, while Europeans were drawn to Japanese culture and art and felt that they understood them, they were repelled, through sheer ignorance, by those of China. As le Blanc de Vernet picturesquely put it in 1880, 'Chez les japonais, une allure absolument libre, vive, riante et fantaste comme leur charactère', while 'chez les chinois, l'art est froidement méthodique et correctement formaliste', a preposterous verdict that was not revised until well into the twentieth century.

Yet the attitude towards Japanese art on the part of its nineteenth-century devotees was somewhat equivocal. On the one hand, they felt that the *Ukiyo-e,* the art of the 'floating world'—which was until the 1880s almost all they knew— was exotic, alluring, exquisitely unreal. On the other, they recognised *Ukiyo-e* as a vigorous, democratic tradition that drew its strength from the newly emerging masses, and its subject matter from the streets, teashops and brothels of rapidly expanding Edo, as Tōkyō was then called. Both views are half-truths. There is a formal and technical discipline in traditional Japanese art that makes a total descent into self-indulgent aestheticism rare, while the almost photographic realism of the Japanese print, which Edmond de Goncourt stressed in his book on Utamaro, lies rather in the choice of earthy subject matter than in the handling of it, which is both stylised and decorative.

When in 1890 Maurice Denis uttered his dictum that 'whether it is a nude or anything else . . . any painting is essentially a flat surface covered with colours assembled in a certain order', the Japanese colour woodcut had for thirty years been undermining the art of the salons. In the Japanese print—Hokusai and Hiroshige in their landscapes are but partial exceptions—there is no atmosphere, the colour has no texture, there are no shadows. Flat areas of pure colour are separated by clear, sharp, rhythmic lines, and the picture area is frankly accepted for what it is, a flat surface. The focal point of the composition may be far

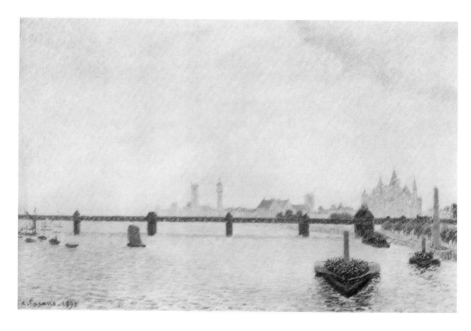

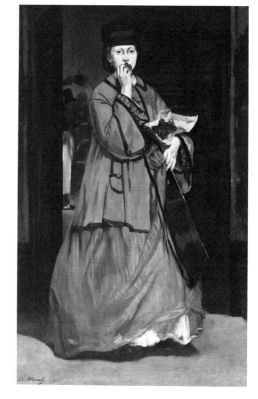

137.
Camille Pissarro (1830–1903). *Chelsea Bridge*. Oil on canvas. 1871. Pissarro, who found justification for his Impressionism in Japanese art, here takes his design from Hiroshige's view of the Eitai Bridge from the second series of Famous Views of Edo, c. 1840.

138.
Edouard Manet (1832–83). *La Chanteuse des Rues*. Oil on canvas. 1863. Bequest of Sarah Choate Sears, Museum of Fine Arts, Boston. Manet's debt to Japan was treated with contempt by the critic Paul Mantz, who wrote of the painting of the face, 'There is nothing more there than the shattering discord of chalky tones with black ones. The effect is pallid, harsh, ominous'.

off centre; objects and figures may be cut off by the edges of the print, in the interest not of visual realism but of effective pattern making. Subject matter counts for little. In these respects the Japanese print is the complete antithesis of all that was taught in the nineteenth-century art school. For the painters banded in revolt against the French Academy, the *Ukiyo-e* seemed at this critical moment to provide not only a vindication of their theories but a practical means of realising them on canvas. 'Damn it all', wrote Pissarro to his son Lucien in 1893, after seeing an exhibition of Japanese prints, 'if this show doesn't justify us! There are grey sunsets there that are the most striking instances of impressionism'. And again, in his next letter: 'These Japanese artists confirm my belief in our vision' (Figure 137).

Japanese art must have been a frequent topic of discussion at the Café Guerbois in the Rue des Batignolles, the meeting place in the 1860s for all the leading figures in the Impressionist movement from Bracquemond and Manet to Gauguin and Cézanne, and for writers and critics such as Astruc, Zola and Duranty. The unquestioned leader of the Batignolles Group, as it came to be called, was Manet. Just when he first encountered Japanese art is uncertain, but he was a close friend of Bracquemond and a frequent visitor to La Porte Chinoise from 1862, the year in which he painted the large *Musique aux Tuileries*. In this richly painted work some writers have detected the first hint of Japanese influence in the tendency to create a pattern of patches of colour, in the effective use of black in the design and in the rather flat schematic drawing of the faces, which has been attributed to Manet's admiration of Hokusai's shorthand figure drawing. If indeed Japanese influence is detectable, it is overwhelmed, as nearly always in Manet's work, by his sheer joy in the medium of oil paint. We would not expect the pupil of Couture and the admirer of Velázquez to surrender without a struggle to so alien an aesthetic.

By the end of 1863, in *La Chanteuse des Rues* (Figure 138), Manet had gone a step further. The model, Victorine Murend, has just emerged from the half-open doorway and seems to hesitate in her forward movement, her voluminous dress swirling about her. Her face is a white blank with the features drawn upon it. The long lines of shadow and dark braid sweep up to her head, both articulating the movement within the figure and giving it unity. The exact counterparts of all these devices can be found in Kaigetsudō's arresting paintings and prints of the beauties of the Yoshiwara, the red light district of Tōkyō (Figure 139). Thus Manet, when the *Ukiyo-e* first began to exert its influence, embraced and reconciled its two apparently conflicting features: social realism and an aesthetic based on the expressive power of line and colour alone. Of all his contemporaries, only Jacques-Emile Blanche understood that Manet, without resorting to obvious japonaiseries, had absorbed and turned to his own use the essential message of Japanese art.

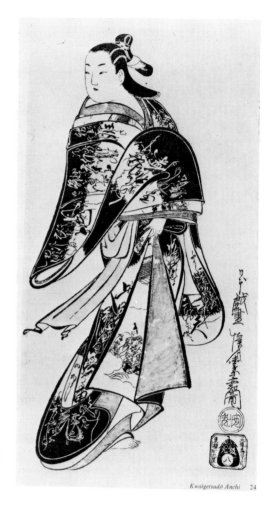

139.
Kaigetsudō Anchi (active 1704–16). *A Beauty of the Day.* Colour woodblock print. British Museum, London. The sweeping black lines of such prints as Kaigetsudō's, the flat patterns of colour and features drawn rather than modelled on the face, are what chiefly stimulated Manet.

Kwaigetsudō Anchi   24

The same almost pure, flat colours and simple forms enclosed by an emphatic line define other pictures that Manet painted at this time, notably the *Dead Toreador* of 1864. The *Olympia* of 1863, which caused such a furore when it was unaccountably accepted for the Salon, is often cited as the apogee of Manet's 'Japanese' period, but it has no Oriental features that are not present in other paintings of the mid-1860s, though they are here brought together with superb assurance in a composition of monumental daring.

Manet's visit to Spain in 1865 helped to renew his old passion for Velázquez. That he did not at once, or wholly, forget the lesson of Japanese art is shown by the *Fifer,* painted in the following year, an almost shadowless figure poised in space, which one critic called 'a costume dealer's signboard'. But in *The Execution of the Emperor Maximilian* there is the beginning of a return to solid three-dimensional forms, while the landscape detail in the background reveals that sensuous handling of oil paint that Manet could not suppress for long. Henceforward, the Japanese elements recur from time to time. We see them in the flatness and tendency to design in patches of colour in the Zola portrait of 1868 (Figure 140), in which the much-discussed Japanese screen and print in the background are of more documentary than pictorial importance, and in the telling use of black as a colour in *Luncheon in the Studio* (1868), and in the grouping of *On the Balcony* (1869). Later still Manet reverts from time to time to a daringly 'Japanese' assymmetry of composition—in *On the Beach* (1873) for instance—or to odd angles and cut-off figures, as in *La Place de la Concorde* (c. 1875) and *Nana* (1877). By this time the lesson of the Japanese print had been totally absorbed—as it never was by Whistler—and had become a natural part of Manet's vision.

Only in one respect did Manet deliberately copy Oriental methods. Some of the plants and animals in his illustrations to Mallarmé's *L'Après-midi d'un faune* are adapted from woodcuts in Hokusai's *Manga*. He seems to have studied Japanese brush painting, and in his swift ink sketches such as *The Bistro* (1877) and *L'Espagnol,* he shows some understanding of *sumi* technique. For a time he liked to write letters on paper on which he had already made a sketch in Chinese ink. The lovely page brushed with sprays of bindweed (Figure 141) must have been inspired by the letter papers used by Far Eastern poets and calligraphers. But Manet's line is seldom as Oriental as theirs; as a European, he is generally too interested in the form that the line encloses to allow it the full calligraphic freedom of Far Eastern ink painting. In the whole of Western art, perhaps only Rembrandt in his pen drawings achieved so perfect a synthesis of the expressive and descriptive functions of the line.

Edgar Degas was twenty-eight when in 1862 he first met Manet and first visited Mme Desoye's La Jonque Chinoise. Over the years he amassed a large art collection that included important prints of Utamaro, Hokusai and Hiroshige, which he bought at first under the guidance of Bracquemond. Everything he did, he did with a cold deliberation. He was a poet, and his sonnets, perfect in form and phrasing, are without human tenderness or passion. The effects in all his pictures are equally calculated and controlled. 'No art', he said, 'was ever less spontaneous than mine'. The beauty is in the poetry of pure form, with no thought to what lies behind it, and in this he is closer to the Japanese printmakers than to his own master, Ingres. The idea of painting the low life of Paris was Japanese also, and he depicted the brothels of Montmartre with the same detachment as the masters of the *Ukiyo-e* had recorded the squalors and delights of the Yoshiwara, transforming them, as they had, through the medium of an exquisitely refined sensibility into harmonies of pure line, colour and tone.

On a few occasions Degas was deliberately, obviously Japanese. He liked to paint Japanese fans for his own amusement, and showed five of them at the

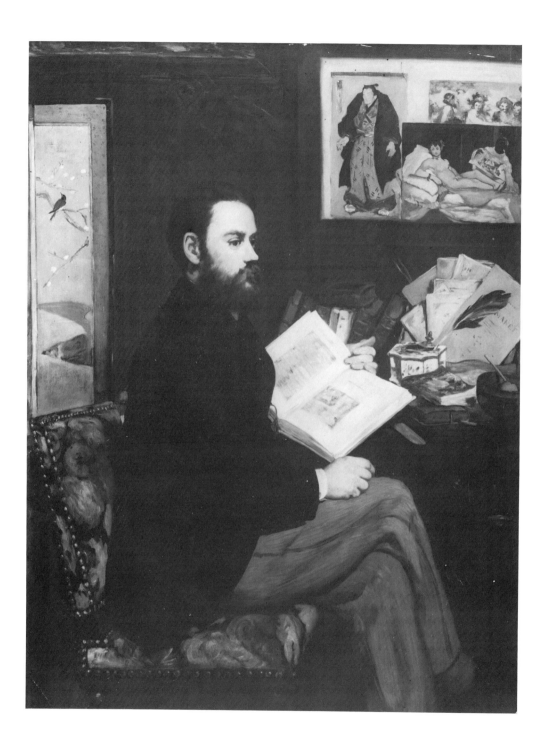

140.
Edouard Manet (1832–83). *Portrait of Emile Zola*. Oil on canvas. About 1868. Musée du Louvre, Paris. Photo by Giraudon. Only the accessories—the screen and the print by Toyokuni—are obviously Japanese, but echoes of the Japanese use of black as a strong element in the design appear both in Zola's coat and in the sketch for the *Olympia* on the wall behind.

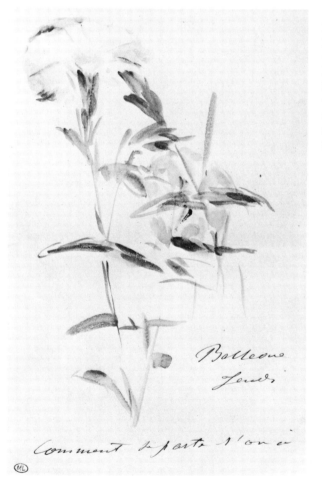

141.
Edouard Manet (1832–83). Page of a Letter Decorated with Sprays of Bindweed. Watercolour. Cabinet des Dessins, Musée du Louvre, Paris. One of the rare instances of an Impressionist practising, without being taught, an Oriental brush technique, although Manet does not seem to be using a Chinese or Japanese brush.

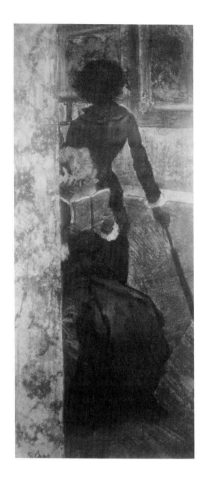

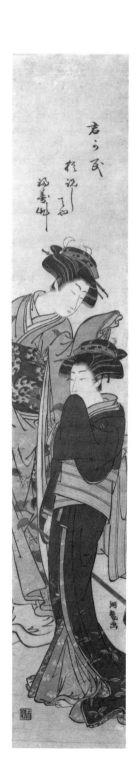

142 (above).
Edgar Degas (1834–1917). *Mary Cassatt at the Louvre*. Chalk, aquatint, drypoint and pastel. 1880. Collection Durand-Ruel. Degas got the idea for his composition and the rear view of the figure from the *hashira-e* (pillar prints) of artists such as Kiyonaga and Koryūsai.

143 (right).
Koryūsai (active c. 1764–88). *Two Geisha*. Woodcut print. c. 1776. Clarence Buckingham Collection, Art Institute of Chicago. A typical *hashira-e* (pillar print) that would have suggested the composition for the Degas in Figure 142.

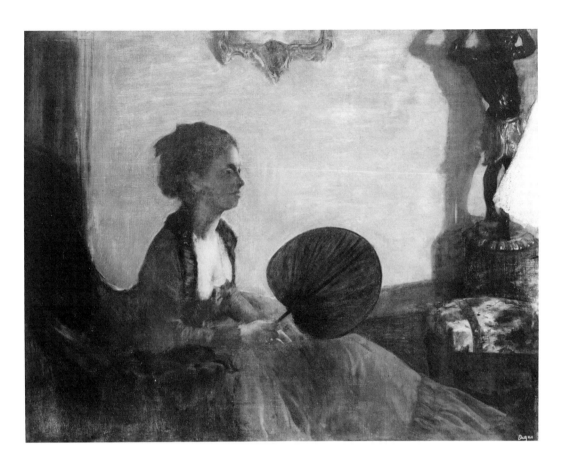

144.
Edgar Degas (1834–1917). *Mme Camus.*
Oil on canvas. 1869–70. Chester Dale
Collection, National Gallery of Art,
Washington, D.C. Degas's concern here
is not to achieve a likeness—Madame

Camus seems somewhat remote—but to
explore the possibilities of pure colour
and tone that he had learned from his
study of Japanese prints.

Impressionist Exhibition of 1870. The composition of his pastel of Mary Cassatt
in the Louvre (1880; Figure 142) is taken straight from the tall, narrow 'pillar
prints' (*hashira-e*) of Koryūsai (Figure 143) and Kiyonaga. His exquisite painting
of Mme Camus (1869–70; Figure 144), wife of the collector of Oriental ceramics, posed holding a fan against a glowing rose pink wall, is perhaps the nearest
he ever came in his oil painting to the kind of japonaiserie that Whistler sometimes indulged in. We have only to compare the portrait of Mme Camus with
Whistler's *The Golden Screen: Caprice in Purple and Gold* (Figure 147), to see what

a gulf separates the two artists. Indeed, Degas deplored the rampant japonaiserie of his day. 'Hélas!' he exclaimed to Bartholomé in 1890, 'Le goût partout!'. As George Moore aptly put it, 'Degas thinks as little of Japanese screens . . . as of newspaper applause. . . . He puts his aesthetics on his canvas'.

Some recent writers have attributed Degas's objective vision as much to the influence of photography as to that of the Japanese print. The invention of the hand-held 'detective camera' in the 1880s has been called in to explain his apparently accidental compositions and the odd angles and cut-off figures that we see in so many of the ballet pictures—notably in *Le Rideau, Aux Courses en Provence* and *La Place de la Concorde*. Some of these pictures were painted in the 1870s before the invention of this particular type of camera, but already in the 1860s there was a vogue for stereoscopic street scenes that showed moving figures, some cut off by the edge of the plate, in instantaneous exposures as fast as a fiftieth of a second. These could have given ideas to Degas and to Manet, as they certainly did to the amateur Impressionist Caillebotte. After Degas's death a large quantity of photographs, about which he had been very secretive, was found in his studio. They must share with the Japanese print the honour of having influenced his attitude towards composition, while they possibly helped him also to establish that subtle unity within a restricted range of tonal values that is unique to his paintings.

If the *Olympia* represents Manet's most successful translation of the Japanese message into French terms, the *Bains de Mer* (c. 1866–67; Figure 145) is undoubtedly Degas's—and for the same reason: in each work the artist has for the moment completely subordinated texture, depth and atmosphere to a flat arrangement of pure colour and line. Having achieved this, Degas returned to his master, Ingres, as Manet did to Velázquez. Thereafter Degas's colour becomes richer and more brilliant, but his later oils and pastels, however solidly painted, are often held together by principles of composition that he had learned in the 1860s from the study of Japanese prints.

On the whole, the Impressionists were concerned chiefly with the rendering of form in terms of the colour of the light reflected from it, and in this particular aspect of their researches they did not feel that they were helped in any way by the Japanese woodcut, although they might point to it as a confirmation of their theories.

Renoir took a rather different view. He felt that a people had no right to appropriate an art that belonged to another race. The Japanese cult disgusted him, as it did Degas, and he remarked once to Vuillard that 'perhaps it's having seen so much japonaiserie that has given me this horror of Japanese art'. It is a rather touching irony that the pupil to whom Renoir was devoted in his last years was the Japanese Impressionist Umehara Ryūzaburō, discussed in a previous chapter.

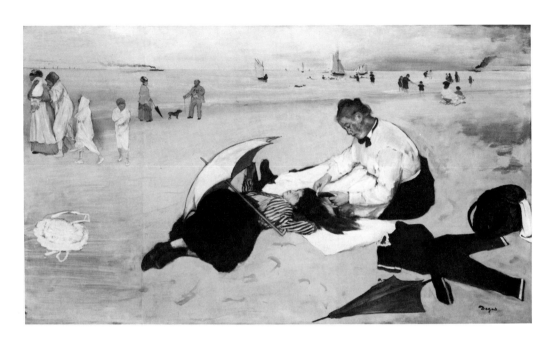

145.
Edgar Degas (1834–1917). *Bains de Mer:
Petite Fille Peignée par sa Bonne.* Oil on
paper mounted on canvas. c. 1866–67.
National Gallery, London. Degas's use
of black and the daring manner in which
objects and figures pull the eye to the
edges of the picture can be found not
only in Japanese prints but also in traditional Japanese painting going back to the
eleventh century.

Monet, although probably one of the first of the Impressionists to buy Japanese prints and a collector of them after he settled at Giverny in 1883, seems to have derived little from the study of them; they were not what he needed in his high Impressionist years. His most ambitious Oriental exercise—*La Japonaise* (1876; Figure 146), representing his wife, Camille, in a theatrical pose, holding a fan against a background of fans and swathed in a preposterous monster-encrusted robe—is a brilliantly vulgar pastiche of the sort that would have horrified the fastidious Degas. Monet himself later regretted it and called it 'trash' (*une saleté*).

During a brief stay in Holland in 1871, Monet bought Japanese prints and painted a few landscapes in bright, flat, pure colours, such as *The Blue House at Zaandam,* but he quickly abandoned this style on returning to Paris. In his later work Japanese elements of design persist, although his rich impasto makes them almost unrecognisable, and they come to final fruition in the great series of paintings of lilies to which he devoted himself in his last years. From about 1892 until he died in 1926 he painted almost nothing but the lily pond and Japanese bridge that he had created at Giverny, culminating in the vast *Nymphéas* series (Colour Plate 20), for which a special oval salon was built in the Musée de l'Orangerie, Paris, after his death. The texture of these huge, coarsely painted canvases of water lilies, wisteria and weeping willow is anything but Japanese, but the conception, although perhaps suggested to him by a friend, puts us in mind of the vast decorative screens and sliding doors of some palatial Japanese halls, while the realisation of the scheme in terms of colour alone, and the very choice of colours—predominantly green, purple, white and gold—remind us of Kōrin. In spite of the obvious roughness of execution, Monet in these panels seems to achieve the impossible: the reconciliation of the conflicting aims of Impressionism and of decorative art. So he too, strictly on his own terms, finally drew Japanese art into the mainstream of the French tradition.

Whistler was one of the first Western painters to fall under the spell of Japanese art, and his surrender was the most complete. He came almost straight from West Point to Paris, the more defenceless against the exotic fashion because he had not been schooled in the Salon tradition. Soon he was buying prints with great discernment—not the crude, aniline-coloured mid-nineteenth-century sheets that everyone was collecting, but the earlier, subtler work of Kiyonaga and his contemporaries. When, after the rejection of *At the Piano* by the Salon of 1859, he moved in 1863 to London, he took the craze with him and soon had infected the Rossettis, with whom he competed for years in friendly rivalry in buying prints and Oriental porcelain. The walls and even the ceiling of his house in Chelsea were covered with fans; he slept in a Chinese bed and ate off blue-and-white.

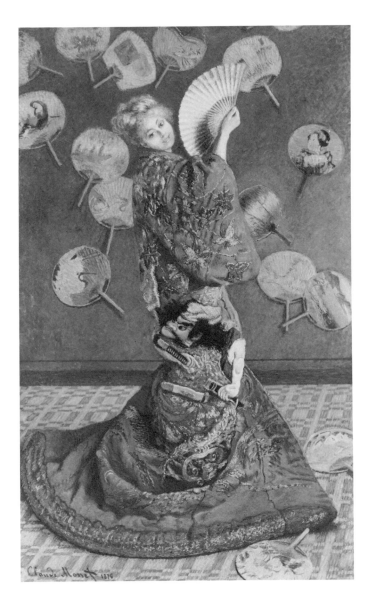

146.
Claude Monet (1840–1926). *La Japonaise*.
Oil on canvas. 1876. Museum of Fine
Arts, Boston. Camille Monet's fantastic
kimono and the prodigal display of fans
illustrate the fashion for japonaiserie then
at its height, but there is nothing Japanese
about Monet's style or technique.

The Rossettis were apt pupils, and William Michael Rossetti's description of a volume of Hokusai's *Manga,* published in *The Reader* in 1863, is full of admiration. He admits that some of the subjects are unedifying: 'The devil in man and the doll in woman seem to be the designer's idea of the radical distinction between the sexes'. But, for the rest, he is all praise for 'Hoxai's' work. 'It assuredly belongs', he writes, 'in various respects to the greatest order of art practised in our day in any country in the world. It has a tenacious grasp of its subject, a majesty of designing power and sweep of line, and a clenching hold upon the imagination'. And he hopes that people who see these books 'may come to recognize their superiority, in some respects, to anything which contemporary European art has to show to us'. Here Rossetti shows an even clearer grasp of the essential merits of the prints than does Whistler himself.

Ruskin, when W. M. Rossetti sent him an album of Japanese prints to look over, was polite about them, but elsewhere if he ever speaks of Japanese art, as opposed to craftsmanship, which he admired, it is with strong antipathy. 'There has long been an increasing interest in Japanese art', he writes in the *Pall Mall Gazette* (1 March 1867), 'which has been very harmful to our painters'; and again, on a gift to the Sheffield Museum in 1876, 'I think this Japanese art, however interesting in itself, not good to be long looked at, or in many examples'. Having once admired, or pretended to admire, Japanese nature drawings, he writes on 23 April 1884 to H. S. Marks that he has been buying Japanese books of birds, 'but only', he explains, 'to study their way of extracting the ugliness of things with vicious veracity, and the way they gloat over black, as if it was blue and gold'. Such comments, scattered through his writings, may help to explain his unremitting hostility to Whistler.

Unlike the Impressionists, Whistler never lost his enthusiasm for things Japanese. As late as 1885, in the celebrated *Ten O'Clock Lecture,* he was putting Japanese art on a par with that of classical Greece. Were another artistic genius, he declared, never to appear again, 'the story of the beautiful is already complete—hewn in the marbles of the Parthenon—and broidered, with the birds, upon the fan of Hokusai—at the foot of Fusiyama'. This was too much for Swinburne. 'The audience', was his waspish comment, 'must have remembered that they were not in a serious world; that they were in the fairyland of fans, in the paradise of pipkins, in the limbo of blue china, pots, plates, jars, joss-houses, and all the fortuitous frippery of Fusiyama'.

Whistler's japonophilia led him inevitably into the kind of pictorial extravagances that Monet indulged in once and later regretted. A series of his most popular paintings depicts European models dressed up in Oriental clothes and surrounded by the sort of bric-à-brac that Lazenby Liberty was now supplying to his London customers by the ton: *Die Lange Leizen* (1864), *La Princesse du Pays de la Porcelaine* (1864), *The Golden Screen: Caprice in Purple and Gold* (1865;

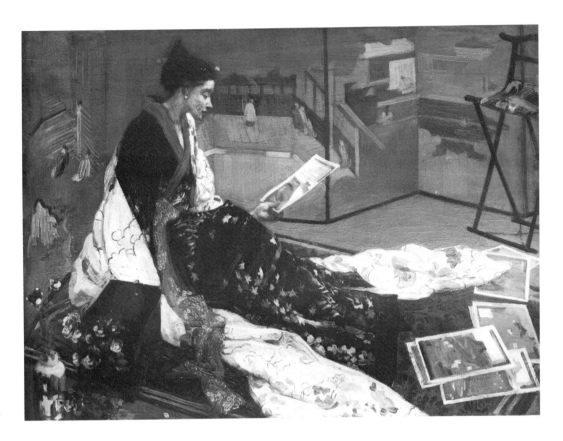

147.
James Abbott McNeill Whistler (1834–1903). *The Golden Screen: Caprice in Purple and Gold.* Oil on canvas. 1865. Smithsonian Institution, Freer Gallery of Art, Washington, D.C. In this rather self-conscious japonaiserie, Whistler's mistress and model, Joanna Hifferman, is studying prints by Hiroshige. The screen in the background does not seem to be copied from a Japanese original.

Figure 147), *The Balcony: Variations in Flesh Colour and Green* (1867–68)—the very artificiality of the titles is revealing. The climax, and Whistler's most spectacular excursion into japonaiserie, was the *Peacock Room* (1876; now in the Freer Gallery, Washington), in which the artist, without the owner's permission, covered F. R. Leyland's priceless Spanish leather hangings with peacocks in blue and gold. This was a tour de force of decorative art, however, and has very little to do with nineteenth-century painting.

In the same years that Whistler was paying these extravagant tributes to fashion, he was painting a series of pictures, entirely un-Oriental in theme, which show a deeper understanding of the Japanese aesthetic than any other

148.
James Abbott McNeill Whistler (1834–1903). *Cecily Alexander.* Oil on canvas. 1874. Tate Gallery, London. Whistler's friend Mortimer Menpes wrote of Whistler's masterpiece, 'The pose of Velázquez, the decoration of Japan, worked out in his own way'.

149.
Andō Hiroshige (1797–1858). *Bamboo Bank, Kyōbashi Bridge.* Colour woodblock print from the *Hundred Views of Edo.* 1857. British Museum, London. This late print of Hiroshige, which provided Whistler with his motif, was itself influenced by European art.

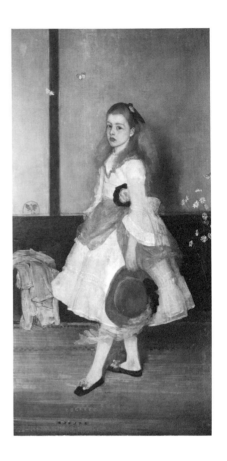

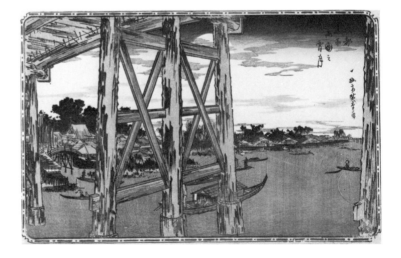

painter except Degas had achieved. In *The Music Room* (1860) black is daringly dominant in a composition indirectly inspired by Kiyonaga; in *The Little White Girl* (1864), a picture that impressed Monet, Whistler's chief concern is with the subtlest harmonies of grey and white; in portraits of his mother (1872) and of Carlyle (1874) Japanese principles of design are applied with serene dignity, while little Cicely Alexander (1874) is portrayed in an exquisite harmony of colour and line, a delicate counterpoint between figure and background, in which even the obviously Japanese elements, such as the butterflies and butterfly signature, seem entirely appropriate to the charm of the subject (Figure 148).

Yet even in this lovely work Whistler was not so much painting what nature presented to him as making the outward reality conform to a preconceived attitude to what a picture should be. Such an approach is both romantic and academic, and Whistler, in rebellion against the Salon, has simply substituted one set of aesthetic principles for another. 'Whistler', wrote George Moore, 'of all artists, is the least impressionist. . . . He thinks of nature but he does not see nature; he is guided by his mind, and not by his eyes'. The Impressionists, guided solely by their eyes, all sooner or later rejected Japanese art—but not Whistler, who once said that nature 'put him out'. The most Japanese of Whistler's later paintings are the many *Nocturnes*, painted from 1875 onwards. Here the sources of his inspiration are very obvious. It is not that the composition of *Old Battersea Bridge* (Colour Plate 21) and the idea for *The Falling Rocket* are taken from Japanese prints—van Gogh borrowed as freely—but that when Whistler saw the Thames wrapped in the fog of a winter evening, he could not help relying on the exquisite pictorial formula that he had evolved, and Hiroshige (Figure 149) hung like a transparent veil between himself and the real world. He lacked the passion of a Monet or a Cézanne, or rather his passion was tinged with a more self-conscious attitude to art than theirs. In London, Hiroshige and Utamaro stood him in good stead, for only by translating Impressionism into pseudo-Japanese terms could he make it palatable to a philistine English public.

Japan and the Post-Impressionists

Just when van Gogh first encountered Japanese art is not certain. Pissarro wrote to his son that van Gogh had seen prints in his parents' home in Nuenen. Writing from The Hague to his friend Anthon van Rappard in July 1883, when he was thirty-one, van Gogh mentions a print by Régamey and comments, 'Beautiful Japanese motifs'. And he had been in Antwerp but a few days when, late in 1885, he exclaimed to his brother Theo, quoting the Goncourts, 'Japonaiserie forever!' and described the docks as 'a famous japonaiserie, fantastic, peculiar, unheard of'. 'My studio is not bad', he goes on, 'especially as I have pinned a lot of little Japanese prints on the wall, which amuse me very much. You know those little women's figures in gardens, or on the beach, horsemen, flowers, knotty thorn branches'.

By March 1886 van Gogh was in Paris collecting prints, and in the following year had acquired enough—some probably borrowed from Samuel Bing—to mount a little exhibition in Le Tambourin, a café in the Boulevard de Clichy frequented by the Impressionists. He spent long hours in Bing's huge establishment rummaging for prints and took a number that he hoped to sell on commission. He suggested to Theo that, after a visit to the south of France, they should go into the print-selling business together.

Nothing came of this project, of course, at least commercially. But the prints had a profound effect on van Gogh as a painter. Together with his reading, especially of Pierre Loti's *Madame Chrysanthème,* they created in his mind a fanciful picture of Japan as a country of clear, simple forms and brilliant colours. No doubt he had also read Duranty's widely quoted declaration that 'the instinct of the people of Asia, who live in the perpetual dazzling light of the sun, has led them to reproduce the constant sensation by which they have been impressed, that is to say, of clear, flat colours'. Confusing the Far East with India is remarkable in a late nineteenth-century critic. But this popular view convinced van Gogh that he would find Japan in the south of France.

Van Gogh left Paris in February 1888, and by September was writing to Theo from Arles, 'Here my life will become more and more like a Japanese painter's, living close to nature like a petty tradesman'. And again, 'If the weather were always fine like this, it would be better than the painter's paradise; it would be absolute Japan'. But winter came, and it was not Japan, and van Gogh knew by now that Provence was very different from what he had imagined. 'There is still present in my memory', he wrote to Henri Bernard, 'the emotion produced by my own journey last winter from Paris to Arles. How I watched to see if it wasn't like Japan! Childish, wasn't it?'. By now the collapse of his dream no longer bothered him, for he was totally absorbed in painting the world around him, and to this end he began to study the methods of the Japanese printmakers and draughtsmen with much closer attention.

While in Paris, van Gogh had made three careful copies in oils of Japanese prints: a teahouse waitress by Eisen Kesai and Hiroshige's *Plum Tree* and *Sudden Shower at the Great Bridge at Atake* (Figure 150; cf. Figure 28) from the *Hundred Famous Views of Edo* (1857). Like Monet and Whistler, at that time he was chiefly interested in Japanese prints as exotic accessories in the backgrounds to his canvases. The Eisen, for example, appears with other prints on the wall, behind the sitter, in one of the two versions of his portrait of the rapacious artists' colourman,

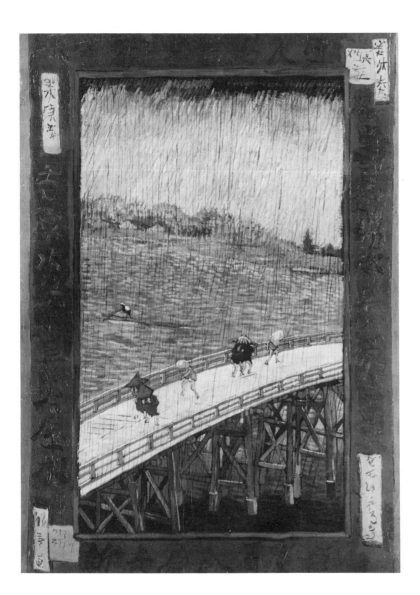

150.
Vincent van Gogh (1853–90). Copy of
Hiroshige's *Sudden Shower at the Great
Bridge at Atake*. Oil on canvas. 1888.
National Museum Vincent van Gogh,
Amsterdam. This is probably the most
striking and obvious illustration of the Im-
pressionists' fascination with Japanese art.

Père Tanguy (Figure 151). But, once in Arles, van Gogh left the cult of japonaiserie far behind. He still hung prints in his bedroom and studio and refers
several times in his letters to the aims of the printmakers, which he now began
to understand much better than he had in Paris. Their absolute clarity of form
and colour cleansed away the rather fuzzy texture that his canvases had acquired
in Paris under Impressionist influence. 'I wish you could spend some time here',
he wrote to Theo, 'you would feel it after a while, one's sight changes; you see
things with an eye more Japanese, you feel colour differently. The Japanese draw
quickly, very quickly, like a lightning flash, because their nerves are finer, their
feeling simpler'. So perfectly is the Oriental influence now integrated into his
work that it is only through his letters that we can be sure that van Gogh is still
thinking about Japanese methods at all. Writing to his brother in October 1888,
he described in detail the 'Japanese' colours in the painting of his bedroom in
Arles (Colour Plate 22) and commented, 'Here colour is to do everything. . . .
The shadows and shadows cast are suppressed: it is painted in free, flat tints like
Japanese prints'.

But it was not only through clear, flat colour that Japanese art spoke to
van Gogh. In mid-June he wrote to Bernard, 'The Japanese . . . express mar-
vellously well the contrast between the dull pale complexion of some girl and
the vivid blackness of her hair, with nothing but a sheet of white paper and four
strokes of the pen. Not to mention their spiky black bushes dotted with a thousand little white flowers'. During the summer of 1888 van Gogh was particularly
absorbed in Japanese drawing and woodcut techniques. He wrote to Theo that he
wanted 'to make some drawings in the manner of Japanese prints' and sketched
for him one of the grasshoppers that swarm over the olive trees, noting that they
were 'like those you see in Japanese sketchbooks'. Another drawing of grasshoppers is strongly suggestive of Hokusai's *Manga,* though probably done from life.

In May and June 1888 van Gogh executed some of his most important landscape drawings (Figure 152), of the Crau and the banks of the Rhône. He described them to Bernard, adding, 'It doesn't look Japanese, yet it is the most
Japanese thing I have done'. Writing to Theo, he was only slightly less emphatic
about how Japanese he felt these drawings were.

We accept so readily the Japanese influence on paintings of van Gogh's Arles
period, such as *The Bedroom, La Berceuse, Les Alyscamps* and *The Fishing Boats,*
that it is a little difficult at first to see in what way the drawings are also Japanese.
But we have only to glance at some of the long, horizontal prints of Hiroshige to
see where van Gogh found his inspiration. The flat landscape, stretching back in
horizontal planes lined with trees, the fences, reeds and grasses drawn with delicately repeated vertical strokes of the pen (replacing his earlier hatching technique), the use of dots to suggest leaves, the 'spiky black bushes dotted with a
thousand little white flowers' can all be found in Hiroshige's long, horizontal

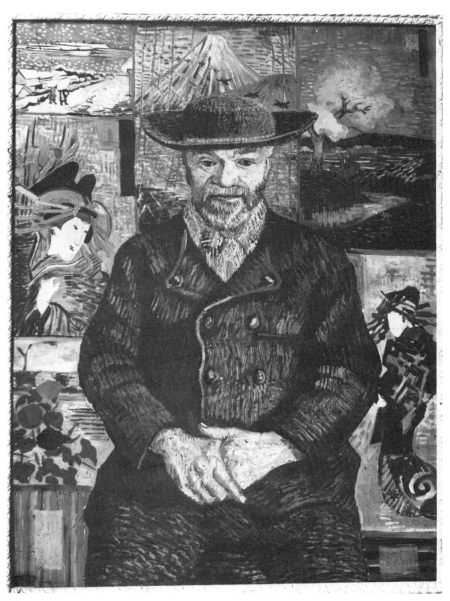

151.
Vincent van Gogh (1853–90). *Le Père Tanguy*. Oil on canvas. 1888. Musée Rodin, Paris. In the lower right corner is the Eisen woodcut of which van Gogh made a careful copy from the cover of the May 1886 issue of *Paris illustrée: Le Japon*.

sheets (Figure 153), and in Hokusai's *One Hundred Views of Fuji*. To make his drawing still more Japanese, van Gogh used a slightly absorbent paper and reed pens of varying thickness, which suggest something of the calligraphic elasticity of the Oriental brush. The notion, put forward by some writers, that he used 'Japanese reed pens' is absurd. There is no such thing. Van Gogh never seems to have experimented, as Manet did, with *sumi* techniques. His new method of painting with short, firm strokes of the brush gave his oils an even more clearly articulated structure, which we see above all in the landscape with the blue cart, called *Jardin de Maraichers* (June 1888), which is very clearly related to the drawings, and so, indirectly, to Hiroshige. Henri Dorra has suggested that the dotting and stippling technique, taken up almost simultaneously by Seurat, Signac and Pissarro, was inspired by the exhibition of Japanese art at the Galerie Georges Petit in 1883. He does not mention van Gogh in this connection, but in his case the influence seems to be even more clearly established by his own letters.

For van Gogh, the northern linear artist thrust into the colourful south, Japanese art was the catalyst. The example of the Japanese print showed him how the apparently conflicting aims of expression through the dynamic line and of expression through composition in colour could be reconciled. The tension between line and colour that runs through his later work is the same as that which gives such visual excitement to the best prints of Hokusai and Hiroshige, yet—and herein lies his genius—the Japanese influence is completely transcended.

Like van Gogh, Gauguin had his own vision of Japan. He had a small collection of Japanese prints; he included prints in the background of several of his portraits; and among the reproductions that he took with him to Tahiti in 1898 were Japanese sketches and works of Hokusai. In *Avant et Après,* the outpouring of notes, reminiscences and anecdotes that he sent back from the Marquesas in 1902 shortly before he died, he included a long and fanciful description, inspired by Loti, of a Japanese peasant family making a cloisonné vase. But the idea of Japan never excited him as it did van Gogh.

For a while Gauguin had thought of going to Java, and he was the first European painter of any importance to admire Buddhist art. At the Exposition Universelle of 1889 he was enchanted by the Indonesian village and the Javanese dancing. He bought photographs of the reliefs on the great ninth-century stūpa of Borobudur (Figure 154), which provided him with motifs for figure paintings for the rest of his life, beginning with the now lost *Eve* painted in Paris in 1890. Several of the standing figures in his Tahiti paintings—*Groupe avec un Ange, Faa Iheihe, Et l'Or de Leur Corps*—are copied from those of worshippers in the Borobudur reliefs, while the girl who holds the centre of his *Contes Barbares* (1902) is seated, rather artificially, in a yogic pose taken from one of the Dhyāni Buddhas on the stūpa. The composition of Gauguin's last and greatest work,

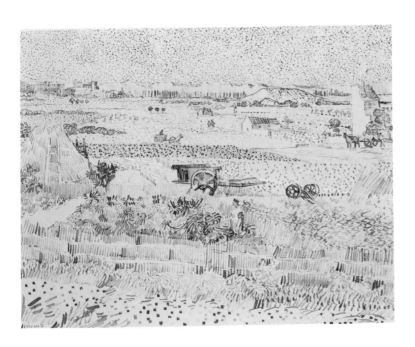

152.
Vincent van Gogh (1853–90). *The Plain of La Crau, Arles*. Pen and sepia ink. 1888. Mr and Mrs Paul Mellon Collection. Of the La Crau drawings, van Gogh wrote to his brother Theo that they did not look Japanese but 'really are, perhaps more so than some others'.

153.
Andō Hiroshige (1797–1858). *Cherry Blossoms at Koganei*. Detail from a colour woodblock print. Late 1830s. Honolulu Academy of Arts, Hawaii. Van Gogh's study of Hokusai and Hiroshige inspired him to imitate, with the reed pen, the effect of dots and short brushstrokes that gave texture to their landscape prints.

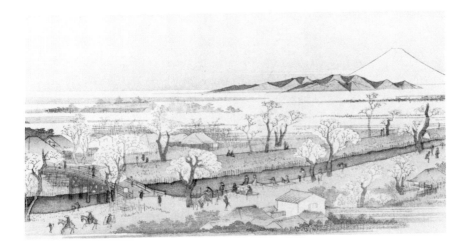

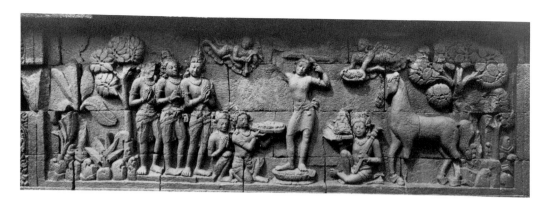

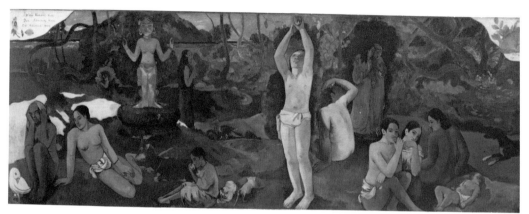

154 (top).
Prince Siddhārta Cuts His Hair, Signifying His Retreat from the World. Relief panel from the great stūpa at Borobudur, Java. Eighth to ninth century.

155 (middle).
Paul Gauguin (1848–1903). *Where Do We Come from? What Are We? Where Are We Going?* Oil on canvas. 1897–98. Arthur Gordon Tompkins Residuary Fund, Museum of Fine Arts, Boston.

156 (bottom).
Paul Gauguin (1848–1903). *The Vision after the Sermon.* Oil on canvas. 1888. National Gallery of Scotland, Edinburgh. Cf. the wrestling figures in Figure 135.

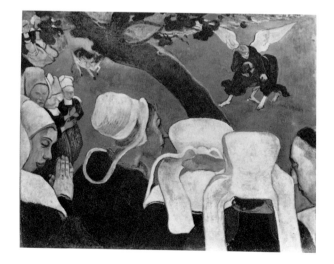

Where Do We Come from? What Are We? Where Are We Going? (Figure 155), may also have been inspired by one of the long narrative panels on Borobudur, and indeed his study of those reliefs—with their heavy, graceful and voluptuous figures, often seated or reclining in languid poses, the anatomy reduced to essentials, the smooth contours harmoniously simplified—provided him with a vocabulary of ready-made images, with which the women he saw in the Marquesas must have seemed miraculously to accord.

Nowhere more successfully than in Buddhist Mahāyāna art have abstract ideas been given visible form. For Gauguin the crypto-Symbolist, the idea generally preceded the form; indeed, he said that he sought forms to match his ideas. The gravely beautiful figures of his Tahitian women have about them an air of mystery, as if the secrets of that dying civilisation could only be suggested in terms of the silent, remote, yet sensuously lovely images that Gauguin took from Borobudur. To suggest the mystery, as Mallarmé said, is the dream—'to choose an object and extract a mood from it by a series of decipherings'. No matter that Gauguin could have had only the smallest notion of the theological complexities of the Borobudur reliefs: the aim of Symbolist art was to evoke ideas that could never, and need never, be put into words.

The road to pure Symbolist art as it was understood in late nineteenth-century Paris, however, was a road to disaster. Indeed, it is a blind alley in any epoch. Three pears on a cloth by Paul Cézanne are moving and sometimes mystical, whereas, wrote Félix Fénéon caustically, 'the entire Wagnerian Valhalla'—when painted by the Symbolists—'is as uninteresting as the Chamber of Deputies'. Gauguin was too good a painter to be a mere Symbolist. He did not need the example of Japanese art to save him, but it certainly helped to refine and intensify his concern with line and colour. At the time when Japanese influence on him was at its height, in about 1888, Gauguin began to speak of abstraction, meaning a synthesis of form and colour, and freedom from the object. 'In Japanese art', he said, 'there are no values', meaning no gradation of tone. And in a letter to Henri Bernard he cited the Japanese for the virtues of painting without shadows: 'I shall get away as much as possible from anything that gives the illusion of an object, and shadows being the *trompe-l'oeil* of the sun, I am inclined to eliminate them. But if a shadow enters your composition as a necessary form that is an altogether different thing'.

Occasionally, as in his depiction of Jacob wrestling with the angel (Figure 156) and in *The Three Puppies* (both 1888), Gauguin took a motif straight out of Hokusai or Kuniyoshi—and incidentally aroused Pissarro's wrath for stealing from another culture. Gauguin's *cloisonnisme,* in which areas of colour flatter and purer even than van Gogh's are bonded by firm dark lines, was inspired by Japanese prints and enamel work. Japanese colour harmonies and principles of design are obvious in *On the Beach* (1902), while the tall, gloriously rich panel *The White Horse* (1898) has in it more than a hint of Kōrin.

Gauguin achieved in his own art a fusion of Post-Impressionism with the decorative ideals of Japan and something of the metaphysical formalism of Hindu-Javanese art. Had this been a conscious process, and an end in itself, it would have been of little significance. But Gauguin's synthesis was produced unconsciously, in the realisation in painting of his own passionate attachment to the world of his senses, the exotic world of Tahiti and the Marquesas. It is this synthesis unconsciously arrived at that makes him a key figure in the confrontation of Eastern and Western art.

Many of the Japanese prints that the Impressionists admired depict the twilight world of the Yoshiwara. But Utamaro and Kiyonaga transmuted the sordid existence of the prostitutes and teahouse waitresses into scenes of quiet and decorous beauty, drained of their poignancy by the abstraction imposed by the woodcut medium. Toulouse-Lautrec found his subjects, his home, in the Yoshiwara of Montmartre. He had a strong feeling for Japan, collected fans, dolls and prints and had himself photographed dressed up as a samurai. He even dreamed of sailing in a yacht to Japan, where he would be less conscious of his shrunken legs. But Lautrec's revelation of the dark side of city life, unlike Utamaro's, is pitiless in its realism. The very harshness of his handling of oil paint ensures that no veil of textural beauty hangs between the subject and the viewer and so obscures the truth. In this his aims are the very opposite of those of the printmakers.

It was not in Lautrec's paintings, however, that his decorative talent fulfilled itself but in his posters and lithographs, for these exacting media presented a challenge and a discipline, forcing him to face the same problems that the Japanese printmaker had to solve, to give full expression to the idea in terms of line and flat colour, to suggest volume without shadows, pictorial depth without atmosphere. The simplification of his design is typical of the *Ukiyo-e*. The use of black masses and sweeping lines in his posters for Aristide Bruant and for the Divan Japonais, for example, recalls the Japanese Primitives and Kaigetsudō; the harmonies of yellow and green in *The Englishman at the Moulin Rouge* and *Reine de Joie* derive from his study of Harunobu; his very signature becomes a Japanese sword-guard.

But there is a difference. The faces in Japanese prints are always formalised, depersonalised; they are not individuals but types. However electrifying in pictorial effect, Sharaku's huge actors' faces are but masks. Lautrec's attitude to his subjects might be psychologically neutral, but he was incapable of generalising, and even when he is at his most abstract and decorative, the eye is arrested by some incisive detail. The faces in the posters are not masks, not even types; they are Jane Avril (Figure 157), La Goulue, the lecherous Englishman caricatured.

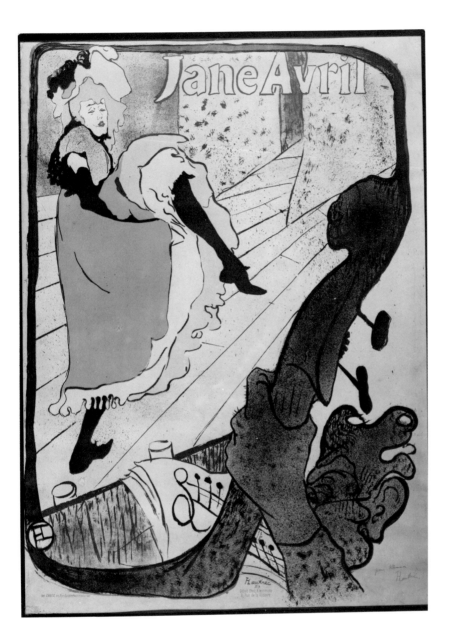

157.
Henri de Toulouse-Lautrec (1864–1901).
Jane Avril au Jardin de Paris. Coloured
poster. 1893. A classic example of Lautrec's very appropriate use of Japanese
strong linear design and flat colour in the
making of a poster.

In Lautrec's household accounts for January 1893, when he was twenty-nine and living with Dr Bourges in the Rue Fontaine, there is the item, 'Kakemonos, fr. 37.50'. We do not know what these Japanese hanging scrolls were, but they were not the first that Lautrec bought. In his portraits of the doctor and of the photographer Paul Sescau, painted in 1891, he had posed his friends in his studio before a Japanese scroll of what appear to be birds and flowers. What he thought of these he does not tell us; his letters, unlike van Gogh's, are remarkably unrevealing about such matters. But he seems to have been one of the first European artists to enjoy Oriental paintings, as opposed to prints, for their own sake.

The hanging scrolls that reached Paris in the 1880s and 1890s were chiefly orthodox works of the Kanō School. They would hardly have affected Lautrec's use of colour, though they may have stimulated his line to a greater freedom, while in some of his hand-coloured lithographs, such as the extraordinary vision of Loei Fuller dancing amid a cloud of veils (Colour Plate 23), Lautrec combines with his sweeping calligraphic line a subtle harmony of graded tones, from blue through grey to violet, that reminds us of Whistler's *Nocturnes*, while by dabbing the sheet with gold dust he gives it a final, almost excessively Japanese, touch. But the lithograph of Loei Fuller is perhaps an extreme example, much closer to Art Nouveau than to Utamaro or Hiroshige.

Oriental Art, the Symbolists and the Nabis

At the turn of the century French art still reverberated under the impact of Japan, but by now the ripples had spread outward and downward into decorative art, particularly into the spidery tendrils and sweeping 'whiplash' rhythms of Art Nouveau. Like chinoiserie, Art Nouveau is in itself an episode in the history of European taste, a compound of earlier *japonismes* and the aesthetics of the Arts and Crafts Movement, and like chinoiserie, it lies outside the scope of this book. Yet it was in the decorative art of the 1890s that there came the first indirect hints of an altogether new awareness of the aesthetic ideals of the East.

In 1890 Maurice Denis had made his declaration, which has already been quoted, that 'any painting is essentially a flat surface covered with colours assembled in a certain order'—a view that Sōtatsu and Kōrin would perfectly have understood. In the previous year a group of young Symbolist painters who called themselves Nabis (prophets, in Hebrew) had come together at the Académie Julian, dedicated, like the Pre-Raphaelites, to the regeneration of art. Their leaders were Denis, Bonnard, Sérusier and Vuillard. They did not deliberately invoke the example of Japan; nevertheless, 'the painter's work', wrote Denis's friend, the monk and artist Verkade, 'begins at that point where the ar-

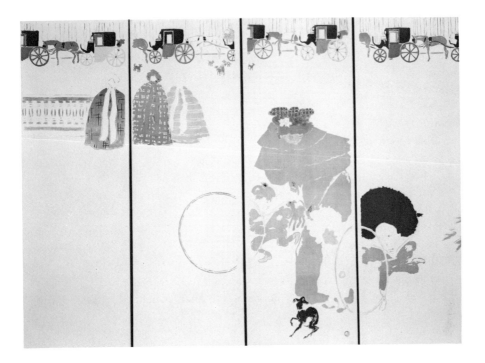

158.
Pierre Bonnard (1867–1947). *Promenades des Nourrices, Frise des Fiacres.* Four-panel screen. Colour lithograph. 1899. Abby Aldrich Rockefeller Fund, Museum of Modern Art, New York. Not only is the design of the screen strongly influenced by Japanese prints, but Bonnard, like the *Ukiyo-e* masters, also finds poetry in the life of the streets.

chitect considers his finished. . . . Down with perspective. . . . The wall must remain a surface. . . . There are no pictures, there is only decoration'. Of the group, Bonnard went furthest in his playful three- and four-panel screens of 1889–92 (Figure 158), which earned him the title 'Le Nabi très japonard'. He took his themes from daily life, made much of empty space and flat textile patterns, used oblique views and slanting planes to suggest depth. But, as with so many French painters, his love of the texture of oil paint soon weaned him away from Japan towards a more plastic and sensuous handling of colour.

With Bonnard's return to the fold, the direct influence of Japan on French painting—'that leaven', as Maurice Denis put it, 'which little by little permeated the whole mixture'—comes to an end. The indirect, and eventually far more

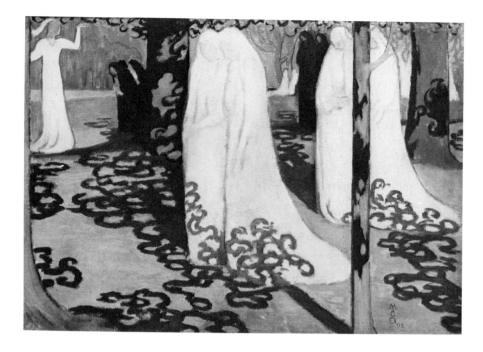

159.
Maurice Denis (1870–1943). *Procession under the Trees*. Oil on canvas. 1892. Arthur D. Altschul Collection, Metropolitan Museum of Art, New York. The art of the Symbolists in its subjects and mysterious meanings is remote from Japan, but its principles of design owe much to the *Ukiyo-e*.

profound, influence of Oriental art, on the other hand, was just beginning. The Symbolists—and the Nabis were all Symbolists—having taken art out of the Academy, having condemned the Impressionists for their concern with mere appearance, had sought to invest form once more with meaning, or rather to create visual 'equivalents', as they put it, for emotional and psychical experience. 'The supreme art', declared their most articulate spokesman, G. Albert Aurier, 'cannot but be ideistic [he reserved the word *idealistic* for classical and neo-academic art], art by definition (as we know intuitively) being the representative materialisation of what is highest and most divine in the world, of what is, in the last analysis, the only existent thing—the idea'. Painting, he went on, aims to express ideas, by 'translating them into a special language'.

But what ideas? Aurier was aware of traditional Asian art and refers admiringly to Buddhist sculpture. But the symbolic languages of Asian art had developed during thousands of years, in company with the ideas they expressed, and within the framework of their own cultures the visual symbols were always understood. The French Symbolist painters, unless like Denis they borrowed their language from Catholicism or Theosophy, sought to express states of feeling too vague and subjective to be translatable. No wonder Verkade said, 'There is only decoration'.

And yet, if the Symbolists failed to create a genuinely symbolic language, they were nevertheless the prophets they claimed to be, for their manifestos, far more than their paintings, which are often dull, hint at an altogether new attitude to the function of art. In 1909 Maurice Denis (Figure 159), looking back over the achievement of the Nabis, said that in their hands, 'art, instead of being representation, became the subjective deformation of nature'. Years earlier he had written that art 'is first and foremost a means of expression, a creation of our minds for which nature merely supplies the pretext'. Even Gauguin never went quite as far as that.

Denis's insistence on the primacy of the artist's inner vision and on art as expression rather than representation carried implications for the twentieth century that he could not have foreseen. On the one hand, they led straight to abstract art and Abstract Expressionism, and on the other, to a view of nature that at last made possible a true meeting of Eastern and Western art. Illumination came with dramatic suddenness in the first two decades of the twentieth century, not as a result of a deeper study of Oriental art but through what now seems an inevitable further step in the trend towards dissociation of the artist from the object, which had begun with Gauguin and the Symbolists.

Oriental Art and Twentieth-Century Painting in the West

So striking seems the accord between Oriental painting and certain key movements in modern Western art that it is natural to conclude that these revolutionary Western developments must have been to some extent at least inspired by Far Eastern thought and art. The parallels between the free existentialist gestures of Pollock, Kline or Soulages and Zen ink painting seem too close to be due to mere chance. After all, it might be argued, if Far Eastern influence had been decisive for the Impressionists in the limited area of the solution of purely formal and visual problems, how much more so must it be for the movements in contemporary art of which not only the methods but the very philosophical basis often seem to be thoroughly Oriental.

Between 1909 and 1920 a barrage of manifestos was launched in Europe aimed at the destruction of traditional beliefs about the nature and purposes of art. The attack came from many directions, chiefly from Munich. The keynote was struck by Kandinsky in 1909 with his famous dictum, *Alles ist erlaubt*, 'everything is permitted'. All forms of imitation, declared the *Futurist Manifesto* of the following year, should be held in contempt. What should inspire the artist, Kandinsky maintained, was not representation of the visible, but 'the inner spiritual side of nature'. In Paris, Matisse was insisting that there is an 'inherent truth' that must be disengaged from the outward appearance of the object to be represented: 'L'exactitude n'est pas la vérité'.

What is this truth? It is not the form, though it is expressed through the form. 'The absolute is not to be sought in the form', wrote Kandinsky. 'The form is always bound in time, it is relative since it is nothing more than the means necessary today in which today's revelation manifests itself, resounds. The resonance is then the soul of the form which can only come alive through the resonance, and which works from within to without. *The form is the outer expression of the inner content*'.

How is this inner content revealed? By absolute spontaneity first of all. The second of Kandinsky's three types of creative art, which he called Improvisation (Figure 160), he defined as 'a largely unconscious spontaneous expression of inner character, of non-material (i.e., spiritual) nature'. André Breton called it Automatism and said that it was 'the only mode of expression which gives entire satisfaction . . . by achieving a *rhythmic unity*'. And Klee described how 'the creative impulse suddenly springs to life, like a flame, passes through the hand onto the canvas, where it spreads further until, like a spark that closes an electric circuit, it returns to the source, the eye and the mind'. Creation, he said, 'must of necessity be accompanied by distortion of the natural form; only in that way can nature be reborn and the symbols of art revitalised'.

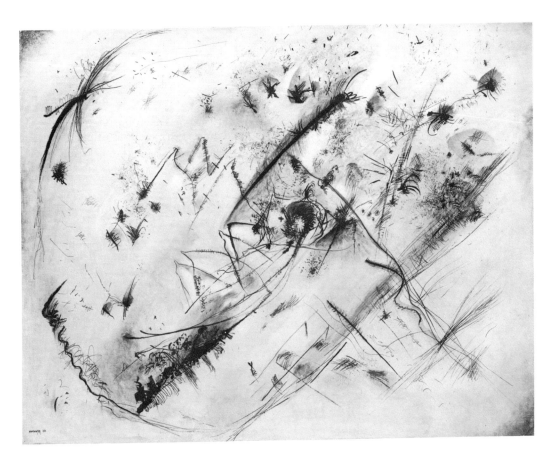

160.
Vasily Kandinsky (1866–1944). *Light
Picture No. 188.* Oil on canvas. 1913.
Solomon R. Guggenheim Museum, New
York. Although Kandinsky had encountered Far Eastern art in Munich in 1909,
it was Oriental metaphysical ideas, which
reached him through Theosophy, rather
than Oriental art, that influenced his idea
of pictorial space.

When representation of the object was no longer the chief aim of painting, the Western artist could abandon the traditionial view that space in a painting could be made real only through the objects that occupy it. This was forcefully expressed by Naum Gabo (Figure 161) in the *Realist Manifesto* of 1920: 'We re-nounce volume as a pictorial and plastic form of space; one cannot measure space in volumes as one cannot measure liquid in yards. . . . What is it (i.e., space) if not one continuous depth?'. And, to emphasise this fundamental point, he re-peated, 'We cannot measure or define space with solid masses, we can only de-fine space by space'. Gabo also proclaimed the idea, which was revolutionary in the West, that the plastic arts could embody through movement a synthesis of space and time: 'We affirm in these arts a new element, the kinetic rhythms, as the basic forms of our perception of real time'. Such pronouncements, which seemed in their day destructive of all artistic values, are now—so profound has been the change in our thinking in the West—taken for granted. To a Far East-ern painter, each of them would have seemed a statement of the obvious.

The creative impulse described by Klee had been the theme of a remarkable long poem, the *Wen fu* (Prose-poem on Literature), written in A.D. 300 by Lu Chi, who analyses with passionate insight the joys and frustrations of literary composition. Here he describes the sudden coming of pure inspiration and its equally sudden vanishing:

> Such moments when Mind and Matter hold perfect communion,
> And wide vistas open to regions hitherto entirely barred,
> Will come with irresistible force,
> And go, their departure none can hinder.
> Hidden, they vanish like a flash of light:
> Manifest, they are like sounds rising in mid-air.
> So acute is the mind in such instants of divine comprehension,
> What chaos is there that it cannot marshal in miraculous order?

Kandinsky's dualism of outer form and inner content had been stressed in the fourth century by the Chinese Buddhist and mystic Tsung Ping, who opened his brief 'Preface on Landscape Painting' (*Hua shan-shui hsü*) with these words: 'The sages cherish the Tao within them, while they respond to the objec-tive world; the virtuous purify their minds, while they appreciate represented forms. As to landscape paintings, they both have material existence, and reach into the realms of the spirit'. And again, 'The divine spirit is infinite; yet dwells in forms and inspires likeness; and thus truth enters into forms and signs'. Forty years later a scholar and musician named Wang Wei (not the famous T'ang painter-poet) wrote a short 'Preface on Painting' (*Hsü hua*) in which he clearly distinguished between representation, which was the 'discipline' of painting, and the animating spirit, which was its 'essence'.

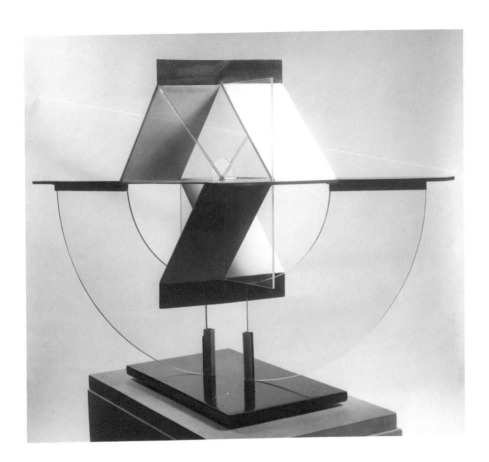

161.
Naum Gabo (1890–1977). *Construction in Space with Balance on Two Points.* Plastic, glass, metal and wood. 1925. Gift of H. Wade White, Yale University Art Gallery, New Haven. Unlike Kandinsky's, Gabo's sense of space expressed in his Constructions was not influenced by the Orient, but was rather a plastic expression of a reality revealed by modern physics. Yet it has more in common with Oriental ideas than with traditional Western concepts of finite space.

The concepts of the 'inner resonance' of the object, which Kandinsky said constituted the 'material of art', and the 'rhythmic unity', which André Breton in *What Is Surrealism?* saw as the aim of painting, have much in common with the first of the six principles of painting set down by the Chinese painter and critic Hsieh Ho between A.D. 530 and 550. This principle, *ch'i-yün sheng-tung* (literally, spirit resonance, life-movement), has become the cornerstone of Chinese aesthetic theory down the centuries. It means, in essence, that the painted forms, which in Far Eastern art are always to some degree conventionalised, must be brought to life by the animating spirit (*ch'i*). Early Chinese painters felt that this 'spirit' was a cosmic force, external to the artist, with which he must intuitively identify himself through the contemplation of the natural world. Later writers held that the *ch'i* was something awaiting release from within the psyche of the individual painter. They would have agreed absolutely with Kandinsky that 'form harmony must rest only on the purposive vibrations of the human soul'. As Will Grohmann has observed, 'The Far East is better equipped to understand Kandinsky than we are'.

Revolutionary ideas put forward by the Symbolists also have their far older Oriental counterparts. The belief expressed in Aurier's statement quoted on page 243, that the painted forms can in some sense stand for ideas, is central to Symbolist theory. The Chinese summed up the theory in two words: *hsieh i* (literally, write ideas), a purpose that gentleman-painters had held up since the Sung dynasty as the true aim of painting: accurate representation could be left to the court painters and professionals. The aesthetics of scholarly painting in China raise pictorial symbolism to a level of subtlety undreamed of by Gauguin and Aurier.

Maurice Denis's belief that nature merely provides the pretext for expression and that form is no more than a vehicle for feeling has also been central to the aesthetic of the Chinese literati since the Sung dynasty, when the poet-painter Su Tung-p'o (1036–1101) said that the gentleman-painter is not attached to material objects; when he paints he merely 'borrows' the form of things in which, for the moment, to 'lodge his feelings'. But he does not leave them there and so form attachments that would burden him. The catalogue of the emperor Hui-tsung's collection contains in an entry on the bamboo painter Wen T'ung (d. 1079) the statement that he 'availed himself of things in order to give lodging to his exhilaration'. Dissociation from the object has a long history in Chinese art.

Even the aims and techniques of the Cubists were, to some extent, anticipated by the Chinese landscape painter Wang Yüan-ch'i (1642–1715), whose method of, as it were, pulling his mountains and rocks apart and reassembling them into a tightly organised mass, with a semiabstract organic unity of their own (Figure 162), has been likened, in its laborious intensity, to Cézanne. Wang

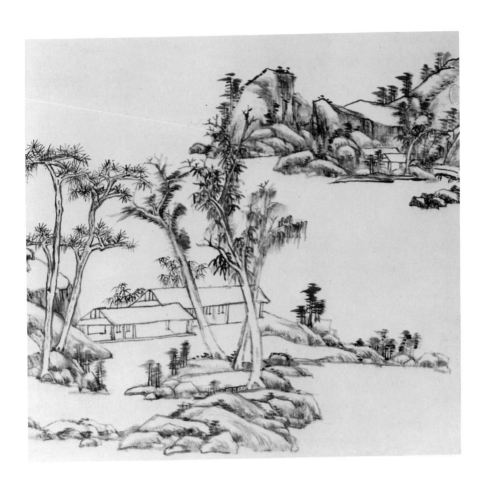

162.
Wang Yüan-ch'i (1642–1715). *Landscape
in the Style of Ni Tsan*. Detail. Ink and
light colour on paper. National Museum,
Kyōto. Wang's tense and expressive distortions of form have been likened to
those of Cézanne, but they never led to
an art of pure form: the Chinese painter
always retained the visible link to nature.

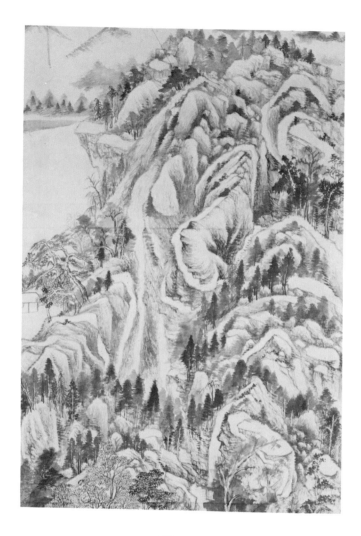

163.
Tung Ch'i-ch'ang (1555–1636). *Mountain Landscape for Sheng-pei*. Detail. Ink on paper. Drenowatz Collection, Rietberg Museum, Zürich. The expressive distortion of landscape forms was practised by Tung Ch'i-ch'ang as a way of putting new life into the tradition. Modern Expressionism has taught the West to appreciate his achievement to a degree that would have been impossible before Cézanne.

Yüan-ch'i's manner of painting was unique in Chinese art, but the distortion of natural forms has been common with Chinese scholar-painters since the Yüan dynasty.

Two centuries after Wang Yüan-ch'i, Paul Klee spoke of the expressive distortion of form as the only way in which 'nature can be reborn and the symbols of art revitalised'. Klee went through a period, roughly from 1917 to 1923, when he steeped himself in Chinese poetry, writing to his wife in 1917, 'J'ai le temps de lire beaucoup, et je deviens de plus en plus chinois'. At this time he painted a series of marvellous landscapes in which the trees and mountains seem, like those in a Chinese painting, to stand for some archetypal forms (Colour Plate 24). Klee's idea of expressive distortion as a path to the revitalisation of a pictorial language reminds us of the great Ming dynasty critic and theorist Tung Ch'i-ch'ang (1555–1636), whose painting and writing illustrate the concepts of distortion and revitalisation to a remarkable degree. In his landscapes the rocks and mountains are twisted and contorted, flat receding planes rise up to confront us, forms interlock and interpenetrate with teasing ambiguity (Figure 163). In later scholarly painting in general, and in Tung Ch'i-ch'ang's work in particular, these are not merely distortions of natural forms; they are, even more, distortions of the forms created by the great early masters such as Tung Yüan and Chü-jan, upon whom Tung Ch'i-ch'ang modelled his style. He acknowledged that no landscape painter could avoid using the schema inherited from his predecessors, but he insisted that the repertoire must be creatively reinterpreted by each successive generation of painters and that this revitalisation inevitably involved distortion both of inherited and natural forms.

In January 1949 Jackson Pollock (Figure 164) described his method of painting in a few now-famous sentences. 'When I am *in* my painting', he said, 'I am not aware of what I'm doing. It is only after a sort of "get acquainted" period that I see what I have been about. I have no fears about making changes, destroying the image, etc., because the painting has a life of its own. I try to let it come through. It is only when I lose contact with the painting that the result is a mess. Otherwise there is pure harmony, an easy give and take, and the painting comes out well'. This might be any Chinese or Japanese calligrapher or Zen painter speaking. We are reminded of Zao Wou-ki's remark to the critic J. D. Ray, 'I like people to be able to stroll about in my canvases, as I do myself when I am painting them'. And here is the Sung dynasty master Wen T'ung, by no means a special devotee of Zen, on his own bamboo painting: 'At the beginning, I saw the bamboo and delighted in it; now I delight in it and lose consciousness of myself. Suddenly I forget that the brush is in my hand, the paper before me; all at once I am exhilarated, and the tall bamboo appears, thick and luxuriant'.

Perhaps even closer to Pollock is the seventeenth-century Individualist Shih-t'ao, who, in his collected comments on painting, the *Hua yü lu,* enunciated the

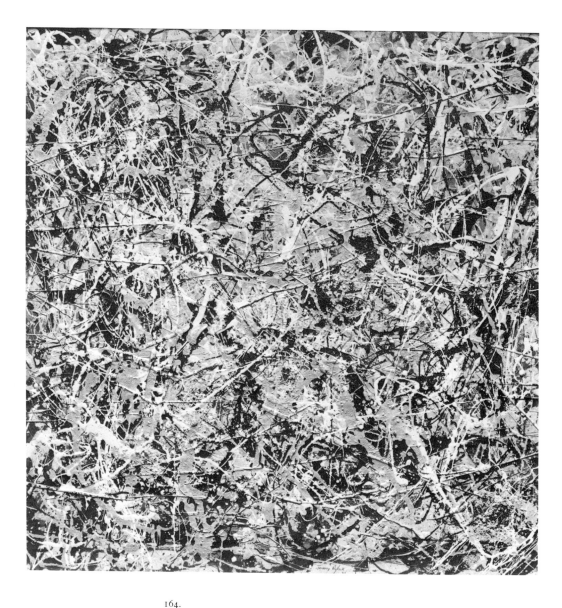

164.
Jackson Pollock (1912–56). *No. 4.* Oil, enamel and aluminum paint with pebbles on cut canvas on composition board. 1949. Katharine R. Ordway Collection, Yale University Art Gallery, New Haven. There is nothing to suggest that Pollock was directly influenced by Oriental art. That Action Painting and the practices of the early Chinese Expressionists have much in common, although it brings East and West together, is pure coincidence.

concept of the *i hua* (literally, one line), whereby the artist's exhilaration carries him through the painting on an unbroken surge of creative power (Figure 165). Shih-t'ao devotes a section to the free movement of the hand holding the brush, fundamental to both painting and calligraphy, and ends, 'If the painter's wrist is animated by the spirit, it produces miracles, and mountains and rivers reveal their soul'. His passage on *yin-yün,* a phrase that in the *Book of Changes* refers to the fundamental unity of Heaven and Earth, concerns precisely that ecstatic losing of oneself in the creative act that Jackson Pollock so wonderfully described.

We may carry the parallel still further. As long ago as the T'ang dynasty (618–906), there were artists in southeast China (in the Nanking-Hangchow region) who practised techniques as wild as those of any modern Action Painter. 'Ink Wang', according to contemporary accounts, would get drunk, then spatter and splash ink onto the silk, then, laughing and singing, stamp on it and smear it with his hands as well as with the brush. He also dipped his hair into the ink and slopped it onto the silk. A certain Mr Ku would cover the floor with silk, then run round and round emptying ink all over the floor and sprinkling colours over it. This must have been a public performance, like Georges Mathieu's spectacular antics before an audience. The works of these men have all disappeared, but something of its quality survives in a scroll attributed to an obscure thirteenth-century artist named Ying(?) Yü-chien (Figure 166), who may have been a Zen monk. The essential difference between the late T'ang eccentrics and the modern Action Painters is that, while the latter left their gestures and splashes as complete statements, their Chinese predecessors of a thousand years ago, by a few deft touches of the brush here and there, turned theirs into landscapes. But Action Painting and Zen expressionism belong to no period. They are moments in time and space that are not linked in any kind of historical continuity. They simply occur, and occur again, in an eternal present.

For the synthesis of space and time that Naum Gabo proclaimed in his *Manifesto* of 1920, and which the exponents of Kinetic Art later realised in practice, there is in the Chinese landscape handscroll a precedent nearly two thousand years old. The handscroll, which is unrolled a little at a time, presents, by means of a continually shifting perspective, a journey in space that, like music, can be experienced only in time. And just as the panoramic handscroll is a world in miniature, so may the time taken to view it represent in miniature the time that such a journey would take in a real landscape.

Chinese painting is imbued with a sense of space, which has no need of a receding ground surface, solid objects or a landscape to suggest it. In Chinese neolithic art, in Han wall painting, as sometimes in mediaeval European art, space is just 'there' whether there are objects in it or not. We are often told by Western writers that the Oriental painter 'invites us to fill up the blank spaces in

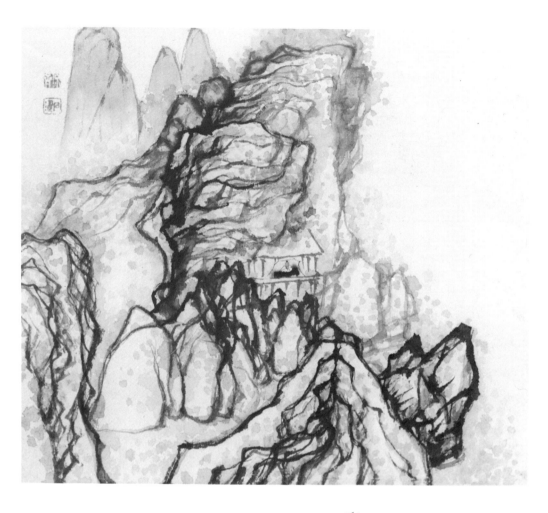

165.
Shih-t'ao (1641–c. 1717). A Man in a
Hut beneath a Cliff. Album leaf. Ink
and colour on paper. Nü-wa-chai Collection, New York. Photo by Bamboo Studio Corp. The suggestion in this very
original work of the projection of the artist's consciousness into the surrounding
landscape and vice versa antedates by two
hundred years the discovery by the West
of such possibilities for art.

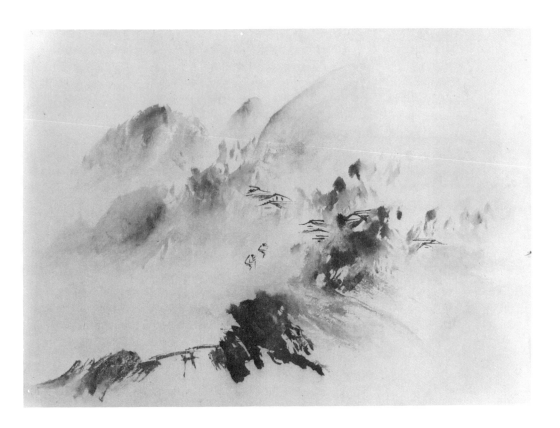

166.
Attributed to Ying(?) Yü-chien (thirteenth century). Mountain Village in
Clearing Mist. One of the *Eight Views
of Hsiao and Hsiang*. Handscroll. Ink on
paper. Commission for the Protection
of Cultural Properties, Tōkyō. Expressionist gestures with brush and ink were
not left by the Chinese painter as pure
abstractions but were always turned into
landscapes by a few small details deftly
added afterwards.

our imagination'. But there are no blank spaces in a Chinese painting. How can there be, when the painting is a picture of space? It defines space, as Naum Gabo put it, by space. A miraculous example of this, and quite typical, is a sketch of a little fish alone in the middle of an album leaf, by the seventeenth-century master Pa-ta Shan-jen (Figure 167). Only the fish is painted; only the fish tells us that the 'blank' part of the paper is water and not air. The unpainted water fills the picture space, indeed goes far beyond it. It will still be there when, with a flick of its tail, the little fish has darted out of sight.

We could go on matching the theories and methods of modern Western artists against those of the traditional Orient, but there is no need to labour the point that what has happened in Western art in the twentieth century has brought it, in certain fundamental respects, into accord with that of the Far East. It is as though the inhabitants of one country, with immense imaginative effort, had succeeded in creating a new language, only to discover that it was the native tongue of another land on the other side of the world.

There are differences, of course. Some movements in modern Western art such as Surrealism, Dada and Pop Art, have no recognisable counterparts outside the West, only imitations of them. Few Western painters have shared Matisse's cosy and very Chinese ideal of 'an art of balance, of purity and serenity devoid of troubling or depressing subject matter, an art which might be for every mental worker, be he businessman or writer, like an appeasing influence, like a mental soother'. Western Expressionism, rooted in the restless, anti-classical psyche of northern Europe, is too full of anxiety and conflict to achieve, except rarely, the inner serenity of even the wildest Zen art. Notable exceptions are the early abstractions of Kandinsky, who was at least partly Asiatic and who, thanks to his Russian temperament, felt, as Herbert Read happily put it, 'at ease in an atmosphere of chaos and intimations of immortality'. Kandinsky may have been stimulated by Madame Blavatsky's Theosophy, but mysticism does not lead inevitably towards abstraction in art; on the contrary, it usually inspires a feeble and insipid symbolic art. Kandinsky's discovery of abstraction, apart from his famous and possibly legendary confrontation with the painting that had been turned on its side in his studio, owes far more to Wilhelm Worringer's very influential thesis of 1908, *Abstraktion und Einfühlung* (Abstraction and Empathy), in which for the first time the 'will to abstraction' is defined as a recurrent impulse in the history of art, than it does to the influence of Far Eastern art.

Yet it is difficult to convince ourselves that Oriental influences were not at work, here and there, in the first decades of the present century. In one or two cases they certainly were. Mark Tobey's moment of truth, discussed further on page 263, came to him one autumn evening at Dartington Hall, in the year following his fruitful visit to the Far East, and though his first exercise in 'white

引此偏懷惟悼人緣何
也下雲自己此明在魚兒
拊米号繁眉金る者

芝室冥旺
∧ⅢⅢ

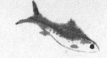

167.
Pa-ta Shan-jen (Chu Ta; 1626–after
1705). Little Fish. Album leaf. Ink on
paper. Sumitomo Collection, Oiso.
A picture not of a fish but of the space
in which the fish is swimming.

writing' looked to him like Broadway, it was unconsciously inspired by his experience of studying calligraphy in Japan. Henri Michaux is another example of direct influence in the 1930s, Morris Graves in the 1940s and 1950s, Sam Francis in the 1960s. But these instances are not of critical importance for the development of modern art for, as Herbert Read wrote in 1959, 'Klee and Kandinsky, in the course of their experimentation, had anticipated all the possibilities that lay ahead; every type of Abstract Expressionism that was to be developed between 1914 and the present day has somewhere its prototype in the immense *oeuvre* of these two masters'.

An important exhibition of Far Eastern art was held in Munich in 1909. Kandinsky wrote an appreciative account of it, which appeared in the same year, for the Moscow art magazine *Apollon*. Yet there is nothing in his own theoretical writings to suggest that he was ever influenced by the Japanese paintings in that exhibition, which included works by the sixteenth-century landscapist Sesson and several Zen masters. If he was affected at all, he seems not to have been aware of it himself.

Worringer in *Abstraction and Empathy* refers but once to Japanese art. His comment is a perceptive one. '*Japonisme* in Europe', he writes, 'constitutes one of the most important steps in the history of the gradual rehabilitation of art as pure forms . . . and on the other hand it saved us from the immediate danger of seeing the possibilities of pure form only within the classical canon'. This is excellent as far as it goes, but it represents a verdict upon the completed Japanese phase rather than the beginning of a new understanding of Oriental aesthetics. Indeed it would be very surprising if Worringer or any of the pioneers of the modern movement—Kandinsky, Klee, Matisse and Gabo—had shown any awareness of the kind of ideals that are expressed in the early Chinese writings on art from which I have quoted. Critical interest in the era of Cubism was focussed almost entirely on the art of Africa and Oceania. Very few of these Chinese texts were translated before the 1930s in any case, and even today some of them, particularly those that concern the detachment of the gentleman-painter from the object, perspective and the methods of the T'ang 'action painters' are known only to specialists in Chinese painting.

The change in Western art in the twentieth century, which has brought it in certain fundamental respects into harmony with that of the Orient, was not due to the influence of Oriental art, nor was Oriental art held up as an example; never did Kandinsky or Klee echo Pissarro's remark about an exhibition of Japanese prints that I quoted earlier: 'Damn it all, if this show doesn't justify us!'. It was due rather to a profound change in Western thinking about the nature of the physical world, most clearly expressed in the physical sciences. No longer do we believe in a finite world or in the permanence of matter. The physicist may describe it in terms of waves, particles or energy, according to the aspect of nature that he is investigating, and he speaks no longer of objects, but of events. 'Physical concepts', Einstein said, 'are free creations of the human mind, and are not, however it may seem, uniquely determined by the external world'. Space and time, we have come to feel, are infinite, and our knowledge of them can be but partial and relative. Solid matter has dissolved into an accretion of particles in an eternal state of agitation. Such a view would seem the natural one to any thinker in the Hindu–Buddhist world. For the basic ambiguity of our concept of matter, and particularly for the illusory nature of sense data, the Buddhist philosopher would use the term *Māyā* (illusion), while, when referring to the idea of continuous change, he would speak of *Sūnyatā* (the Void) or *Saṃsāra* (the chain of existence in which all things are forever coming together, dissolving and coalescing again into new transient patterns). To the Eastern mind, Taoist or Buddhist, the Void is a positive force.

> From ancient times [wrote the Japanese critic Haga Tōru] Being or the Existent, in other words that which makes the appearance of Things as They Are, has been thought of as *Mu* [an approximate term is 'nothingness']. And by *Mu* we do not at all mean a state of absolute zero, but the mysterious core of Being filled with a dynamic, creative energy of infinite scope.
>
> If the light of intelligence is directed from this *Mu,* everything from Man to Nature takes on the same transcendental dimension. Not that Man and Nature thereby come to face each other in an impassive confrontation, but that there occurs a persuasive, mutual interchange of energies between the pair which contributes to the development and growth of both. . . . From the Japanese point of view, it is not Man who draws, but rather the Existent brings forth its own shape.

Or, as Klee put it, 'art does not render the visible, rather it makes visible'. As Western science has been liberated from bondage to visible matter, so has Western art been set free from the necessity of depicting it. What the eye sees at one moment in time is ephemeral, and so illusory. Their awareness of the limiting character of scientific one-point perspective led the Chinese, centuries ago, to reject it. That Chinese painters had a grasp of its principles is shown by the way in which the T'ang dynasty fresco painters of the Paradise compositions in the caves at Tunhuang handled their complex celestial palaces. The tenth-century landscapist Li Ch'eng was severely taken to task by the Sung critic Shen Kua for his very skill in this craft. Why look at a building, said Shen Kua, from only one point of view? Li Ch'eng's 'angles and corners of buildings' and his 'eaves seen from below' are all very well, but only a continually shifting perspective enables us to grasp the whole. Chang Tse-tuan's remarkable long panorama of

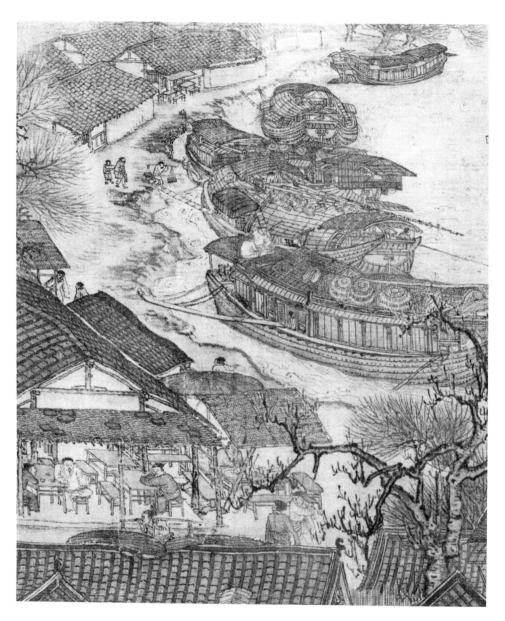

168.

Chang Tse-tuan (active c. 1100–1130). *Going Up River at Ch'ing-ming Festival Time.* Detail of a handscroll. Ink and slight colour on silk. Palace Museum, Peking. This famous scroll of life along the river shows that the Northern Sung painters had mastered realistic drawing, shading and foreshortening by the twelfth century, only to abandon those techniques later as too realistic and not suitable for a scholar-painter.

life outside the Northern Sung capital, *Going Up River at Ch'ing-ming Festival Time* (Figure 168), painted in about A.D. 1120, or shortly after, represents both the climax and the swan song of pictorial realism in the upper levels of Chinese landscape painting. Southern Sung academicians such as Ma Yüan drifted into a dream world of their own, almost into a poetic superrealism, while the gentleman-painters from the succeeding Yüan dynasty onwards showed no interest in realism whatsoever. Today many Western painters have rejected perspective, chiaroscuro, the very picture-frame itself, because they have come to realise, like their Chinese predecessors of the Sung dynasty, that pictorial realism, far from making possible the representation of the Real, actually hinders it. The same liberating process has taken place in Western poetry, music, drama and film, with the result that all these arts are open as never before to influences from the Orient.

So today, for the first time, Eastern and Western artists, instead of merely borrowing from each other for their own immediate ends, as Chinese court painters in the eighteenth century borrowed from the Jesuits, and the Impressionists from the Japanese, have found common ground in a view of reality that reaches far beyond the bounds of art itself. Sometimes in the West we hear painters such as Liu Kuo-sung or Saitō Yoshishige—to take two names at random—being criticised for 'copying' Pollock, Kline or Soulages. But this is quite wrong. On the contrary, many Far Eastern painters, after a brief flirtation with Western realism, are now firmly back on their own ground. That they have to some extent been inspired by the New York School, and all that led up to it from Kandinsky onwards, to achieve a rediscovery of the Abstract Expressionist roots of their own tradition, cannot be doubted, but for this very reason their involvement in it may be deeper and more lasting than that of the Western painters, many of whom have already moved on, before they even began to explore the expressive possibilities of calligraphic abstraction. We should speak not of Western influence on Liu Kuo-sung and Saitō Yohishige but rather of stimulus, or even of provocation.

The American Response to Oriental Art

For Europe to accept the Oriental aesthetic was to deny its own heritage. Modern America has not found it so difficult, for its culture derives part of its strength from its very rejection of Europe. The popularity of Oriental art and thought in America has been partly due to the calibre of the men who propagated it—Fenollosa and Okakura, Coomaraswamy and Suzuki, to name but a few—but their success was also due to the American willingness to look beyond Europe.

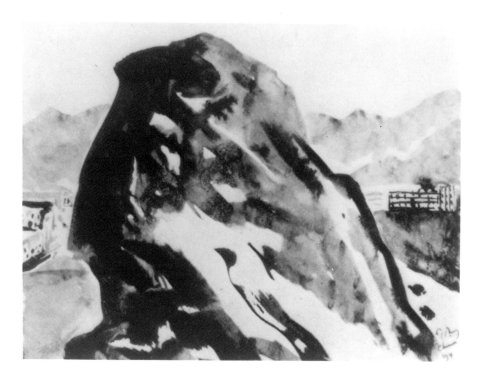

169.
Mark Tobey (1890–1976). *Soochow.* Chinese ink on paper. 1934. Painting under the tutelage of his friend Teng K'uei, Tobey here came as close as he ever got to working in the Chinese manner.

Americans are open and generous, and America suffers not at all from the intellectual complacency of Britain and France. America, moreover, looks westward across the Pacific as well as eastward, and its enthusiasm for things Chinese and Japanese has not been tainted by a sense of cultural superiority to the East.

For twenty years before the New York Armory Show in 1913 opened American eyes to modern art, Arthur Dow, Fenollosa's close friend and travelling companion in Japan, had been promoting a system of art education that stressed not the realism of the salons, but essentials of pictorial form, rhythm and construction. 'I confess', he wrote with great insight, 'to sympathy with all who reject traditional academicism in art. . . . Japanese art had done much towards breaking the hold of this tyranny, the incoming Chinese art will do more, but it may remain for modernist art to set us free'. Some critics have seen the Oriental landscape at work in Dow's most distinguished pupil, Georgia O'Keeffe, but after early experiments in *sumi* she developed a style that owes little or nothing to the Orient. Ever since she abandoned those experiments, her inspiration has been New Mexico—'my country', as she said, 'terrible winds and a wonderful emptiness'. Nothing could be further from the Oriental ideal of a paintable landscape than the glaring light and windswept plains of New Mexico.

'I have often thought', wrote Mark Tobey in 1957, 'that if the West Coast had been as open to aesthetic influences from Asia, as the East Coast was to Europe, what a rich nation we would be'. Though America continued through force of habit to look to Europe, it was in the Pacific Northwest, in the work of Tobey himself, that Oriental art first struck a responsive chord in an American painter. On Tobey the influences were cumulative. First, his conversion, in about 1918, to the syncretic faith Baha-i; then, in 1923, his encounter with Japanese prints in Seattle and his meeting with the Chinese painter and critic Teng K'uei, who gave him his first lessons in handling the Chinese brush (Figure 169). Ten years later he stayed with Teng K'uei in Shanghai, then moved on to Japan, where he spent a month in a Zen monastery, painting and practising calligraphy, and trying to meditate. Like the fourth-century Chinese landscape painter Tsung Ping, he found that he was not very good at meditating, but, like Tsung Ping, he felt that the act of handling the brush gave him the same feeling of spiritual release.

Tobey's experience in Japan left him feeling very much an Occidental—or so he thought. But after he had returned to England in 1935, one autumn evening in his studio in Dartington Hall he began to weave on paper an endless web of white lines on a brown ground. When he had finished, the result did not look to him in the least Oriental (Figure 170); it looked like Broadway, or Shanghai, of which he had written in his *Journal* of April 1934, 'Shanghai seems like New York, congested, crazy, and almost any kind of life. . . . There are dance halls

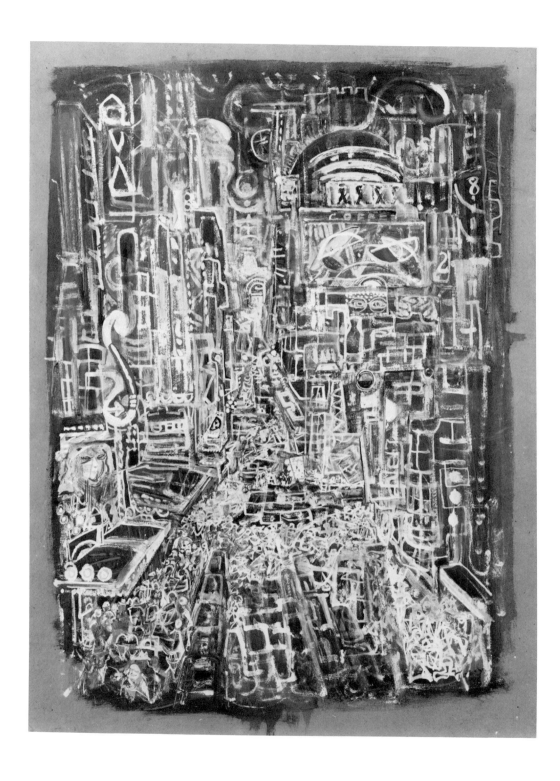

and dance halls, traffic and neon signs, especially red ones, twisting and turning over everything'. As he later remembered this climactic experience, 'Of its own accord', he said, 'the calligraphic impulse I had received in China enabled me to convey, without being bound by forms, the notion of the people and the cars and the whole vitality of the scene'. The scales fell away. In a sudden flash, he had broken through the Western conventions of pictorial space into a new world.

But at this point in our enquiry such labels as 'Oriental in appearance' are beginning to lose their meaning, and we find ourselves in a realm in which East and West are inextricably interwoven. However strong the influences from the East, Tobey's declared aim was to express an essentially American experience. 'Artistically speaking', he wrote, 'I have already had several lives. Some critics have accused me of being an Orientalist and of using Oriental models. But this is not so, for I knew when in Japan and China—as I struggled with their *sumi* ink and brush in an attempt to understand their calligraphy—that I would never be anything but the Occidental that I am. But it was there that I got what I call the calligraphic impulse to carry my work on into some new dimensions. . . . With this method I found that I could paint the frenetic rhythms of the modern city, the interweaving of lights and the streams of people who are entangled in the meshes of this net'. Just as Shiba Kōkan had had to call in the aid of Dutch realism to paint his beloved Mount Fuji, so now did Tobey turn to Oriental calligraphy to help him to convey his feelings about Manhattan.

It is often said that what is Oriental about Tobey's famous 'white writing' pictures is their calligraphic quality. But his line, endlessly moving or agitated in jerky rhythms though it may be, is seldom in these paintings really calligraphic; unlike the line in Oriental calligraphy, it cannot be pulled out of the picture to stand as an expressive form on its own. Rather is it a means to an end—namely, the evocation of a feeling of continuous space, which became for Tobey 'a kind of living thing—like a sixth sense'. The line, as he puts it, brings about 'the dematerialization of form by space penetration'.

170.
Mark Tobey (1890–1976). *Broadway.*
Tempera on fibreboard. Arthur H. Hearn
Fund, Metropolitan Museum of Art,
New York. Tobey is able to suggest the
frenetic life of the modern Western city
by means of the feeling for space and
movement he had learned from his study
of Oriental brushwork.

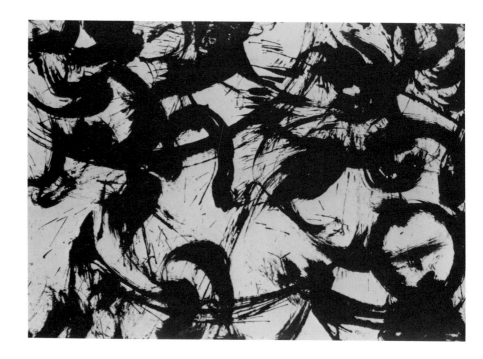

171.
Mark Tobey (1890–1976). *Composition.*
Chinese ink. 1957. Galerie Beyeler,
Basel. Here Tobey carries his breakthrough into the realm of pure abstraction, suggesting limitless space beyond
the confines of the picture.

Much later, in 1957, Tobey experimented briefly with pure calligraphic ink
gestures (Figure 171), but while these pictures are obviously Oriental in appearance, they are less deeply Oriental in feeling than those miraculous hints of a
world beyond time and space revealed in the most lyrically abstract of his 'white
writing' pictures. In the 1950s a number of artists, such as Pollock, Dubuffet,
Michaux (Figure 172) and Cuppa, arrived at a similar type of all-over composition composed of endlessly moving lines or dots or agitated vermicular forms or
calligraphic gestures. But what may appear to be Oriental influence is the natural
way of the Abstract Expressionist. In answer to enquiries from Gordon Washburn, set down in Yamada's *Dialogue in Art,* Soulages, Mathieu and Hartung all

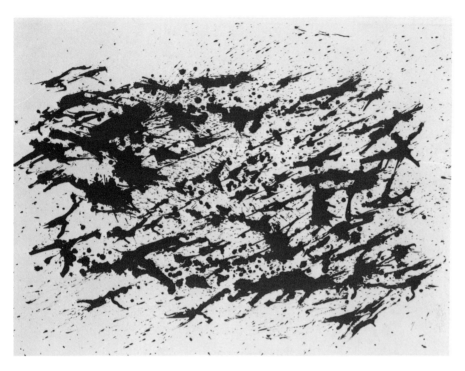

172.
Henri Michaux (1899–1984). *Painting*. Chinese ink. 1960–67. Galerie le Point Cardinal, Paris. Many Abstract Expressionists—among them Zao Wou-ki's friend, the poet-painter Henri Michaux, who travelled in Asia—have claimed that their style was a natural evolution in Western modernism, so there is no need to look for direct Oriental influence here.

denied any Oriental influence in their work. When it does appear, it is, with few exceptions, in the work of minor artists, such as William Barker, whose *I-ching* series of oil paintings was inspired by the Shang oracle bones (as was Zao Wou-ki in one phase of his career), and Ulfert Wilke, an exponent of Abstract Calligraphy who spent a year in Japan, part of it in a Zen temple.

The work of Morris Graves, another Seattle painter, may seem at first sight more Oriental than Tobey's. For not only did he borrow Tobey's 'white writing', but the subjects of some of his most striking pictures are taken from the Chinese ritual bronzes in the Seattle Art Museum. He is a profound admirer of Tobey and a student of Zen, has visited the Orient and creates around himself a

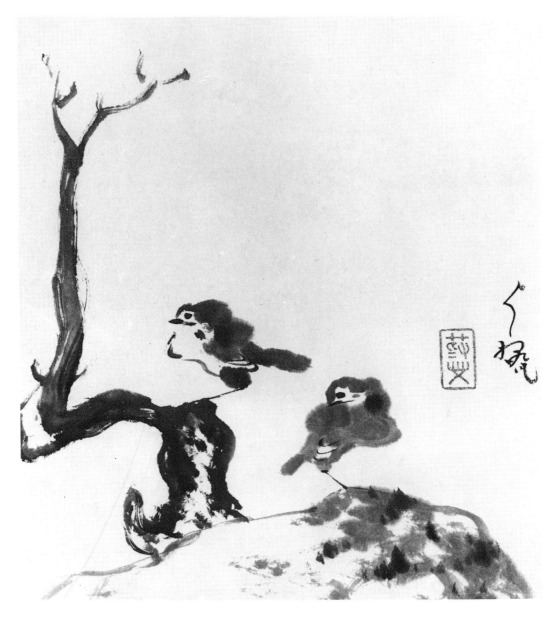

173.
Pa-ta Shan-jen (Chu ta; 1626–after 1705).
Little Birds. Album leaf. Ink on paper.
Sumitomo Collection, Oiso. Here Pa-ta
reduces form to essentials, seeing the
birds poised in space as redolent of the
life of nature.

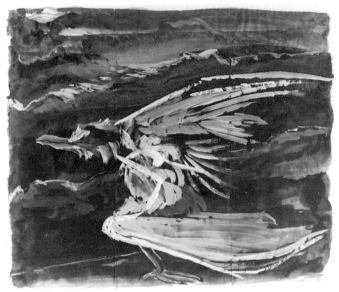

174.
Morris Graves (b. 1910). *Wounded Gull*.
Gouache on paper. 1943. Phillips Collection, Washington, D.C. Although
Graves was fascinated by Oriental art
and took many of his themes from it, his
haunting image of the dying gull depicts
an aspect of nature that no Chinese artist
would consider a suitable subject for
painting.

thoroughly Japanese ambience. But his work is very different. While in Tobey's
paintings forms dissolve into space, Graves's archaic bronzes and wounded gulls
loom out of the night, bathed in an unearthly luminosity, as if possessed by
some magic, animating force. Space is not the subject of his pictures, but only
the matrix out of which the forms become manifest with a dreamlike clarity.
A parallel has been drawn between his birds and those painted by the Chinese
seventeenth-century eccentric Pa-ta Shan-jen, which have something of the
same compelling power (Figure 173). But while Graves's birds dwell in a twilight world, Pa-ta's belong to the day. They may sometimes look bad-tempered,
but never are they, like Graves's, threatening, wounded, blind or dead. Such a
view of nature would be unthinkable to a Chinese painter.

   Morris Graves said of his *Wounded Gull* (Figure 174) that 'the dying image
will soon be one with the vast, infinite forms of the ocean and the sky around it',
and felt that this was a Zen idea. But in Zen the union of the spirit with Eternity
is attained not by the dissolution of the physical body but by the conscious
mind. It is an ecstatic thing, and Zen art above all is an art of release and joy. An
American critic wrote of Graves's tortured *Owl of the Inner Eye*, '*Vainly* [my ital-
ics] it attempts, through its outer calm and inner intensity, to unite itself with
the void and attain Satori'. No Zen painter would depict the spiritual agony and
loneliness of a being unable to find union with God. In spite of his Oriental
themes and occasional Oriental techniques, Graves's mysticism seems somewhat
Western in character.

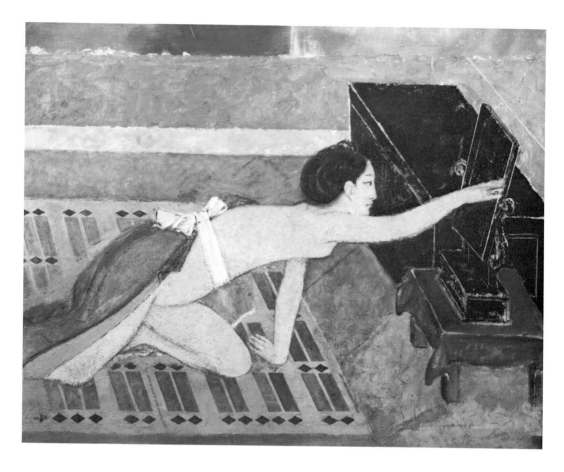

Balthus. *Japanese Girl with Black Mirror.*
1967–76. Oil. Private Collection. Photo
courtesy of Pierre Matisse Gallery.

Some Reflections on the East-West Dialogue

We have come to a point in our enquiry into the East-West confrontation where it is legitimate to ask whether one can discern any pattern or principle governing the process of artistic influence between cultures, and what the significance of this interaction is for the future of art. I should say at once that there are no complete or satisfying answers to either of these questions: we know very little about the psychology of artistic stimulus in the individual and still less about how it operates between cultures, while it is idle to speculate about the future. Yet it may still be of some use to set down some of the factors that seem to be involved in this process and are beginning, even now, to reshape the art of the major civilisations. If these comments seem disconnected and inconclusive, that is because this is a theme that too easily inspires high-sounding generalisations. All I can offer is a few thoughts on the subject.

What, first of all, are the conditions under which artistic influences operate? Styles in art may travel under their own colours, so to speak, or be carried by forces or events that in themselves have nothing to do with art. Japanese influence on the Impressionists was a case of direct transmission from one group of artists to another through the neutral medium of commerce; Western art, on the contrary, was adopted by Meiji period painters under pressure from the Japanese government, who deliberately promoted it as an instrument of modernisation and nation building. Painters were encouraged, even forced, to paint and draw in the Western manner whether they liked it or not. That some of them liked it very much does not contradict the fact that its introduction to Japan was an act of political policy.

Religion is a particularly sensitive conductor of artistic style. Religious art carries style on its wings, and unlike court art takes no account of class, while its appeal goes beyond art itself. More specifically, the power that resides in a religious image may depend precisely on what it looks like—on its style. The more closely the image resembles the particularly potent icon from which it derives, the more of the original's power will seem to emanate from it. The history of Buddhist art is full of instances of copying of famous images, the best known being the statue of Śākyamuni reputedly made by King Udyāna in the Buddha's lifetime, which sired a vast family of replicas throughout Buddhist Asia for over a thousand years. Such an icon is recognised at once by the devotee, who feels its potency through its style. Even in religious art the medium is, to some extent, the message.

So potent a vehicle is style, indeed, that the archaeologist and art historian may be tempted to interpret the appearance of similar forms in different places as evidence of deeper or more direct contact than actually occurred. In primitive communities a type of image may be shared by two tribal groups that have nothing else in common, and may even be traditional enemies or separated by hostile tribes. Techniques and skills, moreover, can travel great distances, leaving no trace of their passage. The painted pottery of neolithic China, for example, may have been influenced by that of Mesopotamia, for some of the decorative motifs it employs appeared rather earlier in the Near East, but the two cultures were not only unaware of each other's existence, they were also separated by nomadic peoples who apparently did not make pottery themselves. There is no need to infer direct contact between prehistoric Mesopotamia and China or the vast, slow Völkerwanderung that was once taken as the only possible explanation of the similarity. Besides, similarity in motifs does not necessarily mean transmission. Some basic designs are common to the painted pottery and textiles of totally unrelated cultures, such as those of China and Peru. Is it possible that a culture may, like an organism, act as a 'carrier' without itself being affected?

But when artistic transmission does occur, clearly the receiving culture must be at least neither hostile nor totally indifferent. At the most superficial level, a turn of the wheel of fashionable taste may make acceptable what last year, or next year, would be ignored. 'Sick of Grecian elegance and symmetry, or of Gothic grandeur and magnificence', wrote Lady Mary Wortley Montagu in 1740, 'we must all seek the barbarous gaudy gout of the Chinese'. In T'ang China, fashion had a good deal to do with the wholesale borrowing of western

Asiatic art, while fashion may have been the vehicle in an even more literal sense. Father Bouvet, like Athanasius Kircher before him, published his copies of Chinese figure paintings in *L'Estat présent de la Chine en figures* not as examples of Chinese art, but as models to the court of how to dress with more dignity and modesty. Any artistic message these prints carried was merely accidental.

The reasons for the acceptance of foreign art may go much deeper. Generalisations about cultures are always dangerous, but I think it can safely be said that the Indian mind is perfectly at home in the realms of metaphysics and religious experience, worlds into which comparatively few of the down-to-earth Chinese care to wander. Until the coming of Buddhism, there was no true religious art in China. Buddhist doctrine and art gave Chinese culture a new dimension, filling an empty space, as it were. Perhaps their discovery that there was a space to be filled created in the Chinese the need that made them receptive to all that Buddhism brought with it. Once China felt that need, Buddhism in time became an integral part of its civilisation.

The view that influence operates in response to a conscious or unconscious need is supported by the truth of its opposite, namely, that where no need is felt, influence may not be transmitted. Cultures, like neighbours, can live next door to each other and scarcely exchange a word. China and India have felt from time to time that they ought to understand each other, but in things of the mind they are worlds apart. Once the empty space I spoke of had been filled by Buddhism, there was little that China could take from India. When Rabindranath Tagore lectured in Peking in 1924, his message fell on deaf, not to say hostile, ears, while Bertrand Russell and John Dewey were heard with rapt attention. They brought to China the hard good sense that China needed and understood, while Tagore preached a transcendental aestheticism that was no help at all to China in its painful progress into the modern world.

While foreign forms and techniques in the arts might be borrowed to fulfil a particular role, there was, at least in China, a tendency for them to be kept firmly in their place. The 'foreign realism' in the art of the early Ch'ing dynasty was confined largely to the Nanking painters and professional artists; the scholars in general ignored it. Buddhist art had brought with it to China a number of foreign techniques such as shading, chiaroscuro, 'relief painting' and some peculiar drapery conventions, which were assiduously applied by Chinese painters to the figures in Buddhist banner and wall painting, but these techniques and conventions were, as far as we know, very little used, if at all, by scholarly masters such as Yen Li-pen and Li Lung-mien. The Chinese evidently felt that foreign techniques were appropriate only to foreign subject matter. In fact, these techniques were gradually forgotten as Buddhism lost its hold over China. The Japanese, as we would expect, have not taken so uncompromising a view. It would be interesting to enquire whether the principle of reserving foreign techniques for foreign, or 'second-class', subject matter has been applied in any art that was not Chinese.

Yet the work of art, while outwardly the product or illustration of a cultural situation, is in the final analysis the creation of an individual. Where East and West meet is in the mind of the artist himself, and the processes of acceptance and transformation depend ultimately on the choices that he makes. What governs these choices? The answer is partly historical, for the fact of his encountering of a particular style or object can usually be accounted for. At the same time his choices are governed by the way in which he 'sees', and this is in part the product of tradition and training, which, too, are historical facts. As Sir Ernst Gombrich pointed out in *Art and Illusion,* the artist sees and paints what he has learned to see and paint. Beyond that point again, the choices that the artist makes are determined by the pressures upon him, as a creative individual, from personal circumstances and human relations, and by other factors, even more mysterious, that often seem to the observer to be utterly arbitrary or random.

As with a civilisation, whether or not an artist responds voluntarily to the challenge of an alien form, style or technique depends ultimately on whether it fulfils a need for him. Where no specific need exists, it can be created artificially by confrontation with the new object, as experts in advertising well know. The effect then is likely to be transient. Sasanian art had appealed to T'ang China through its richness and novelty and rapidly went out of fashion when China became culturally isolationist after the middle of the dynasty. So with chinoiserie, which found its natural place in Rococo ornament, to disappear entirely with the coming of Neoclassicism.

Very different was the impact of European art on certain Chinese painters in the seventeenth century, for when they encountered it, they recognised not simply a new style of painting but a new kind of vision. Until they saw the engravings brought by the Jesuits, they had, so to speak, no idea what they were missing. The realism of Northern Sung painting was by then long forgotten, and the Western pictures stirred anew in certain painters of the Nanking School a desire for greater realism that had lain dormant, or perhaps had survived only at the level of popular art. The difference here is that the stimulus offered by fanciful pseudo-Chinese art evoked no response in European painters, while that offered by Western realism to certain Chinese painters of the late Ming and early Ch'ing was eagerly taken up, suggesting that the 'need' was a genuine, if unconscious, one.

How is that need felt? We would give much to know what thoughts—I mean, in the first place, purely professional thoughts about composition, form, line and colour—passed through the mind of a Ming artist such as Tung Ch'i-ch'ang when, as seems very possible, he thumbed through the exquisite engravings in Nadal's *Evangelicae Historiae Imagines* and other books brought by the Jesuits. And what did Boucher feel when he took in his hands the Chinese albums in the collection of his engraver friend Jacques-Gabriel Huquier? Did these pictures say nothing to him? If so, then that can only be because he did not really see them, because he was prevented from giving them his full critical attention by the feeling that, while they were exotic and enjoyable—and all the more enjoyable for being exotic—they could not be taken seriously as art, for they could not be profited from. As the Chinese court painter Tsou I-kuei put it, speaking of Western artists, 'These painters have no brush manner whatsoever; although they possess skill, they are simply artisans and cannot consequently be classified as painters'. Some such feeling too may have prevented the Catholic convert and landscape painter Wu Li from making any attempt to paint in the Western manner. The practice of Western art, whatever its merits, was for artisans; it could have no message for him and make no claim on him as a scholar and a gentleman. If this was indeed the case, the influence of European engravings on some of the gentleman-artists in Nanking needs to be explained. It may be that their interest in brush methods, which produced that famous handbook for art students, *The Painting Manual of the Mustard-seed Garden* (1679), made them particularly predisposed to examine different techniques, no matter where they came from.

The most fruitful responses seem to have occurred when the alien art had helped to fulfil a need of which the artists at the 'receiving end' were already fully aware, or, to put it another way, when they were already searching in that particular direction. The influence of the Japanese print on the Impressionists is the most obvious example of this. The Impressionists were groping towards something, and the *Ukiyo-e,* by showing them in part at least what it was they were groping for, helped them to articulate their aims, and they freely acknowledged their debt. Contrary to what many people think, this is not true of the relationship between Cubism and African tribal sculpture. Cubism was a natural development beyond Cézanne, and only when that point had been reached did the solutions to formal problems arrived at by the carvers of African masks suddenly become interesting and meaningful to Cubist painters and stimulate their art. It was Cubism, moreover, that opened the eyes of the public to the aesthetics of African sculpture, not the other way about.

It is, of course, quite unnecessary for the meaning and purpose of the original art to be understood for it to be influential. The Cubists were interested only in the formal qualities of African sculpture; the Impressionists, only in those same aspects of the *Ukiyo-e*. Also, the imported art might be put to quite different uses or given a different interpretation. Japanese artists, for instance, have employed Surrealism not so much to reveal the subconscious as to express the idea of spiritual freedom, and, indirectly, as a form of political protest.

The response, when it does occur, does not involve the wholesale adoption of a foreign art or style. That is simply copying. The artist's response is a process of ingestion and transformation, often of distortion. All the major examples I have given in this book involve this process, ranging from the splendid adaptation of a European compositional convention in Hokusai's *View of Yotsuya* to the complete transformation of Japanese aesthetic principles that we see in van Gogh's *Bedroom at Arles*. The translation of a style from one medium to another is also of crucial importance. Western realism becomes something subtly different when expressed in the ink and washes of a *Nihonga* painter such as Kaihō Yushō; the aesthetic of the *Ukiyo-e* undergoes an astonishing transformation when translated into oil paint or Lautrec's lithographs.

The creative frisson that develops between cultures in contact with one another derives in part at least from the differences between them. So we cannot leave the subject of the confrontation of Eastern and Western art without giving some thought to just what is confronting what. I approach this topic with some misgivings. Comparisons of this sort involve making sweeping generalisations about beliefs and attitudes, which must at best be very superficial and to which obvious exceptions at once leap to mind. But it is worth the attempt, because East and West have traditionally felt very differently about the world and have expressed their feelings in very different ways. Only when we realise how great these differences are, can we fully appreciate the achievement of the creative men and women who have tried to wrestle with these differences and have in some cases achieved, without deliberate intent, a triumphant resolution of them.

Many attempts have been made to describe the differences between Eastern and Western concepts and modes of expression, of which one of the most thoughtful was F. S. C. Northrop's *The Meeting of East and West*. The East, as Northrop put it, dwells in an 'undifferentiated aesthetic continuum'; the West, in a 'differentiated logical continuum'. In the East, the 'aesthetic' component dominates; in the West, the 'theoretic'. We can think of many aspects in which this is not true: the West has its poets and mystics, the East its pragmatists. But the differences are sufficiently striking for a comparison like this to be helpful. Fully aware that the canvas is being painted in very crude colours and that China and Japan cannot be lumped together, I should like in the few remaining pages to see if this contrast holds good in the world of art. Japan is indeed a special case, for while aspects of the Far Eastern tradition are expressed in the unique qualities of Japanese art, they are by no means all native to Japan. Japan has played a special role in the confrontation of Eastern and Western culture, which I will discuss later. In the meantime my comparisons will be drawn between

China on the one hand and Europe on the other and will stress traditional concepts rather than the increasingly similar attitudes of modern times.

If such statements have any validity at all, it may be said that the Western outlook is traditionally theistic, the Far Eastern atheistic. The West sees God as centre; to the East there is no centre. The mainstream of Western art, embodying both the classical and Christian traditions, is one of figure painting; that of China, at least since the Sung dynasty, one of landscape painting. To the West, Man is God's supreme creation; to the East he is but part of a total, if not clearly understood, pattern. Western man conceives of God, as it were, from below, reaching upwards from his experience of the human father towards the transcendental, and makes God in his own image.[1] China, having never seen the need of a personal God, does not attempt to describe the Divine except in the vaguest metaphysical terms. The West sees the working out of God's purposes in finite time; China has no eschatology. Western man, in attempting to explain God's purposes, creates insoluble philosophical problems for himself, such as that of the existence of evil, which is quite meaningless to the Chinese mind. Working outwards from the directly observed and experienced, the Western mind sets itself the heroic task of discovering meaning through the cumulative understanding of separate parts; the Chinese, indeed the Eastern, mind less strenuously seeks through intuition a grasp of the whole.

It follows from this that the 'typical' traditional Western work of art, if there is such a thing, is more likely to be a record or representation of a particular experience or form, while the typical Eastern painting is a generalisation from experience, the distillation of an essential form. Exceptions abound: Christian art before 1200, for example, shares with Buddhist art a heiratic formalisation utterly different from the realism of Western classical, late mediaeval, Renaissance and post-Renaissance art. But the kind of art that is the product of particularised experience is typically Western, the general statement typically Eastern. When Cézanne spoke of his 'little sensation', he meant a reaction to a quite specific stimulus at a particular time and place; when the Sung master Fan K'uan spoke of observing the effect of moonlight upon the snow, he was speaking of the cumulative storing up of experience that he could draw on whenever he wanted to paint a winter landscape. Even the titles of paintings illustrate this difference; compare, for instance, the precision of *Mont Sainte-Victoire, La Maison du Pendu* and *Dr. Tulp's Anatomy Lesson,* on the one hand, with the delib-

---

1 This is a typical point at which a generalisation has to be explained before it can be accepted. While the Buddha image is not, and never was, truly anthropomorphic, the popular gods of China were all too human, being embodied in a kind of celestial civil service modelled on a system with which the Chinese were very familiar. They belong, however, not to the realm of higher religion but to the world of folklore and superstition.

erately generalised *Travelling amid Mountains and Streams, Early Spring* and *Scholars Collating the Classics,* on the other.

Thus while the West approaches reality through the particular instance, the Far East sees the instance as an aspect and hence as a symbol of the whole. The processes are complementary, and each has its limitation. Western art—a good deal of Dutch painting, for example—can cling so close to the object as never to take wing at all. Oriental art, by the continual restatement of general truths, can become wearisome, unless the statement is enlivened by the artist's excitement communicated through his brush.

The Western work of art, like the Western body of knowledge itself, is the product of a careful process of analysis and building up. The composition of the picture is the solution to a problem that the painter has set himself, and our recognition of the challenge and of the artist's triumphant solution of it is an important part of our pleasure in his achievement. When the Far Eastern artist first puts brush to paper, he knows, in a general way, what he will do, and the act of painting—I am speaking of course of paintings in which the brushwork is expressive rather than merely descriptive—is a kind of performance in which he is no more concerned with overcoming technical problems than is the concert pianist. The composition may be conventional; our appreciation of it rests, as with music, upon the quality of his performance and upon the subtlety and depth of his interpretation, rather than upon the novelty of it. Originality in itself has never counted for very much in Chinese art.

The traditional art of China and Japan, far more than that of the West, depended on a set of pictorial conventions that were eventually codified in painters' manuals such as the *Mustard-seed Garden,* which I mentioned on page 115. There were no 'words' in this vocabulary for foreign and unfamiliar things or for things not considered suitable for painting. We can see the difficulty that this still presents today when a contemporary 'realist' in China attempts to paint, in the traditional style, what is before his eyes; when Lo Ming, for example, puts a row of beetlelike lorries on his *Highway to Tibet,* or when a traditional painter visiting Switzerland tries to depict a mountain village. Either the lorries and chalets are drawn correctly, in which case they are out of key with the conventional language of the rest of the picture, or they are translated into Chinese conventions and lose contact with reality, and hence any interest for the viewer.

The solution to this problem is either to do away with the conventions altogether, and hence to abandon the fundamental basis of Chinese pictorial representation, or to create a new vocabulary of 'type-forms'. That the latter course, taken by Li K'o-jan and a host of modern traditional painters working in the Mao Tse-tung period, was in direct contravention to one of the basic tenets of Socialist Realism to which they were ostensibly committed is one of the more intriguing aspects of art in the first three decades of the People's Republic. It may be partly because they recognised the impossibility of reconciling the two approaches that more and more artists who want to express their own experience have turned to Western art.

Because Western viewers derive so much of their pleasure from the artist's mastery of purely formal problems, they can enjoy a work of art of which the subject matter may be unedifying, if not positively repulsive. Asians, and particularly educated Chinese, are often appalled at the slaughter, martyrdoms and rapes that fill our galleries and upon which we gaze with such delight: they see our separation of form and content as evidence of a deplorable lack of spiritual and moral wholeness. Their condemnation of the work of an artist like Francis Bacon would be total. They have no sympathy for a point of view that sees subject matter as a mere vehicle for form; even the well-known modern painter Huang Yung-yü could dismiss Western abstract art as 'meaningless' because he could not accept the form as the subject matter. To him, an abstraction was an incomplete work of art. Communist Party theorists couple this age-old Chinese view with an ideological condemnation summed up in the label 'bourgeois formalism'.

Japan here, as elsewhere, is a special case, and much closer to the West: the dramatic cruelty of some of the great fourteenth-century narrative scrolls depicting the horrors of the civil wars is a source of added excitement to the viewer and intensifies their impact. No Chinese artist would paint such subjects.

Because the East sees Reality as indivisible, it holds out for many people in the West a view of the world that is more 'whole' than the one they grew up believing in. Yet at the same time the East is rapidly acquiring the disciplines of logic and the scientific outlook that the West developed. This reversal of roles may be temporary and is certainly partial: there are whole areas, notably in social behaviour and the more intangible realms of thought and feeling, that remain unchanged on both sides. But it constitutes a revolution in both Eastern and Western civilisation greater than either has experienced in the whole course of world history. Modern art, in which China discovers realism and particularisation while the West moves towards abstraction and the general statement, is only one aspect of this revolution.

The effect of this upheaval is of course more apparent now on the East than on the West, for it is Western technology that still sets the pace. It is flattering for Westerners to see the rest of the world modelling itself in their image. We take it for granted that the Chinese, Japanese and Koreans wear Western clothes, keep the Christian calendar and are accomplished violinists. It is the East, we think, that must adapt to our ways, not we to its. But traditional Oriental values, social modes and artistic techniques are beginning to find expression in the West, often in the most unexpected places, and are beginning to work subtle changes in our culture. If this fact is not more widely recognised, it is because Occidentals, so much less well-informed about the East than the East is about them, often do not realise where these ideas and forms came from.

And what of Japan? By now it must be clear that the Japanese artistic tradition cannot be broadly defined and compared with that of the West, as can that of China. Japan is a restless, dynamic blend of conflicting cultural forces, its native temperament and religion, Shintō, its love of nature and its reverence for craftsmanship sometimes combining with, and sometimes reacting violently against, the overwhelming pressure of successive waves of cultural influence from abroad. Japan developed a remarkable skill in coping with these pressures, which has not been impeded by a coherent, deeply rooted philosophical system of its own against which foreign influences had to be measured.

Japanese writers have noted, for example, how readily Japanese artists have accepted Abstraction, partly because in their architecture and crafts they are already surrounded by abstract art of great refinement and subtlety, but partly also because they have seen no need to understand Abstract Art intellectually. The critic Kawakita Michiaki has spoken of the 'mannerism of superficial abstract painting' after the Second World War and observes, 'It is true that while Japanese painters have often displayed an unusual facility for sensibility, their intellectual base has often been deficient'. As I have suggested in an earlier chapter, the adoption of an alien style or technique often occurs too quickly and too easily to permit, or demand, that imaginative reworking which is the only means whereby China and the West can come to terms with each other's art.

There was yet another reason for Japan's rapid and wholesale adoption of Western culture. Since the late nineteenth century many progressive Japanese have believed, with Fukuzawa Yukichi, that Japan's salvation, meaning its development into a modern power, lay in 'getting out of Asia' and attaching itself to the technological West, thereby so strengthening itself that it could show the rest of Asia the way into the modern world. The swift, skilful adoption of every development in Western culture as soon as it appeared was an essential part of this process. It even became a patriotic duty. Japan's success in fulfilling this self-appointed role can be seen from the fact that it was Japanese painters who first taught Western techniques in China before 1920 and Japanese Abstract Expressionists in the decade after the Second World War who translated the idiom of the New York School into a style for the whole of the Far East, not by means of a philosophical reinterpretation of its basic theory, but purely in visual and stylistic terms.

As I have suggested, almost every style practised by Chinese avant-garde painters in Hong Kong and Taiwan before the late 1970s had its antecedents in postwar Japan. When, in Hong Kong in 1972, I put this to a group of modern painters which included Lui Show Kwan, Liu Kuo-sung, Hon Chi-fun and Lawrence Tam, they strenuously denied it. At first I put this down to the artists' understandable Sino-centrism. But on reflection I realised that so confidently were they rooted in their own tradition that they were not satisfied simply to copy a foreign style. It had to establish its credentials in Chinese terms before they could make use of it. If we find the best works of Chu Teh-Chun or Wu Kuan-chung more satisfying than those of Dōmoto Inshō (and this is the personal opinion of a China-oriented writer), it may be because they seem to be less decorative, less on the surface, more deeply thought through.

Modern Japanese art, nevertheless, has an important historical part to play as a catalyst for the cultures of East and West. That indeed is the role in which Japan has cast itself in other realms than art. The great Meiji period liberal and innovator Okuma Shigenobu believed that 'Japan had the ability and duty to arbitrate between East and West, erasing barriers between races and cultures. . . . Japan had the unique capacity to graft the scientific civilisation of the West, having its origin in Greek knowledge and analysis, onto the substratum of ancient civilisation of China and India, based on intuition and sentiment'. By fulfilling this task, Okuma felt, Japan would also be able to repay its ancient cultural debt to China. Such was his belief in Japan's future in the world that he could confidently claim that 'on the Japanese alone devolves the mission of harmonising the civilisations of East and West'.

In proposing their country primarily as an intermediary, these writers are doing Japan less than justice. In one area at least, that of garden and environmental design, Japan's contribution is unique. While the art of the garden was created in China, the Chinese never used it to express their highest philosophical concepts; that office they reserved for poetry and landscape painting. But for the Japanese the garden has become the most subtle and eloquent statement of the relationship between man, nature and art. Today, as Westerners begin to revolt against the machine society they have created and artists seek tangible ways— through Environmental Art, for example—of expressing their rediscovery of their relationship with nature, they must look to the Japanese example if they hope to advance beyond the somewhat crude or merely infantile forms that this movement seems, so often, to have taken.

With an infinity of media and style open to today's artists throughout the world, just what choices the artist makes in any given work may be less interesting—at least to the art historian—than his or her conscious or unconscious motivation. We cannot tell from year to year what specific forms art will take, but it may be possible to discern a general trend. Kawabara Sumio foreshadowed a new awareness on the part of Japanese artists when he wrote in 1973, 'Japanese art which has for the past one hundred years looked earnestly towards Europe and America . . . must rediscover an Oriental consciousness shared with the nations of the East. It is time that Japanese art took up the new work of confronting common problems shared with the rest of Asia. It is in this direction that a new possibility will be opened up in art'.

Ten years later, the challenge has been taken up. Japanese artists today are intensely interested in what their contemporaries are doing in South Korea, Hong Kong, Taiwan and the People's Republic. Exhibitions are being exchanged between the major East Asian cities with increasing frequency. No longer does Japan look to the West for guidance or inspiration. No longer does she see her destiny in 'getting out of Asia'. An East Asian consciousness is coming into being, and though—such is the unity of technological culture—the forms and media may not look uniquely Chinese, or Japanese, or Korean, the sensibility, the references to tradition, however deeply embedded will, it seems, give the work an increasingly national character and strength. The West, having led the world for so long, may well, as we move towards the twenty-first century, look with envy on the enormous creative possibilities that this newly awakened consciousness is creating for the arts of Asia.

Meanwhile, the interaction between East and West becomes ever closer and more intense, and there is no turning back. A number of writers have envisaged an eventual synthesis. Fenollosa as early as 1898 was foreseeing a new, loftier world culture born out of the fusion of Far Eastern spirituality and Western science, a view echoed in Northrop's vision of a future society in which 'the higher standard of living of the most scientifically advanced and theoretically guided Western nations is combined with the compassion, the universal sensitivity to the beautiful, and the abiding equanimity and calm joy of the spirit which characterises the sages and many of the humblest people of the orient'. Today, such an attitude cannot help but seem to come too pat. Not only does there lie behind it the philistine presumption that, since what Asia brings to the bargain is intangible, the West, bringing tangible benefits, must assume the natural leadership, but it also suggests a very short-sighted view of history. Only since the Industrial Revolution has the West seemed to be the leader. When 'spiritual' Asia catches up with the 'scientific' West, as Japan has done and China soon will do, what becomes of the dichotomy then?

I have not once used the word 'synthesis' in this book—not, at least, with this larger meaning—for the notion of synthesis implies something final and therefore static. To the Chinese view, it is not the synthesis of *yang* and *yin* but the eternal, dynamic interaction of these opposite but complementary forces that is life-giving. So also should we regard the interaction between East and West as a process in which the great civilisations, while preserving their own character, will stimulate and enrich each other. Such a condition for the meeting of Eastern and Western art seems to offer far more creative possibilities than a synthesis, which would be sterile if it were consciously pursued.

But today the nature of that interaction is changing, as ideas, forms and techniques in the arts move with lightning speed across the world. In rapid succession they are borrowed, absorbed, made use of, adapted, distorted, forgotten, but they cannot be shut out for long. Each artist dwells in his or her own imaginary museum, the art of the whole world being instantly accessible through books and reproductions. If today his choice is limited, the cause is likely to be political control or censorship rather than his own ignorance.

This instant communication means that artists take up ideas and styles from abroad that they barely understand. The new openness of China in the 1980s has exposed her younger artists all at once to a plethora of art movements that have developed in the West over a period of forty years. The result is that at the time of writing (1988) nontraditional art in China is in a state of utter confusion. Only the strongest creative personalities have a clear idea of what they are doing and why.

Another effect of this rapid flow of art from culture to culture, which we are now coming to take for granted, is that what would once have been thought of by the art historian as an exotic or fascinating event—such as, for instance, the influence of Pozzo's perspectives in eighteenth-century Chinese painting, or of Hiroshige on the Impressionists—is no longer surprising or even historically very important. When Japanese erotic prints become the starting point for paintings by Balthus or for a series of drawings by Picasso, that their inspiration is Japanese seems hardly worth mentioning. It happens too easily, and too often. The age of mutual discovery, of wonder and revelation, is almost over.

But this does not mean that the interaction between Eastern and Western art is any less dynamic and fruitful. It may indeed be more so, as it takes place deeper and deeper within the psyche of the individual artist. At this point, the art historian steps aside, and the artist who has achieved a reconciliation of East and West in his own creative imagination speaks to us direct, needing no interpreter.

Notes on Sources

Chapter 1

Useful general works on early European influence in Japan include the following: Sir George Sansom, *The Western World and Japan* (London, 1950); C. R. Boxer, *The Christian Century in Japan* (Berkeley and Los Angeles, 1967) and *Jan Compagnie in Japan, 1600–1817* (The Hague, 1950); also C. R. Boxer, 'Some Aspects of Portuguese Influence in Japan, 1542–1640' (*Transactions of the Japan Society* 33 [1936]: 13–64). For art, a useful survey is Calvin French, *Through Closed Doors: Western Influence on Japanese Art, 1639–1853* (Rochester, Michigan, 1977). Donald Keene, *The Japanese Discovery of Europe, 1730–1830*, rev. ed. (Stanford, 1969), contains material on Shiba Kōkan. See also Calvin French, *Shiba Kōkan: Artist, Innovator and Pioneer in the Westernization of Japan* (New York and Tōkyō, 1974), from which the quotation on p. 21 is taken.

On early Christian art in Japan, see Mishimura Tei, *Namban Bijutsu* (*Namban Art*; Tōkyō, 1958), and the volumes on *Namban* art published by the Kōbe City Museum of Namban Art. See also Johannes Laures, S.J., *Kirishitan Bunko, A Manual of Books and Documents on the Early Christian Missions in Japan* (Tōkyō, 1957); G. Schurhammer, 'Die Jesuitenmissionäre des 16. und 17. Jahrhunderts und ihr Einfluss auf die Japanische Malerei' (*Jubiläumsband der Deutschen Gesellschaft für Natur- und Völkerkunde Ostasiens* 2 [Tōkyō, 1933]); and Michael Cooper, S.J., ed., *The Southern Barbarians: The First Europeans in Japan* (Tōkyō and Palo Alto, 1971). Kenji Toda, *Descriptive Catalogue of Japanese and Chinese Illustrated*

Books in the Ryerson Library of the Art Institute of Chicago (Chicago, 1931), is a useful work, dealing chiefly with Japanese books.

The most influential art manual in Tokugawa Japan was Gérard de Lairesse, *Groot Schilderboek, waarin de Schilderkunst in al haar deelen grondig word onderweezen* (various editions, 1707, 1728–29, 1746, etc.). See also Jan Vredeman de Vries, *Perspective* (New York, 1968).

Of the extensive literature on the Japanese print I have found particularly helpful Kikuchi Sadao, *A Treasury of Japanese Wood Block Prints* (New York, 1969). On particular artists and aspects, see John Hillier, *Hokusai: Paintings, Drawings and Woodcuts* (London, 1955), *Hokusai Drawings* (London, 1966) and *Utamaro: Colour Prints and Paintings* (London, 1961); Theodore Bowie, *The Drawings of Hokusai* (Bloomington, 1964); and B. W. Robinson, *Kuniyoshi* (London, 1961). On Nagasaki and Yokohama prints, see G. Kuroda, *Nagasaki-kei yōgwa* (Ōsaka, 1932), and N. H. Mody, *A Collection of Nagasaki Colour Prints and Paintings Showing the Influence of Chinese and European Art on That of Japan*, 2 vols. (London and Kōbe, 1939); Tamba Tsuneo, *Yokohama ukiyoe* (Tōkyō, 1962); and H. P. Stern, 'America: A View from the East' (*Antiques* 79, no. 2 [February 1961]: 166–69).

Chapter 2

An essential reference book on Ch'ing dynasty personalities is A. W. Hummel, *Eminent Chinese of the Ch'ing Period*, 2 vols. (Washington, 1943). Harold Kahn, *Monarchy in the Emperor's Eyes* (Cambridge, Mass., 1971) contains information on the Ch'ien-lung emperor as an art patron.

Of the very extensive literature on the missions in China, I have consulted chiefly the following: Louis Pfister, *Notices biographiques et bibliographiques sur les Jésuites de l'ancienne mission de Chine, 1552–1773*, 2 vols. (Shanghai, 1934); various authors, *Lettres édifiantes et curieuses*, 4 vols. (Panthéon ed., Paris, 1843); and George H. Dunne, S.J., *Generation of Giants* (Notre Dame, 1962). The prime source on the early period is Pasquale M. D'Elia, S.J., *Fonti Ricciane: Documente originale concernante Matteo Ricci e la storia delle prime relazioni tra l'Europa e la Cina, 1579–1615*, 3 vols. (Rome, 1942, 1949). For the French missions, see P. H. Havret, S.J., *La mission du Kiang-nan, son histoire, ses oeuvres* (Paris, 1900), and *Histoire de la mission de Pékin*, 2 vols. (Paris, 1933).

On individual missionaries relevant to this book but not themselves artists, see G. Deshaines, *Vie du Père Nicolas Trigault de la Compagnie de Jésus* (Tournai, 1864); Edmond Lamalle, S.J., 'La Propagande de Père Nicholas Trigault en faveur des missions de Chine (1616)' (*Archivum Historicum Societatis Jesu* 9 [1940]: 49–120); and A. Vath, *Johan Adam Schall von Bell, S.J.* (Cologne, 1933). The last phase of mission activity is covered in C. de Rochemonteix, *Joseph Amiot et les derniers survivants de la mission française à Pékin (1750–1795)* (Paris, 1915).

On the beginning of Christian art in China, the chief sources are Pasquale M. d'Elia, S.J., *Le origine dell'arte cristiana cinese (1583–1640)* (Rome, 1939); Henri Bernard, 'L'art chrétien en Chine' (*Revue d'histoire des missions* 129 [1935]: 199–299); Paul Pelliot, 'La peinture et la gravure européenes en Chine au temps de Mathieu Ricci' (*T'oung Pao* 20 [1921]: 1–18); and S. Schüller, 'P. Matteo Ricci und die christliche Kunst in China' (*Katholische Missionen* 69 [1936]). Berthold Laufer, 'Christian Art in China' (*Mitteilungen des Seminars für Orientalische Sprachen* 13 [Berlin, 1910]), concerns the six copies of European engravings, allegedly by Tung Ch'i-ch'ang, which are also discussed in J. Jennes, 'L'art chrétien en Chine au début du XVIIIe siècle' (*T'oung Pao* 33 [1937]: 129–33).

Material on European painters in China between 1600 and 1800 is drawn chiefly from the following: Feuillet de Conches, 'Les peintres européens en Chine et les peintres chinois' (*La revue contemporaine* [Paris, 1856]: 216–60); George Loehr, 'Missionary Artists at the Manchu Court' (*Transactions of the Oriental Ceramic Society* 34 [London, 1962–63]: 51–67); Giovanni Gherardini, *Relation du voyage fait à la Chine . . . par le Sieur Giov. Gherardini* (Paris, 1700). Du Halde, *A Description of the Empire of China*, 2 vols. (London, 1741), contains a long account, drawn from Jesuit sources, of Gherardini's illusionistic wall paintings and painted 'dome' in the cathedral at Peking and of the impression that they made on Chinese visitors. Matteo Ripa, *Memoirs of Father Ripa during Thirteen Years' Residence at the Court of Peking,* trans. Fortunato Prandi (London, 1844), contains all the parts about his artistic activities in China that are in his three-volume account of the founding of the Chinese College in Naples, published in Naples in 1832; see also Kneeland McNulty, 'Matteo Ripa's Thirty-six Views of Jehol' (*Artist's Proof: The Annual of Prints and Printmaking* 8 [1968]: 87–92).

The main work on Castiglione is Ishida Mininosuke, 'A Study on the Life of Lang Shih-ning (Giuseppe Castiglione)' (*Bijutsu kenkyū* 10 [October 1932]: 1–40), with additional notes and corrections in *Sansui* (1947) and in *Ishihama sensei koki kinen tōyōgaku ronsō* (1959): 18–22. See also George Loehr, *Giuseppe Castiglione* (Istituto per il Medio ed Estremo Oriente, Rome 1940); and Gustav Ecke, 'Sechs Schaubilder Pekinger Innenräume des achtzehnten Jahrhunderts nebst zwei Blumenstueckchen von Castiglione' (*Bulletin of the Catholic University of Peking* 9 [1934]). Michael Sullivan, 'The Night Market at Yang-ch'eng' (*Apollo* 88 [November 1968]: 330–35), contains material on Attiret. For Panzi, see Henri Cordier, 'Giuseppe Panzi, peintre italien à Pé-kin (XVIIIe siècle)' (*Mélanges offerts à M. Emile Picot* 1 [Paris, 1913]: 429–43).

For a detailed discussion of the illustrated books and engravings brought to China by the missionaries and their possible influence on Chinese painting, see Michael Sullivan, 'Some Possible Sources of European Influence on Late Ming and Early Ch'ing Painting', which also includes the Chinese comments on Western art mentioned in this chapter, with sources (*Proceedings of the International Symposium on Chinese Paintings* [Taipei, 1972]: 595–633), and James Cahill, *The Restless Landscape: Chinese Painting of the Late Ming Period* (Berkeley, 1971), in the latter of which Yoko Woodson discusses the problem of Western influence, *The Compelling Image: Nature and Style in Seventeenth-Century Chinese Painting* (Cambridge, Mass., 1982), and *The Distant Mountains* (New York and Tōkyō, 1982). For Chinese sources, see Hsiang Ta, 'Ming Ch'ing chih chi Chung-kuo mei-shu so shou Hsi-yang chih yin-hsiang' (Western influences upon Chinese art in the Ming and Ch'ing periods; in Chinese) (*Tung-fang tsa-chih* 27, no. 1 [1939]: 19–38; tr. in *Renditions* 6 [Spring 1976]: 152–78).

The contents of the former Jesuit libraries in Peking are discussed in von J. Laures, S.J., 'Die Bücherei der alteren Jesuitenmission im Pei-t'ang zu Peking' (*Monumenta Nipponica* 2, no. 1 [1939]: 124–39); see also P. Verhaeren, C.M., 'L'ancienne bibliothèque du Pét'ang' (*Bulletin catholique de Pékin* [1940]: 80–86). An important analytical study is Henri Bernard, S.J., 'Les adaptations chinoises d'ouvrages européens: Bibliographie chronologique depuis la venue des Portugais à Canton jusqu'à la mission française de Pékin' (*Monumenta Serica* 10 [1945]: 1–57 and 309–88; 19 [1960]: 349–83). See also Henri Cordier, 'L'imprimerie sino-européenne en Chine, XVII et XVIII s' (*Publications de l'Ecole des Langues Orientales* ser. 5, tom. 3 [1901]).

Two important articles deal with Wu Li, neither of which present any evidence that he was influenced by European art: M. Tchang and de Prunelé, 'Le Père Simon a Cunha, S.J.' (*Variétés sinologiques* 37 [Paris, 1914]), and Ch'en Yüan, 'Wu Yu-shan. In Commemoration of the 250th Anniversary of His Ordination to the Priesthood of the Society of Jesus', trans. Eugene Feifel (*Monumenta Serica* 3 [1937–38]: 130–70b).

On the influence of Western perspective on Chinese painting, see O. Franke, *Keng tschi t'u* (Hamburg, 1913), George Loehr, 'Missionary Artists at the Manchu Court' (*Transactions of the Oriental Ceramic Society* 34 [London, 1962–63]: 51–67), and Paul Pelliot, 'A-propos du Keng tche t'ou' (*T'oung Pao* [1913]: 65–67).

On engraving in China, see Walter Fuchs, 'Der Kupferdruck in China vom 10. bis 19. Jahrhundert' (*Gutenberg Jahrbuch* 25 [1950]: 74–78), and 'Die Entwurfe der Schlachtenkupfer der Kienlung- und Taokuang-Zeit: mit Reproduktion der 10 Taokuang-Kupfer und der Vorlege für die Annam-Stiche' (*Monumenta Serica* 9 [1944]: 101–22). The most exhaustive study of the first Conquests series is Paul Pelliot, 'Les "Conquêtes de l'empereur de la Chine"' (*T'oung Pao* 20 [1921]: 183–274).

Chinese painting in the European manner has not yet received much attention. A useful sourcebook is James Orange, *The Chater Collection: Pictures Relating to China, Hong Kong, Macao, 1655–1860* (London, 1924). See also C. Toogood Downing, *Fan Qui in China in 1836–37*, 3 vols. (London, 1838; my quotation is taken from vol. 2., 108–9), and W. C. Hunter, *The Fan Kwae in Canton before Treaty Days* (London, 1911).

On Chinnery, see Robin Hutcheon, *Chinnery: The Man and the Legend* (Hong Kong, 1975), and Francis B. Lothrop, *George Chinnery, 1774–1853, and Other Artists of the China Scene* (Peabody Museum, Salem, 1967). Both include useful bibliographies.

Chapter 3

Among the books that helped to form Europe's view of the arts of China are Athanasius Kircher, *China monumentis qua sacris qua profanis, nec non variis naturae et artis spectaculis, aliarumque rerum memorabilium argumentis illustrata* (Antwerp, 1667), and Joachim von Sandrart, *Teutsche Academie* (Nuremburg, 1675–79), the first Western history of art to include a section on Chinese painting; see also Michael Sullivan, 'Sandrart on Chinese Painting' (*Oriental Art* 1, no. 4 [Spring 1949]: 159–61).

On general cultural contacts with China, see A. Reichwein, *China and Europe: Intellectual and Artistic Contacts in the Eighteenth Century* (New York, 1925), and Henri Cordier, *La Chine en France au XVIIIe siècle* (Paris, 1910). There is an extensive literature on chinoiserie, including Hugh Honour, *Chinoiserie: The Vision of Cathay* (London, 1961); J. Guérin, *La chinoiserie en Europe au XVIIIe siècle* (Paris, 1911); H. Bélévitch-Stankévitch, *Le goût chinois en France au temps de Louis XIV* (Paris, 1910); and A. Brookner, 'Chinoiserie in French Painting' (*Apollo* 65 [June 1957]: 253–57). A scholarly study of early Italian collections of Oriental art is R. W. Lightbown, 'Oriental Art and the Orient in Late Renaissance and Baroque Italy' (*Journal of the Warburg and Courtauld Institutes* 32 [1969]: 228–78).

On Chinese wallpapers, see Margaret Jourdain and Soame Jenyns, *Chinese Export Art in the Eighteenth Century* (London, 1950).

On cultural contacts between Europe and China before the arrival of Ricci, see Henry Yule, *Cathay and the Way Thither*, 2 vols. (London, 1866); Leonard Olschki, *Guillaume Boucher: A French Artist at the Court of the Khans* (Baltimore, 1946); and Ronald Latham, ed., *The Travels of Marco Polo* (London, 1958). I. V. Puzyma, *La Chine, l'Italie et les débuts de la Renaissance* (Paris, 1935), attempts on the basis of the similarity of some landscape conventions to show that Chinese art brought by missionaries and merchants influenced early Renaissance painting. There is no evidence that Chinese paintings reached Europe before the six-teenth century, though it is just possible that some Chinese motifs were trans-mitted—and transmuted—through Islamic art. Donald F. Lach, *Asia in the Making of Europe,* vol. 2: *A Century of Wonder* (Chicago and London, 1970), re-produces as Plates 4 and 5 two Chinese paintings (called 'Indian' in an inventory of 1596) that were in the collection of Archduke Ferdinand of Austria (1520–95) at Ambrass and are now in the Kunsthistorisches Museum in Vienna. One is a fanciful palace-in-a-landscape; the other, geese amid reeds and lotuses; both are by anonymous Ming artists. A third, now lost, depicted 'Indian [*sic*] houses in which the Indians are sitting down together while one of them, clad in a red coat, is writing'. This book contains a mass of material on Oriental art in Eu-rope in the sixteenth century, but in the total absence of any documentary proof to support it, I find it difficult to accept the author's suggestion that the buildings in the work of Hieronymous Bosch and the fantastic landscapes in that of Niccolo dell'Abate and Pieter Brueghel the Elder were inspired by Chinese painting. As Professor Lach himself points out (page 74, n.89), although there were a number of Chinese illustrated books in Europe at the time, the pictures in them were mostly figure subjects. Jacques Bousquet, in his discussion of affinities with Chinese painting (*Mannerism,* New York, 1964, 270–71), cautiously, and I think rightly, remarks that 'to make these comparisons is not in any way to insist upon direct influence of Oriental painting. Rather, these visual analogies are cited to underscore the fact of a new sensibility to nature in Western artistic expression in the sixteenth century'.

On Chinese visitors to Europe, see J. Dehergne, S.J., 'Voyageurs chinois venus à Paris au temps de la marine à voiles et l'influence de la Chine sur la lit-térature française du XVIIIᵉ siècle' (*Monumenta Serica* 23 [1964]: 372–97).

On Chinese books in seventeenth- and eighteenth-century France, see Abel Rémusat, *Mémoire sur les livres chinois de la bibliothèque du Roi . . . avec des re-marques critiques sur le catalogue publié par Fourmont, en 1742* (Paris, 1818), and Henri Cordier, 'Catalogue des albums chinois et ouvrages rélatifs à la Chine conservés au Cabinet des Estampes de la Bibliothèque Nationale' (*Journal asiati-que* [September–October 1909]). On Chinese European-style drawings in the Bibliothèque Nationale, see also George R. Loehr, 'Peking-Jesuit Missionary-Artist Drawings Sent to Paris in the 18th Century' (*Gazette des beaux arts* 60 [Oc-tober 1962]: 419–28).

On individual artists referred to in this chapter I have found the following especially useful: Robert Schmidt, 'China bei Dürer' (*Zeitschrift des Deutschen Vereins für Kunstwissenschaft* [Berlin, 1939]: 103–8); Kenneth Clark, *Rembrandt and the Italian Renaissance* (London, 1966), which contains the inventory of Rem-brandt's bankruptcy sale; Christopher White, *Rembrandt as an Etcher,* vol. 1 (London, 1969), 15–17, on his use of Japanese and Chinese papers. On Watteau, see de Fourcaud, 'Antoine Watteau' (*La revue de l'art ancien et moderne* [November 1904]); J. Mathey, *Antoine Watteau; Peintures réapparues* (Paris, 1959); Séries Cabinet du Roi, *Jean de Julienne et les graveurs de Watteau* (Paris, 1921). Hélène Adhémar, *Watteau, sa vie—son oeuvre* (Paris, 1950), reproduces the harpsichord panel in Figure 68.

The possible Chinese source of the new informality of eighteenth-century garden design is discussed in Arthur O. Lovejoy, 'The Chinese Origin of a Romanticism' (99–135) in his *Essays in the History of Ideas* (Baltimore, 1948); see also Christopher Hussey, *The Picturesque* (London, 1927); Osvald Sirén, *China and the Gardens of Europe in the Eighteenth Century* (New York, 1950), and *Gardens of China* (New York, 1949); and Rudolf Wittkower, 'English Neo-Palladianism, the Landscape Garden, China and the Enlightenment' (*L'arte* 6 [June 1969]: 18–35).

Early European sources quoted or referred to are João Rodrigues, S.J., ed., *Arte da Lingoa de Iapam* (Nagasaki, 1608); Sir William Temple, *Upon Heroick Virtue* (London, 1683); Sir William Chambers, *Dissertation on Oriental Gardening* (London, 1772); C. C. Hirschfeld, *Theorie der Gartenkunst* (Leipzig, 1779); and G. L. le Rouge, *Détails de nouveaux jardins à la mode: Jardins anglo-chinois,* 20 *cahiers* in 2 vols. (Paris, between 1776 and 1787).

Chapter 4

On Japan's response to the West since 1868, see Sir George Sansom, *The Western World and Japan* (New York, 1950); Edmund Skrzypczak, ed., *Japan's Modern Century, A Special Issue of Monumenta Serica, Prepared in Celebration of the Meiji Restoration* (Tōkyō, 1968); Marius B. Jansen, ed., *Japan's Changing Attitudes toward Modernization* (Princeton, 1965); Joyce C. Lebra, 'Okuma Shigenobu: Modernization and the West', in Edmund Skrzypczak op. cit., 27–40. See also Donald Keene, ed., *Modern Japanese Literature, An Anthology* (New York, 1956), and Kokusai Bunka Shinkokai, ed., *Introduction to Japanese Literature, 1902–1935* (Tōkyō, 1935).

On Fenollosa and Okakura: E. F. Fenollosa, *Epochs of Chinese and Japanese Art,* 2 vols. (London, 1912), contains an account of his work by his widow, Mary; the most complete study is Lawrence W. Chisholm, *Fenollosa: The Far East and American Culture* (New Haven and London, 1963); see also Taro Odakane, 'Ernest F. Fenollosa's Activities in the Field of Art' (in Japanese; *Bijutsu kenkyū* 110, 111, 112 [1941]); Okakura Kakuzō, *The Awakening of Japan* (New York, 1905); and Horioka Yasuko, *The Life of Kazukō, Author of Book of Tea* (Tōkyō, 1963).

Much has been published on art of the Meiji period during and since the centenary of 1968. I have found the following especially useful. Uyeno Naoteru, *Japanese Arts and Crafts in the Meiji Era,* English adaptation by Richard Lane (Tōkyō, 1968); Serge Elisséef, *La peinture contemporaine au Japon* (Paris, 1923); Fernando Gutierrez, 'Artistic Trends in the Meiji Period', in Edmund Skrzyp-czak, ed., *Japan's Modern Century* (Tōkyō, 1968). See also M. Bernardi, 'Antonio Fontanesi in Japan' (*Eastern World* 4 [1953]: 109–16); R. G. Jerry, 'European Influence on Japanese Design' (*Antiques* 73 [May 1948]: 452–58); John M. Rosenfield, 'Western-style Painting in the Early Meiji Period and Its Critics', and Toru Haga 'The Formation of Realism in Meiji Painting: The Artistic Career of Takahashi Yuichi (1828–1894)', in Donald H. Shively, ed., *Tradition and Modernization in Japanese Culture* (Princeton, 1971). Toru writes that when in 1893 Takahashi organized a retrospective show of Japanese oil painting, portraits of Shiba Kōkan, Kawakami Tōgai and Fontanesi were displayed at the front of the hall, and bottles of sake were offered to them.

Wallace Baldinger, 'Takeuchi Seihō, A Painter of Post-Meiji Japan' (*Art Bulletin* 36, no. 1 [March 1954]: 45–56), is one of the few studies in English of a modern *Nihonga* painter. Baldinger gives an odd and tragic instance of the lengths to which Seihō would go 'in attempting to follow the nineteenth-century European custom of representing nothing until it was first consulted in nature'. In 1910 the Nishi Honganji temple in Kyōto commissioned Seihō to decorate the ceiling of the main gate with flying angels. The master insisted on drawing his figures from nude models who were suspended in the air as if flying. He worked through the winter with only a *hibachi* (charcoal brazier) to keep the unfortunate girls warm, with the result that one fled and two died of pneumonia. The ceiling was never painted, but the temple has preserved Seihō's studies.

There is a vast literature on Japanese painting since the Second World War. I have found the following particularly useful: National Committee for the International Association of the Plastic Arts, *Who's Who among Japanese Artists* (Tōkyō, 1961); Nakamura Tanio, *Contemporary Japanese-style Painting,* trans. and adapted by Ito Mikio (New York, 1969); David Kung, *The Contemporary Artist in Japan* (Honolulu, 1966); Oliver Statler, *Modern Japanese Prints* (Rutland, Vt., and Tōkyō, 1956); S. Takashima, Y. Tono and Y. Nakahara, *Art in Japan Today,* vol. 1 (Tōkyō, 1974); Y. Nakamura and Minimura Toshiaki, *Art in Japan Today,* vol. 2, 1970–83 (Tōkyō, 1984). Oriental Art Press Company Limited, *Masterpieces of Modern Art* (Tōkyō, 1967), contains the most penetrating critique of modern Japanese art, from which I have quoted. See also Michel Tapié and Toru Haga, *Continuité et avant garde au Japon* (Turin, 1961). A rich and well-illustrated source of ideas and material on mutual influences between Japanese and Western art is Chisaburoh F. Yamada, *Dialogue in Art: Japan and the West* (London, Tōkyō and

Paris, 1976), particularly stimulating being the contributions by Kawakita, Ya-mada and Gordon Washburn.

Among innumerable exhibition catalogues: Department of Education, Tōkyō, *Catalogue of the Exhibition of Fine Art Held by the Department of Education,* 4 vols. (Tōkyō, 1937), and other similar official publications; National Museum of Modern Art, Tōkyō, *Living of Nineteen Japanese Artists* [*sic*] (1955), *Exhibition of Japanese Artists Abroad: Europe and America* (1965) and *Modern Japanese Art,* foreword by Kobayashi Yukio (1969); Museum of Modern Art, New York, *The New Japanese Painting and Sculpture,* foreword by William S. Lieberman (1965); Solomon R. Guggenheim Museum, New York, *Contemporary Japanese Art,* Fifth Japan Art Festival Exhibition, introduction by Edward F. Fry (1970); and Kawa-kita Michiaki, *Japanese Expressionism,* pamphlet catalogue for exhibition (Tōkyō, 1960), from which the quotation on *Mu* (nothingness) is taken (p. 259).

On individual artists, see Atsuo Imaizumi and Lloyd Goodrich, *Kuniyoshi,* catalogue of Kuniyoshi's posthumous exhibition at the National Museum of Modern Art, Tōkyō (Tōkyō, 1954); Kawakita Michiaki, *Kobayashi Kōkei (1883– 1957),* English adaptation by Roy Andrew Miller (Tōkyō and Rutland, Vt., 1957); various authors, *Inshō Dōmoto* (Kyōto, 1965); Isamu Noguchi, *Isamu Noguchi: A Sculptor's World,* foreword by R. Buckminster Fuller (London, 1967).

Chapter 5

Only in the last ten years has modern Chinese art become the subject of much serious critical and historical study, and yet very little is accessible to the Western reader. Michael Sullivan, *Chinese Art in the Twentieth Century* (London, Berkeley and Los Angeles, 1959), covers the period up to 1955, while particular aspects are dealt with in two doctoral theses at Stanford University, California: Mayching Kao, *China's Response to the West in Art, 1898–1937* (1972), and Shirley Sun, *Lu Hsün and the Chinese Woodcut Movement, 1929–1936* (1974). See also L. Hájek, A. Hofmeister and Eva Rychterova, *Contemporary Chinese Painting,* trans. Jean Layton (London, 1961); and Chu-tsing Li, *Trends in Modern Chinese Painting* (*Artibus Asiae Supplementum* no. 36, Ascona, 1979). Arnold Chang, *Painting in the People's Republic of China: The Politics of Style* (Boulder, Co., 1980) deals with propaganda art under Mao. T. C. Lai, *Three Contemporary Chinese Painters* (Seattle and London, 1975), discusses Chang Ta-ch'ien, Ting Yen-yung and Ch'eng Shih-fa.

As interest in twentieth-century Chinese art increases, so does the number of exhibitions, of which the following, among others, have useful catalogues: Alan Priest, *Contemporary Chinese Painting* (Metropolitan Museum of Art, New

York, 1948); C. Vadime Elisséef, *La peinture chinoise contemporaine* (Musée Cernuschi, Paris, 1948); Michael Sullivan, *Trends in Twentieth-Century Chinese Painting* (Stanford University Museum of Art, 1969); Wu T'ung, *Chinese Painting
since the Opium Wars* (Museum of Fine Arts, Boston, 1980); Hugh Moss, *The
Experience of Art* (Hong Kong, 1983). Lucy Lim, James Cahill and Michael Sullivan, *Contemporary Chinese Painting: An Exhibition from the People's Republic of
China* (Chinese Culture Center of San Francisco, 1983) contains a bibliography
of selected sources in Chinese, including periodicals published in the People's
Republic and Hong Kong.

Articles on modern Chinese painting were published in Shanghai between
1936 and 1940 in *T'ien Hsia Monthly.* Among more recent and accessible articles
are the following: Lucy Lim, 'A Hundred Flowers Blooming' (*Portfolio* [April–
May, 1980]); Michael Sullivan, 'New Directions in Chinese Art' (*Art International 25*, nos. 1–2 [1982]). Tsung Pai-hua's essay, 'The Abstraction and Reality in Chinese Art' appeared in translation in December 1961, in the Peking
monthly *Chinese Literature,* which regularly publishes articles on the more orthodox trends in contemporary Chinese art. Chu Kuang-ts'ien's article, 'The
Problem of Formal Beauty' appeared in *Eastern Horizon,* Hong Kong, May 1964.

Chapter 6

On nineteenth-century painting, John Rewald, *The History of Impressionism,* rev.
ed. (New York, 1961), and *Post-Impressionism from van Gogh to Gauguin* (New
York, 1950), are the most convenient general surveys; I have found Aaron
Scharf, *Art and Photography* (London, 1968), suggestive. A number of the
themes developed in this chapter are discussed in Chisaburoh Yamada, ed., for
the Society for the Study of Japonisme, *Japonisme in Art: An International Symposium* (Kodansha International, Tōkyō, 1980).

On individual artists I have consulted chiefly the following. On Bracquemond, see L. Bénédite, 'Félix Bracquemond' (*Art et décoration* [February 1905]),
and Gabriel P. Weisberg, 'Félix Bracquemond and Japanese Influence in Ceramic
Decoration' (*Art Bulletin 51* [September 1969]): 277–80).

On Whistler, see E. R. and Joseph Pennell, *The Life of James McNeill Whistler,*
2 vols. (London, 1909); Denys Sutton, *James McNeill Whistler* (London, 1966),
which includes the *Ten o'Clock Lecture,* and *Nocturne: The Art of James McNeill
Whistler* (London, 1963); and L. Bénédite, 'Whistler' (*Gazette des beaux arts 33*
[1905]: 403–10, 496–511; 34 [1905]: 142–58, 231–46).

On Manet, see Gotthard Jedlicka, *Edouard Manet* (Erlenbach-Zürich, 1941);
Nils Gösta Sandblad, *Manet: Three Studies in Artistic Conception,* trans. Walter

Nash (Lund, 1954); J. Richardson, *Edouard Manet* (New York, 1961); Alain de Leiris, *The Drawings of Edouard Manet* (Berkeley and Los Angeles, 1969); and Ann Coffin Hanson's review of de Leiris's book (*The Art Bulletin* 4 [December 1971]: 543–45).

On Degas, see Julius Meier-Graefe, *Degas,* trans. J. Holroyd-Reece (London, 1923); Pierre Cabanne, *Edgar Degas* (Paris, 1958); and Jean Bouret, *Degas* (Paris, 1965).

For other Impressionists, see William C. Seitz, *Claude Monet* (New York, 1966); John Rewald, ed., *Camille Pissarro: Letters to His Son Lucien* (New York, 1943).

Robert Goldwater, *Paul Gauguin* (London, 1957); Paul Gauguin, *Avant et après* (Leipzig, 1919) and *Intimate Journals,* trans. van Wyck Brooks (London, 1923); Bernard Dorival, 'Sources of the Art of Gauguin from Java, Egypt and Ancient Greece' (*Burlington Magazine* [April 1951]: 118–22).

On van Gogh, see J. B. de la Faille, *L'Oeuvre de Vincent van Gogh, Catalogue Raisonné,* 4 vols. (Paris and Brussels, 1928); Vincent van Gogh, *The Complete Letters,* 3 vols., 2nd ed. (Greenwich, Conn., 1959); Douglas Lord, ed., *Vincent van Gogh: Letters to Emile Bernard,* 2 vols. (New York, 1938).

On Toulouse-Lautrec, see Jean Bouret, *The Life and Work of Toulouse-Lautrec,* trans. Daphne Woodward (New York, 1966); Fritz Novotny, *Toulouse-Lautrec* (London, 1969); Douglas Cooper, *Toulouse-Lautrec* (Paris, 1955). Charles Chasse, *The Nabis and Their Period,* trans. Michael Bullock (London, 1969).

Very influential in developing a taste for things Japanese was Samuel Bing's monthly magazine, *Le Japon artistique,* founded in 1880, with the help of Burty, Duret, Edmond de Goncourt, Louis Gonse and others. An English version appeared in the same year. The wide variety of responses by French critics (as opposed to artists) to Japanese art is explored in Elisa Evett, *The Critical Reception of Japanese Art in Late Nineteenth Century Europe* (UMI Research Press, Ann Arbor, 1982).

The quotations from Ruskin will be found in Cook and Wedderburn, *The Complete Works of Ruskin* (1906, 1912), vol. 17, 340; vol. 28, 576; and vol. 38, 334.

The literature on Japanese influence on the Impressionists and Post-Impressionists is very extensive. I have found the following particularly useful: Ernest Chesnau, 'Le Japon à Paris' (*Gazette des beaux arts* 18 [1878]: 385–97, 841–56); Y. Thirion, 'L'Influence de l'estampe japonaise dans l'oeuvre de Gauguin' (*Gazette des beaux arts* 47 [1956]: 95–114), and 'Le Japon en France dans le seconde moitié du XIXe siècle, à la faveur de la diffusion de l'estampe japonaise' (*Cahiers de l'Association Internationale des Etudes Françaises* 13 [1961]: 117–30); H. Focillon, 'L'estampe japonaise et la peinture en Occident' (*Congrès d'Histoire de l'Art* [Paris, September–October 1921]: 367–76; Ernest Scheyer, 'Far Eastern Art and

French Impressionism' (*Art Quarterly* 6 [1943]: 117–43); M. E. Trabault, 'Van Gogh's Japonisme' (*Mededelingen van der Dienst voor schone Kunsten der gemeente s'Gravenhage* 1–2 [The Hague, 1954]: 16–40); S. H. Levie, Willem van Gulik and Fred Orton, *Japanese Prints Collected by van Gogh* (Amsterdam, 1978); Clay Lancaster, 'Oriental Contributions to Art Noveau' (*Art Bulletin* 34 [December 1952]: 297–310; T. S. Madsen, *The Sources of Art Nouveau* (Oslo, 1956); John Sandberg, 'Japonisme and Whistler' (*The Burlington Magazine* 106 [November 1964]: 500–507), and 'The Discovery of Japanese Prints in the Nineteenth Century before 1867' (*Gazette des beaux arts* [June 1968]: 295–302); Henri Dorra, 'Seurat's Dot and the Japanese Stippling Technique' (*Art Quarterly* [Summer 1970]: 109–13); Cleveland Museum of Art, *Japonisme: Japanese Influence on French Art, 1854–1910* (1975); Chisaburo (or Chisaburoh) Yamada, ed., *Japonisme in Art: An International Symposium* (Tōkyō, 1980); and Klaus Berger, *Japonismus in der Westlichen Malerei* (Munich, 1980). Mark Roskill, *Van Gogh, Gauguin and the Impressionist Circle* (chap. 2, 57–85) (London, 1970), deals with Japanese influence in some detail. Roskill also notes that van Gogh's notion of Japanese art was partly based on Théodore Duret's essay of 1884, 'L'art japonais', reprinted in his book, *Critique d'avant garde* (Paris, 1885). On Monet's Japanese prints, see G. Aitken and Marianne Delafond, *La Collection d'estampes japonaises de Claude Monet à Giverny* (Paris, 1983).

On Kandinsky, see Wassily Kandinsky, *The Art of Spiritual Harmony,* trans. M. T. H. Sadler (London, 1914), and *Concerning the Spiritual in Art* (New York, 1947). See also Hilda Rebay, *In Memory of Wassily Kandinsky* (New York, 1945); J. Eichner, *Kandinsky und Gabriel Munter: von Ursprungen moderner Kunst* (Munich, 1957); Will Grohmann, *Wassily Kandinsky: Life and Work* (New York, 1958).

The Chinese sources cited in this chapter are drawn from the following. On Lu Chi: Ch'en Shih-hsiang, 'Literature as Light against Darkness', *National Peking University Centennial Papers,* No. 11 (1948; rev. ed., Portland, Maine, 1952). On Tsung Ping, Wang Wei and Hsieh Ho: Michael Sullivan, *The Birth of Landscape Painting in China* (London, Berkeley and Los Angeles, 1962). On the Sung scholar-painters: James Cahill, 'Confucian Elements in the Theory of Painting', in Arthur Wright, ed., *The Confucian Persuasion* (Stanford, 1966). On Tung Ch'i-ch'ang: James Cahill, *Fantastics and Eccentrics in Chinese Painting* (New York, 1967), 16–22. On Wen T'ung: Osvald Sirén, *Chinese Painting,* vol. 2 (London, 1956), 14. On Shih-t'ao: Pierre Ryckmans, *Les 'Propos sur la peinture de Shitao',* *Mélanges chinois et bouddhiques,* no. 15 (Brussels, 1970). On the T'ang eccentrics: S. Shimada, 'Concerning the I-p'in Style of Painting', trans. James Cahill (*Oriental Art,* New Series, 7.2 [1961]: 66–74.

Most of the key texts on twentieth-century art from which I have quoted in this chapter are conveniently assembled in Herschel B. Chipp, *Theories of Modern Art: A Source Book by Artists and Critics* (Berkeley and Los Angeles, 1968). I have also found the following useful and suggestive: Herbert Read, *A Concise History of Modern Painting* (New York, 1966); Wilhelm Worringer, *Abstraction and Empathy,* trans. Michael Bullock (London, 1953); Maurice Raynal and others, *History of Modern Painting: Fauvism, Expressionism,* trans. Douglas Cooper (Geneva, 1950); Bernard Dorival, *Twentieth Century Painters: Nabis, Fauves, Cubists,* trans. W. J. Strachan (New York, 1958); Michel Seuphor, *Abstract Painting* (New York, 1961); André Fermigier, *Pierre Bonnard* (New York, 1969); Renata Negri, *Bonnard e i Nabis* (Milan, 1970); Charle Chasse, *Les Nabis et leur temps* (Lausanne, 1970); Emile Nolde, *Jahre der Kämpfe, 1902–1914* (Flensburg, n.d.), and *Welt und Heimat: Die Sudseereise, 1913–1918* (Cologne, 1965); and Constance Naubert-Riser, 'Paul Klee et la Chine' (*Revue de l'art* 63 [1984]: 47–56).

On the relationship between modern art and science, see particularly C. H. Waddington, *Behind Appearance* (Edinburgh, 1969), and Peter Blanc, 'The Artist and the Atom' (*Magazine of Art* [April 1951]: 145–52).

On America and Oriental art, I have consulted Clay Lancaster, *The Japanese Influence in America* (New York, 1963). Constance Perkins, 'Fact or Fiction? The Legacy of Oriental Art' (*Art in America* 53, no. 1 [1965]: 42–47), deals chiefly with architecture, however, a subject that I have not touched on in this book, for it is a topic that would require a volume in itself.

On individual American painters, see Mark Tobey, 'Reminiscence and Reverie' (*Magazine of Art* 44 [October 1951]: 228–32); William C. Seitz, *Mark Tobey* (Museum of Modern Art, New York, 1962); Fred Hoffman, 'Mark Tobey's Paintings of New York' (*Art Forum* [April 1979]: 24–29); Henry J. Seldis, 'Exhibition Preview: Pacific Heritage' (*Art in America* 53, no. 1 [1965]: 27–33); Frederick S. Wight, J. J. H. Baur and Duncan Phillips, *Morris Graves* (Berkeley and Los Angeles, 1956); George Michael Cohen, 'The Bird Paintings of Morris Graves' (*College Art Journal* 18 [Autumn 1958]: 3–19). Shortly before this book first went to press, I reread Benjamin Rowland's *Art in East and West* (Cambridge, Mass., 1954) and found that although I did not agree with all his interpretations, particularly those of Chinese painting, our views on the allegedly Oriental qualities in the work of Morris Graves were substantially the same.

A number of exhibitions have been devoted to the fruits of the East-West interaction, notably that organized by Professor Theodore Bowie at Indiana University in 1965, which resulted in a fascinating volume, *East-West in Art: Patterns of Cultural and Aesthetic Relationships* (Bloomington, 1966), with an introduction by Rudolf Wittkower and contributions by Bowie and other scholars. See also *Orient Occident, Rencontres et influences durant cinquante siècles d'art* (Musée Cernuschi, Paris, 1959).

Designer: Steve Renick
Compositor: G & S Typesetters, Inc.
Text: 10/13 Bembo
Display: Bembo
Printer: Malloy Lithographing, Inc.